GOVERNMENT IS US

I don't know . . . there seems to be a lot of talk . . . about reinventing citizenship; what it means. What is this group that bombed the building in Oklahoma really saying? . . . isn't government really us? I don't think that people really understand that . . . it affects their lives and that they get to have a say in what it does. They seem so helpless. If only they knew how much power they really had.

–Karen Verrill
President, Washington State League of Women Voters
(Frankus, 1995)

GOVERNMENT IS US

Public Administration in an
Anti-Government Era

Cheryl Simrell King
Camilla Stivers

in collaboration with Richard C. Box, Linda W. Chapin,
Dolores Foley, Joseph E. Gray, Ralph P. Hummel, Margaret M. Kelly,
Walter W. Kovalick, Jr., Renee Nank, Deborah A. Sagen,
Mary M. Timney, and Lisa A. Zanetti

SAGE Publications
International Educational and Professional Publisher
Thousand Oaks   London   New Delhi

For information:

 SAGE Publications, Inc.
2455 Teller Road
Thousand Oaks, California 91320
E-mail: order@sagepub.com

SAGE Publications Ltd.
6 Bonhill Street
London EC2A 4PU
United Kingdom

SAGE Publications India Pvt. Ltd.
M-32 Market
Greater Kailash I
New Delhi 110 048 India

Printed in the United States of America

Library of Congress Cataloging-in-Publication Data

King, Cheryl Simrell.
    Government is US: Public administration in an anti-government era
/ Cheryl Simrell King and Camilla Stivers in collaboration with
Richard C. Box ... [et al.].
        p. cm.
    Includes bibliographical references and index.
    ISBN 0-7619-0881-1 (cloth: acid-free paper). — ISBN
0-7619-0882-X (pbk.: acid-free paper)
    1. Political participation—United States. 2. Political planning—
United States—Citizen participation. 3. Bureaucracy—United
States. 4. Democracy—United States. I. Stivers, Camilla.
II. Box, Richard C. III. Title.
JK1764.K55 1998
323'.042'0973—dc21   97-33823

This book is printed on acid-free paper.

04 10 9 8 7 6 5

Acquiring Editor:	Catherine Rossbach
Editorial Assistant:	Kathleen Derby
Production Editor:	Astrid Virding
Production Assistant:	Karen Wiley
Typesetter/Designer:	Rebecca Evans/Ravi Balasuriya
Indexer:	Teri Greenberg
Cover Designer:	Candice Harman
Print Buyer:	Anna Chin

Contents

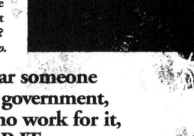

Public servants, ordinary citizens, heroes all
Responding to the call of duty.

Isn't it time to end the constant
attacks on the people who
serve us? Who knows what the
twisted mind of a terrorist
might think?
Or do.

Next time you hear someone viciously attack our government, and the Americans who work for it, tell them— STOP IT. THIS IS OUR GOVERNMENT.

AFSCME.
in the public service

Preface

Cam:

Although negative feelings about government have been growing in the
United States for some time, this book had a specific genesis: the bombing
of the Alfred P. Murrah Federal Building in Oklahoma City on April 19,
1995. For Americans who weren't living in or near Oklahoma City at the
time, the bombing had, at least initially, a sort of unreal quality to it. It was
too big, too horrible, and too far away to seem real.

Perhaps that's why, as a teacher and theorist of public administration
sitting in my office some 2,000 miles from the site of the event, I sent an
e-mail to a colleague then teaching at the University of Oklahoma, something to the effect that the bombed building with its ruined, sagging facade
seemed an apt symbol of the current condition of the administrative state.
The colleague, Ralph Hummel, e-mailed back: "To us here in Oklahoma,
Cam, it's not a symbol. Everyone here either knows someone who was in
the building, or who had a family member or close friend in the building,
or who worked to pull the dead and the still-living from the wreckage. We
live with it, and we will for a very long time."

Ralph's reminder about what's real and for whom was underscored a
few days later when the American Federation of State, County and Municipal Employees (AFSCME) published an advertisement in newspapers
around the country, showing pictures of the police, firefighters, physicians,
nurses, counselors, and other workers who joined in the emergency rescue.
Accompanying the photos was the message: "This is *our* government."

AFSCME sought to remind the American public what they seemed, and seem, in danger of forgetting: that government isn't an abstraction and government bureaucrats aren't nameless, faceless robots, but real people with families they love and who love them, who went into public service to serve the public.

Over the weeks following the bombing, I continued to reflect on its meaning, all the while trying to keep from falling again into thoughtless conceptualizing. It seemed as if the sad state of government-citizen relations, which the bombing drove one to contemplate, came down finally not to theories of American government but to relationships among people, and particularly between government workers and the citizens they aim to serve. If there was something gone radically awry with citizens' perceptions of government, perhaps one of the keys to improving their feelings was to change the quality of the interactions between the two: to restore a sense of connection between ordinary people and their governments—to make it possible for them to say, and mean, that "Government is us." This, it seemed, could not be done theoretically; it would have to occur in practice, for relationships aren't concepts, they are intersubjective experiences. They involve working together and engaging in conversation on a sustained basis.

On consideration of what has been written for general as well as scholarly readers, it seemed that whereas there was quite a bit of material on the nature of citizenship, the role of the public administrator in governance, and even "how-to" advice to citizens about getting government to do what you want, there was very little that appeared to help practicing administrators figure out how to work more productively with citizens. Yet conversations with them revealed again and again how perplexed they were about the barrage of criticism, how disappointed they were in their working lives, especially considering the high aims and hopes that brought them to public service to start with, and how much they wanted to improve not just the way citizens feel but the practical options available to them. Still committed underneath their superficially low morale, government workers wanted fresh ideas about how to work with citizens.

Gradually the idea of a book emerged, and wouldn't go away. Although a book seemed, once again, like an awfully abstract reaction to a concrete situation, books can have consequences (think, for example, of Rachel Carson's *Silent Spring*, or Osborne and Gaebler's *Reinventing Government*, or any number of others—pick your own favorite). But what kind of book? A visit with Cheryl King at her home in Kent, Ohio, and the conversations that took place there, began putting a rather vague idea into tangible form.

Cheryl:

Cam and I were walking on the campus of Kent State University when we first talked about this book. We visited the memorial for the students killed and injured by the Ohio National Guard in May 1970. From the vantage point of 25 years later, we were both struck with the weight and importance of that event. Like the Oklahoma City bombing, the Kent State incident could also be seen as an apt symbol of the state of the relationship between government and its citizens. However, as in Oklahoma, for many people in my community the incident is not symbolic—it remains very real. For some of us, particularly those who were there (either on campus, injured in the event, in town, or in Vietnam), our daily lifeworld is shaped by that event. Indeed, the community itself, at least partially, takes its shape from that event; the incident put Kent, Ohio "on the map."

As the result of this powerful experience of viewing the memorial, Cam and I began talking about the contemporary state of citizens' relationships to their governments and governments' relationship to their citizens. This provided me an opportunity to air my frustrations about the lack of scholarly work focusing on what administrators *do*. Many of our respected colleagues and friends have written about the current anti-government era, but their focus is primarily on defending or grounding the legitimacy of the administrative state. This is good work that is needed but it fails, unfortunately, to address the question of what administrators can do about the anti-government era and fails to connect with the lived experience of administrators, some of whom have stopped identifying themselves as government workers out of fear for their lives and livelihoods. The legitimacy literature also illuminates a serious problem in our field that has not been addressed: If we are so disconnected from the notion of *we the people* that we must defend ourselves as a legitimate part of government, then the problem is not one of legitimacy. The need for legitimacy is a symptom of a much deeper, chronic, and potentially fatal problem.

At the time of our walk, I was wrapping up a qualitative research project that examined citizen participation efforts from the perspective of citizens, administrators, and activists. After listening to the many stories of the participants in our research, talking with subject-matter experts from across the country, and conducting an extensive review of the literature, I was beginning to see that the key to effective participation lies in human relationships. The big question for me became the following: How do we shift attention in our field away from its fixation on efficiency, professionalism, objectivity, and neutrality and toward relationships? Then I attended a talk by Carol Gilligan in which she framed her past and present research as taking place in what she calls a "disassociated culture." In such a culture, we are emotionally distanced and disconnected from those things that have the potential to connect us with ourselves and others. I began to wonder if it is even possible to practice relational administration in our current context. Luckily, the answer to this question is *yes,* as we believe this book shows.

As Cam and I spoke on our walk, the seed for this book was planted. We realized that it had to be a book, not an article. Although we wanted to ground our work in solid scholarship and theory, we would be writing primarily for those who are out in the trenches and needed a way to reach people that was not mired in scholarly garb. We were hesitant about doing a book. Cam was on her way to Washington, D.C. for the first leg of her sabbatical which she was using to research another book, one that she has put aside in the short run to pursue this, and was feeling as if she could not make another book commitment. I was not sure that pursuing a book was a good idea early in my academic career. On further discussion, we realized we simply had no choice. We had to do this and it could not be an ordinary book project. Both the process and outcome had to reflect what we are advocating: collaborative work that comes out of a deep, full relationship. The relationship would not always be harmonious because we wanted all the collaborators to be who they were, even when it meant disagreement. But it would entail authentic connection out of which, we believed, new possibilities would emerge.

Cam and Cheryl:

We enlisted a team of collaborators; some are currently working in public agencies, others are currently teaching public administration. Most have a combination of practical and academic experience. We were looking for people who had stories to tell that we thought would illuminate the issues involved in administrator-citizen collaboration—and we found them. The stories draw on experiences in large federal agencies, at the state level, and in local governments. Each gave us all food for reflection.

Sage Publications, in the person of Catherine Rossbach, encouraged us in our desire not to produce a conventional edited volume, but to strive for true collaboration that would involve lots of interchange among contributors. As we finalized our proposal to Sage, many of those who became members of the team, as well as others who were interested in the project, gave us ideas and critiqued the prospectus.

To perpetuate the interchange, we created an electronic bulletin board, through which all the collaborators could share ideas, give one another feedback on our draft chapters, and argue. Over the months between the organization of the bulletin board and the submission of the manuscript to Sage, the interchange wove the collaborators all together. In the book, we have tried to give the flavor of that relationship by interspersing excerpts of the conversations in sidebars at appropriate places.

Implicitly following Follett's (1924) ideas of taking our orders from the situation, the project has evolved considerably since our first conversations. As Follett suggested, by continuing to talk, we achieved a sort of "integration" in which the final product, we believe, is better than either of us or any of our collaborators could have come up with individually. As we proceeded, we realized that we couldn't, as originally planned, divide up and single-author the chapters that provide the framework for the stories. Trying to write individually just didn't work. Like the collaboration we are advocating for citizens and administrators, our work required equal ownership, writing and thinking together, and a great deal of deliberation and exchange. The alphabetical listing of our names reflects the depth of our collaboration.

The hubbub over anti-government rhetoric seems to have died down over the last year or so. Less attention has been paid in the media to anti-government activities post-Waco, Ruby Ridge, the Oklahoma City bombing, and the Jordan, Montana separatist standoff. In fact, a friend recently commented that there was no need to do a book focused on helping administrators cope in an anti-government era; the anti-government era was over. We know this is not true.

During the last two months of coordinating this effort our work has taken on a special resonance. The book idea was planted as a result of the Oklahoma City bombing; the book came to fruition during the time when Timothy McVeigh was on trial for the bombing. We were continually pulled back to the level of real life by the vivid and heartrending stories told by many of the witnesses at the trial who had either lost family members or who climbed into the wreckage as rescue workers. Cam had several experiences on visits to Oklahoma where she sat in Masters of Public Administration classrooms and heard class members talking about their experiences at the time of the bombing. It was clear that, to them, the event was not over and probably never would be. Although there may not have been radical manifestations of anti-government fervor over the last few months, anti-government feeling remains and the effects on government workers are long lasting.

There are a few people we'd both like to thank: Larry Luton for sharing his file of newspaper clippings; Catherine Rossbach for her support and her vision of doing something "different;" Cheryl's co-researchers—Kathryn Feltey and Bridget O'Neill Susel—who contributed because so much of what is here was influenced by our work together; the Ohio Urban University Inter-Institutional Program, which funded King, Feltey, and Susel's work; Tony Copeland at AFSCME, who enthusiastically supported the idea; and our colleagues and friends (in addition to the collaborators) who helped shape this work: Guy Adams, Bob Denhardt (who led us to Joe Gray and Linda Chapin), Ken Dolbeare, Bob Letcher, and Kevin Snape. In addition to being a coauthor, Renee Nank also did a great deal of the library reference work and securing of permissions.

Cam:

I want to thank the community residents that I worked with during my years in Washington, D.C., who taught me what true community and true participation are. Thanks also to Ralph Hummel, whom I owe more than it is possible to say.

Cheryl:

Thanks to my daughter Kate, for her enduring patience and support. And to Hugh Miller for the myriad of ways he has contributed to my ideas about citizens and administrators.

This book is dedicated to the memory of the men, women, and children who had to die in order for us to pay attention.

Cheryl Simrell King
Camilla Stivers
Spruce Head Island, Maine

PART I

THE ANTI-GOVERNMENT CONTEXT

Chapter 1

INTRODUCTION

The Anti-Government Era

Cheryl Simrell King and Camilla Stivers

Over the past decade or so, we've seen a lot of cynicism on the part of citizens about their government. I truly believe that the only way you can rebuild a relationship of trust and of working together is to do it over a long period of time, investing a lot of effort and a lot of patience in the process. . . . One of the reasons citizens are so cynical is because we don't have a very good history of involving them in the process and listening to their concerns.

—Linda W. Chapin
Chairman: Orange County, Florida
("Targeted Community Initiative," 1997)

Americans have always been somewhat skeptical about government. After all, one of the most enduring images in our political life is a "tax revolt"—the infamous Boston Tea Party. Over the course of 200 years American citizens have tended to tolerate government rather than to support it with enthusiasm. Yet in recent decades, distaste for government seems to have deepened.

As we near the turn of the millennium, citizens of the United States are expressing what seem to be unparalleled levels of discontent, distrust, and anger. Although, as we will try to show, these feelings have a variety of sources, the blame is concentrated in one place. According to Susan Tolchin (1996), "The unifying theme behind the otherwise free-floating anger of

3

the 1990s is the target: government. Government has suddenly become the scape-goat for all that is wrong with society" (p. 6).

To some degree the current situation is predictable. In many ways, Americans' current distrust and anger are what one would expect of a country where "Don't tread on me" (or its equivalent) has been, since revolutionary times, a cherished watchword. Then, too, the United States is a large, diverse, and relatively young nation with political, social, and geographic boundaries that have been in flux throughout our history. We have fewer deep-rooted traditions than longer established societies— excepting, of course, the American passion for individual freedom. As Marin (1996) indicates, it is hard to overestimate the degree to which individual liberty shapes our public and private lives:

> Freedom unfortunately invites into the world not only sweetness and light, but every excess, mania, . . . passion, . . . peculiarity, and grotesque imagining that inhabits the psyche or that men invent in liberty and solitude. . . . We have always been a divided nation. . . . The crises and cultural clashes now splitting us apart simply trace out the fault lines of our society laid down long ago, along which it fractures in times of stress. (p. 43)

A nation grounded in such strong commitment to individual liberty can be expected to reflect ongoing doubts about government power. Yet the current situation seems unique in important ways, particularly for public administrators.

BASHING BUREAUCRATS

Public attitudes about bureaucrats have been largely reduced to negative stereotypes, as illustrated by numerous examples in the media. The magazine *Chicago* gives an annual "Big Onion Award For Greed, Sloth, and Exceptional Idiocy by the People Whose Salaries You Pay" ("Big Onion Award," 1997). *Reader's Digest* indicates that you know you are a bureaucrat if you count pencils, know your retirement date, and favor many rules to control employees ("You Know You're a Bureaucrat," 1997). Poking fun at government has become a staple of comic strips that both reflect and shape popular culture. In Figure 1.1 *Cathy* embodies the disgruntled tax-payer, fuming over government waste and inefficiency. Or take *Blondie,* which recently turned the years-long series of collisions between a late-to-work Dagwood and the postman into deliberate anti-government aggression. In this particular story, which stretched across several weeks, Blondie had been forced to navigate a mire of bureaucratic red tape as she moved

cathy® by Cathy Guisewite

Figure 1.1. *Cathy* as Taxpayer

Figure 1.2. Postman Herb as Target

forward with her plans for opening a deli and catering business. Blondie and Dagwood became increasingly irritated over endless paperwork, confusion, red tape, and regulations. In the culminating episode, Dagwood once again runs down the mailman, but this time on purpose (see Figure 1.2). Dressed and ready for work, waiting and watching out the window, Dagwood says to Blondie: "Boy, that hassle you're going through with the government is really getting to me!" The strip ends with a battered postman stretched out on the ground, asking "Why do I get the idea he was lying in wait for me this morning?"

A more sinister image of the government is reflected in the hit TV series *The X-Files*. The two heroes, both of them FBI agents, find that their main challenge is not the strange paranormal phenomena they are supposed to investigate, but the machinations of evil men inside their own agency, in cahoots with powerful outsiders. The disaffection of the two federal agents, particularly Agent Mulder, and the focus on internal corruption seem to play to the American paranoia about government. At any rate, it is difficult to imagine a hit series based on heroic bureaucrats furthering the aims of an effective, public-interested agency.

Negative images of bureaucrats in the media are only the tip of the iceberg. Many citizens in the United States feel alienated from government as a whole. The signposts are everywhere. A 1994 Roper poll found that two thirds of Americans picked big government as the country's gravest peril and agreed that "government creates more problems than it solves" (Zinsmeister, 1995). Fully 80% of the respondents see government as wasteful and inefficient and 79% believe that tax dollars are spent on the wrong things (Morin & Balz, 1996). Disaffected Americans fault government for reasons that include the following: Government has let too many jobs go overseas (76%); failed to reduce the deficit (76%); not done enough to create new and better jobs (75%); and done too much for the rich (67%). Only 27% say that government's efforts to help the poor is a major reason for their dissatisfaction (Pearlstein, 1996).

Politicians like Jimmy Carter, Ronald Reagan, and Newt Gingrich have traded on these sentiments by campaigning on anti-government platforms. As Gary Wamsley (1990) recalls, Jimmy Carter's administration descended on Washington, D.C. "as a victorious army conquering an alien city, intent on dealing bureaucracy and 'red tape' a mortal blow" (p. 9). Both the Carter and Reagan administrations, for all their differences, represented themselves as vengeful forces intent on occupying Washington and "making the Potomac run red with the blood of slain bureaucrats" (Wamsley, 1990, p. 9). The 1992 Republican "Contract With America" made anti-government fervor and bureaucracy bashing its central theme, promising not just to do more with less, but to do less with less. Political battles are fought at the expense of administrative agencies and their work, as in the 1995 federal budget stalemate that led to a prolonged shutdown with more than 280,000 federal workers furloughed. One person commented that politicians were "holding people hostage for political gain" (Gay, 1995, p. 12a). President Bill Clinton recently announced to approving applause that the era of big government was over, suggesting that the solutions to the country's social problems lie instead in getting more people to engage in volunteer activities in their communities, an approach that was tried and found inadequate a century ago.

The spectacle of presidents and members of Congress leading the charge against bureaucracy, of course, contains a distinct irony. As James Q. Wilson said, "Congress is certainly the architect of the bureaucracy" because it has passed the laws that govern what administrative agencies do. "For Congress to complain of agency red tape is akin to an architect complaining of a home owner who finds it necessary to walk up five steps before he can get from his bedroom to the bathroom" (1989, pp. 236-237). This irony unfortunately goes unnoticed as the public continues to complain about current regulations that were put in place precisely in response to earlier cries for reform.

Many administrative leaders, as well, sustain their constituencies by perpetuating public disaffection. For example, the elected manager of Montgomery County, Maryland issued an order removing the word *government* from county stationery, publications, and vehicles, saying it was "off-putting" to citizens (Vick, 1995). Bureaucrats, for their part, disavow their identities and try to keep a low profile, as when Dr. Richard Klausner, newly appointed head of the National Cancer Institute, firmly declared, "I am not an administrator . . . I am a scientist and a physician" (Kolata, 1995, p. C1).

There are signs that attitudes about government may be getting more negative over time. Regularly conducted polls provide a clear picture of these changing attitudes. In 1958, when asked by pollsters how much of the time citizens could trust government in Washington to do what is right, 75% of those polled believed you could trust government all or most of the time. By 1993 this had dropped to 25%, with 75% now believing you could only trust government to do the right thing some of the time (Roper, 1993). Perceptions of who benefits from government activities have undergone a similar shift. In 1958, less than one in five American adults thought that government represented mainly the interests of the few. By 1972, two out of three answered "yes" to this question (Wiebe, 1995, p. 230). Ironically, at the same time that they profess high levels of mistrust, 89% of Americans continue to define themselves as very patriotic: 80% say their love for America is very or extremely strong, 90% believe it is one's democratic duty to vote, and 96% say they are proud to be an American (Flanigan & Zingale, 1994).

As Ban and Ricucci (1991) state: "One of the great paradoxes of American public service is that the citizenry, which regularly depends upon government's services, has a cynical view of government. No group is more maligned by the public than those who serve the public" (p. 7).

WHY IS GOVERNMENT THE TARGET?

Berman (1997) argues that citizens question their relationship with government and experience a sense of disenfranchisement under three conditions: (a) when citizens believe government is using its power against them or not helping them; (b) when citizens find policies and services to be ineffective, inefficient, or otherwise problematic; and (c) when citizens do not feel a part of government, feel ignored, or feel misunderstood by government (pp. 105-106). This framework helps organize some of the immediate conditions and sources of citizen discontent.

Government Using Power Against Citizens

The perception that government is exercising illegitimate power is most clearly reflected in separatist and militia movements, especially those centered in the midwestern and western United States. In a series of articles in *The Spokesman Review* that reported anti-government movements in the Pacific Northwest, the head of Spokane, Washington's Libertarian Party said that "the uprising [of anti-government feeling] reflects people's sense that the federal government wants to control them, not listen to them. Many people out here feel no more connection with the government than Americans felt for King George in 1776" (Lynch, 1995, p. H2).

Although vehement anti-government feelings are most likely to be voiced among fringe groups like the militia, anti-government tendencies are not limited to these groups. Populists, Christian fundamentalists, gun owners, home schoolers, loggers, small government advocates, Constitutionalists, and individual rights advocates all coalesce to a greater or lesser extent around anti-government perspectives. As Tolchin (1996) points out, the difference between the anti-government movement of the 1990s and those in the past is that today "anger at government intrusiveness crosses economic and ideological lines" (p. 78).

Negative attitudes about the use of governmental power take several forms. First is the perception of a trampled U.S. Constitution, a view that crosses ideological boundaries in a sometimes surreal manner—gun control opponents can find themselves on the same side of the line as abortion-rights advocates, both arguing against the use of government power to curtail individual liberty. A good example is the unlikely alliances forming around the issue of government "takings"—that is, government actions that reduce the value of private property, an issue that, according to the *New York Times,* is uniting "an anti-pornography preacher in Mississippi, the cultural elite in New York City, and families living . . . in the cozy towns of the Cascade foothills" of Washington State (Egan, 1995, p. A1). In addition, the feeling of being strangled by regulations, especially environmental regulations, fuels anti-government fervor. A recent news article described how landowners in the Ruby Valley of Montana (many of them wealthy people who have moved in recently from out of state) are putting up fences and even shooting at would-be fishermen to keep them from getting to trout streams that cross private property but that are, by law, open to the public below the high water mark (Robbins, 1997). Perceptions of a federal police state, symbolized for many by Waco and Ruby Ridge, and of a one-world economy, which many people see as a threat to local and individual capacities, are other forms of the negative feelings about government. At a gun-rights rally in Michigan, one World War II veteran commented, "In the schools, they're teaching kids that they're world citizens. They're not learning about America" (Janovsky, 1995, p. A6). Many who are not members of what TV news broadcasts term "fringe groups" believe that the government wants to micromanage their lives and livelihoods, meddling in issues that are seen as personal or none of the government's business. As one rancher stated, "A true bureaucracy, that's what we're living under today. Unelected people are dictating how we live and that's wrong" (Lynch, 1995, p. H2).

Ineffective or Inefficient Government Policies and Services

Anger at, and discontent with, the government is also related to people's perceptions of the ineffectiveness and inefficiency of government policies and services. Some of this is no doubt warranted; people are fed up with government inefficiencies, red tape, apparently bloated bureaucracies, and with what some perceive as an endless stream of regulations that cost money to follow and administer. Right or wrong, citizens see government inefficiency as a problem and administrators and political leaders often agree.

Indeed, it seems as if politicians have perfected the anti-government platform in the 1990s, ironically contributing to a movement that works against their own effectiveness. Anti-government campaigning seems to break through citizen apathy in ways that other platforms appear unable to do. Candidates actively court the support of anti-government voting blocs, especially in the Northwest where an anti-government candidate can draw a standing-room-only crowd in a local rally (Lynch, 1995). A national campaign advertisement that arrived in the coupon section of a Sunday newspaper in November 1995 (see Figure 1.3) states in bold letters: "Who should have to pinch pennies—your family or the Washington bureaucrats?" "Washington Bureaucrats" is circled in red. The text below the headline says that the Republican party thinks bureaucrats, not families, should pinch pennies, and a vote for the Republican plan can save a family of four a great deal of their "hard-earned money." Two coupons at the bottom of the page promise how much one could save per week or month by voting Republican.

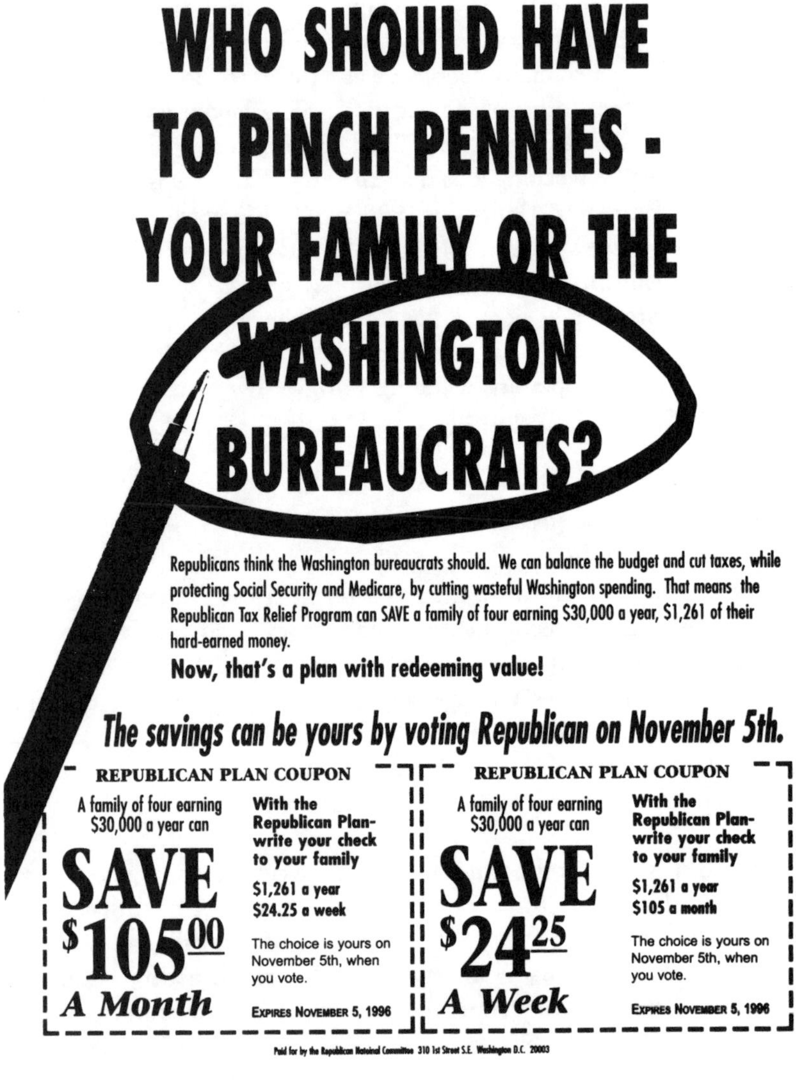

WHO SHOULD HAVE TO PINCH PENNIES - YOUR FAMILY OR THE WASHINGTON BUREAUCRATS?

Republicans think the Washington bureaucrats should. We can balance the budget and cut taxes, while protecting Social Security and Medicare, by cutting wasteful Washington spending. That means the Republican Tax Relief Program can SAVE a family of four earning $30,000 a year, $1,261 of their hard-earned money.

Now, that's a plan with redeeming value!

The savings can be yours by voting Republican on November 5th.

REPUBLICAN PLAN COUPON		REPUBLICAN PLAN COUPON	
A family of four earning $30,000 a year can **SAVE $105⁰⁰ A Month**	With the **Republican Plan**– write your check to your family $1,261 a year $24.25 a week The choice is yours on November 5th, when you vote. Expires November 5, 1996	A family of four earning $30,000 a year can **SAVE $24²⁵ A Week**	With the **Republican Plan**– write your check to your family $1,261 a year $105 a month The choice is yours on November 5th, when you vote. Expires November 5, 1996

Paid for by the Republican National Committee 310 1st Street S.E. Washington D.C. 20003

Figure 1.3. Anti-Government Rhetoric in the Sunday Coupon Insert

The mainstream media are both architect and expositor of anti-government charges of inefficiency and ineffectiveness. Consider, for example, the U.S. media reaction to the 1995 three-and-a-half week general strike of thousands of workers and students in France, which literally brought the country to a standstill. Instead of rallying behind a successful effort on the part of French public servants, the U.S. press castigated them as spoiled and wasteful. As Pollitt (1996) points out, the U.S. press railed against the "dangers to all those beloved institutions—not to mention European unity—posed by 'coddled' public-sector workers (*Time*) unwilling to make 'sacrifices' (*New York Times*) of their 'luxuriant' benefits (*Newsweek*) and 'cushy social programs' (*Business Week*) in the cause of 'improving competitiveness' (*New York Times*)" (p. 9). This reaction to an event in France reflects all too well the press's attitude toward U.S. government workers.

Disconnected Government

Perhaps the most fundamental of Americans' negative feelings about government is that government has nothing to do with them. Not only does government exercise too much power and in the wrong ways, not only is it inefficient and wasteful, but it appears to care little about ordinary citizens, their lives, and their problems. Citizens feel that they have little if any impact on what government does. As one resident of Mexico, Missouri commented, "My senator and representative are way out of my loop, and the President might as well be on another planet" (Apple, 1995, p. A13). From 33% to 50% of Americans (depending on their level of knowledge about government) strongly agree that public officials don't care what people like them think (Morin, 1996). Because they feel powerless to affect government actions, it is no wonder that they see government as heavy handed and bloated. Because they have no hand in shaping policies, they are forced to focus on who gets what—and to feel discriminated against when they don't benefit from specific programs.

To make matters worse, citizens' feelings of disconnection from government produce an apparent apathy that itself reflects a profound lack of knowledge. According to the *Washington Post* series, "Reality Check: The Politics of Mistrust," more than 50% of those asked could not name either of the U. S. senators representing their state, and 58% thought that the U.S. government spends more on foreign aid than on Medicare (military and other foreign aid accounts for less than 2% of the federal budget, Medicare about 13%). Some 34% believed that the number of federal employees had increased over the previous three years, whereas 28% believed the number had decreased, and 35% didn't know (the number has decreased). Lack of knowledge about government is closely correlated with feelings of powerlessness: 69% of respondents who knew little about government agreed that politics and government were so complicated that they could not really understand what is going on; only 33% of respondents who knew a great deal about government felt this way (Morin, 1996).

To summarize, it appears that when citizens voice anti-government feel-ings, what they mean is one or more of three things: Government has too much power and does not use it in the interest of most of its citizens; government is inefficient and wastes the taxpayers' money; government is remote and disconnected from ordinary life. Government workers—"bureaucrats"—have taken the lion's share of the blame for Americans' frustration and declining hopes, but the sources of the problem generally lie elsewhere.

ATTITUDES IN HISTORICAL CONTEXT

Are these contemporary attitudes new? Although suspicion of government is an enduring feature of American political culture, in some respects the current situation is different from the past.[1] As Michael Nelson (1982) observes, the birth of the American nation was marked as much by anger against government—in this case, the British monarchy—as by a positive desire for something new. King George "has erected a multitude of new offices and sent hither swarms of officers to harass our people and eat out their subsistence," proclaimed the Declaration of Independence. Leading colonists complained about the continuing presence of British soldiers, about public jobs going to friends of the King, and of course, about "taxa-tion without representation." But the early Americans were even skeptical about representation itself. Assemblies were tolerated only because it was impractical, even at that time, for all the people to act "directly and per-sonally," in Thomas Jefferson's words (Morone, 1990, p. 40).

Although the emergence of the new Constitutional government soothed a few of the fears Americans had about governmental power, the founders' careful efforts to restrict the exercise of authority to the elite groups they believed to be qualified to govern left simmering resentment on the part of the average citizen. These ill feelings were the base on which Andrew Jackson's presidency forged a more popularized approach. Jackson ar-gued that the duties of public officials were so simple that virtually anyone could do them, and ordinary Americans agreed. As Nelson (1982) suggests, Jackson's idea that the selection of personnel for government jobs should be based on party loyalty—what has become known as the "spoils system"—helped to make the government legitimate in the eyes of ordinary citizens as well as to assimilate vast numbers of immigrants during the course of the 19th century.

During much of the 19th century, Americans exhibited relatively posi-tive attitudes toward government. As most property restrictions on the franchise were dropped and virtually all white males became eligible to vote, electoral turnouts soared. At the state level, as Morone (1990) reports, "voting turnout surged to between 60% and 98% [of eligible voters] in the first two decades" of the 19th century (p. 84). In presidential elections while less than 27% had voted in 1824, percentages rose to about 57% for the Jackson and Van Buren elections and then to more than 80% in 1840. Voting turnouts remained high throughout the balance of the 19th century. The high water mark was the election of 1896, after which a decline began that in the case of presidential contests, eventually stabilized at around 50% with only modest deviations.

As Alexis de Tocqueville's well-known observations attest, mid-19th-century America was marked by a high level of public activity on the part of ordinary citizens, one that seems extraordinary from the vantage point of the late 20th century:

> Everything is in motion around you; here the people of one quarter of a town are met to decide upon the building of a church; there the election of a representative is going on; . . . in another place, the laborers of a village quit their plows to deliberate upon the project of a road or a public school. Meetings are called for the sole purpose of declaring their disapprobation of the conduct of the government; while in other assemblies citizens salute the authorities of the day as the fathers of their country. . . . The great political agitation of American legislative bodies . . . is a mere episode, or a sort of continuation, of that universal movement which originates in the lowest classes of the people and extends successively to all the ranks of society. It is impossible to spend more effort in the pursuit of happiness. (de Tocqueville, 1830/1945, Vol. I, p. 259)

As Robert Wiebe's (1995) recent history of American democracy notes, 19th-century politics was "a vibrant public process: marching, chanting, disputing, debating, voting." For white men, party politics was a defining feature of masculine identity; it constituted what Wiebe calls "lodge democracy," a mode of participation based in the many fraternal organizations and clubs to which they belonged (p. 68). Far from being a facet of life that people felt was remote or unrelated to their lives, politics was a matter of central interest and active involvement. For example, as late as 1896, 750,000 people—some 5% of the electorate—traveled to Ohio to hear William McKinley, the Republican presidential candidate, speak from his front porch (Morone, 1990).

Public activity was, of course, not simply a matter of rallying around governments. Participation often came out of profound disagreement with government policies. In the 1870s and 1880s, midwestern and southern farmers drove many miles in their farm wagons to hear Populist speakers vociferously criticize the federal government's failure to help farmers borrow money and to join in crafting alternative policies (Goodwyn, 1978).

Such active participation in politics reflected a different attitude toward public life than the one with which we are familiar today. Governments, including the federal government, were small, and most people thought of them as "an agent of the people," as Populist William Peffer said in 1891 (quoted in Wiebe, 1995, p. 202), a perception that could take root because there were few policies that conferred benefits on narrowly defined groups with specific interests. Tocqueville noted the extent to which active American citizens believed that their actions shaped governments:

> However irksome an enactment may be, the citizen of the U.S. complies with it, not only because it is the work of the majority, but because it is his own, and he regards it as a contract to which he is himself a party. . . . It is the opulent classes who frequently look upon law with suspicion. . . . The people in America obey the law, not only because it is their own work, but because it may be changed if it is harmful. (1830/1945, Vol. I, p. 256-257)

Given this level of involvement and support, what factors led to the change in attitudes of Americans toward their government? Some of this change can be attributed to measures instituted in the late 19th century that erected barriers to the exercise of the franchise and to public life in general: literacy tests, poll taxes, voter registration, Jim Crow laws of all kinds, and laws that barred immigrating Asians from citizenship. In addition, a variety of local ordinances and practices began to close off the public space, especially to the poorer members of society: vagrancy laws, increased surveillance of street life, laws requiring permits for public gatherings, and anti-labor injunctions. Such steps to regulate public life led to what Wiebe (1995, p. 136) calls "the sinking of the lower class," that is, their disappearance from the public space.

The restrictions on gathering in groups also led to gradual atomization of the electorate, a trend exacerbated by the introduction of the Australian or secret ballot, which turned voting from a public act, a declaration made by citizens in the presence of their fellows, to a secret act performed alone in the privacy of the voting booth. For many ordinary people, the collapse of the Populist movement after its fateful "fusion" with the Democratic Party in the election of 1896 contributed to the loss of belief in the efficacy of group action.

The development of clientele politics in the latter half of the 19th century added to the change in public attitudes, shifting political participation from broad-based parties rallying in public to the organization of much narrower groups around particularized interests. These groups began to press governments, especially the federal government, to respond to their special needs. The growth of the federal government took place in response to these claims, beginning with the formation of the Agriculture Department in 1862 and followed by departments or bureaus of education, labor, business, and veterans' affairs. As those familiar staples of current-day public life, namely lobbies and interest groups, coalesced and government policies were passed one by one to respond to these groups, the average citizen's perception of government's purposes began to change. Citizens began to view government more as the source of largesse than as a mechanism for ensuring the good of all. Democracy began to be measured more by economic criteria—who got what—than by political criteria, such as how things were decided. As the federal government grew in response to the claims of interest groups, politics changed from a public process rooted in the open-air rally to a matter of invisible negotiations conducted in government offices by public officials and private interests. "Ordinary citizens, one by one, had no access to these offices, no legitimate business with their government. . . . Citizens were cast in the role of tourists" (Wiebe, 1995, p. 206). As a result, the latent citizen suspicion of government, which had been slumbering since the founding, began to reemerge.

While the crisis of the Depression in the 1930s made Americans turn to the national government for help, the form taken by New Deal policies did nothing to reverse the sense that politics had become a matter of specific benefits tailored to discrete interest groups. As President Roosevelt sought to cope with dramatic growth in the task of public administration, the public's fear of administrative power, so visible at the time of the American Revolution but at relatively low ebb during the 19th-century era of small governments, reasserted itself in force. When the Presidential Commission on Administrative Management (the Brownlow Commission) issued its 1937 report calling for steps that would enable the president to function somewhat like a national chief executive officer, vehement protests erupted. One member of Congress said that the bill to implement the Commission's recommendations "plunged a dagger into the very heart of democracy," and 100 men dressed as Paul Revere galloped on horseback to Washington, D.C., each with a banner proclaiming "No one man rule." More than 300,000 telegrams were received, most of them overwhelmingly negative. In a statement reminiscent of Richard Nixon's "I am not a crook" speech, President Roosevelt declared, "I have no inclination to be a dictator" (Morone, 1990, pp. 137-139).

World War II brought American patriotism back to the fore and postwar abundance kept negativism at a relatively low ebb; however, a surge in government activism in the late 1960s and early 1970s triggered a new wave of negativity among ordinary Americans. Perceptions that Lyndon Johnson's War on Poverty delivered benefits to a relatively narrow group about which middle- and upper-class Americans had their doubts exacerbated feelings that government, especially the federal government, existed for the purpose of doling out largesse to a favored few. Another war, this time in Vietnam, sharpened the American sense that not only did the federal government practice favoritism (sending working-class boys to fight while the sons of the elite managed to avoid military service), but it was incapable of getting anything done except to waste the public's tax dollars in dubious large-scale efforts. The eruption of the Watergate scandal, hard on the heels of these other events, did nothing to restore public trust (Schell, 1975).

In the 1970s, a virtual grass-roots revolt against government at all levels appeared to burst forth. Beginning in California with Proposition 13, Americans began to take aim at existing levels of taxation and at the authority of governments to set these levels without direct approval from the citizenry at large. Proposition 13 reduced local property taxes in California by an average of 57% overnight (Schrag, 1994). Even more important, it moved from the local to the state level the decision about how property taxes should be allocated. Not only did this weaken local governments, but, because California's constitution already included a provision requiring a two-thirds vote for passage of the state budget or the approval of an appropriation, it led to severe stalemate at the state level as well, because relatively small minorities now had the power to block measures that might otherwise have had wide support. Similar steps have since been taken in many other states, with similar results.

The irony in the tax revolt has been considerable. As Schrag (1994) points out, immediately after Proposition 13 was passed, people in California talked about how wonderful it was that ordinary citizens could take on big government and win:

> But the real outcome is precisely the opposite. Although there are always deals to be cut and favors to be sold, government as a whole—which was complicated enough before in such areas as taxation, water policy, and insurance—has become nearly incomprehensible to both citizens and legislators. Few understand the bizarre tangle of special districts created to cope with the state's spending and tax limits; those who do are likely to be government technicians and lobbyists. (p. 55)

The result of the citizen-led tax revolts of the 1970s and 1980s is a confusing administrative and political mire with a high degree of disconnection between the citizenry and their government. Turnouts in state-level elections in California have declined because the issues are so difficult to understand. Lowered spending has produced near-crises in public institutions and services, including libraries, museums, schools and universities, public health, swimming pools and playgrounds, hospitals, and child protective services. Governments across the United States have traded the mid-1960s rhetoric of social investment and high government purpose for the rhetoric of disinvestment, devolution, and gridlock. Mandatory spending limits, mandatory sentences, term limits, and other "auto-pilot" measures meant to rein in government, to bring it under popular control, instead threaten to put government completely beyond any control.

THE ROOTS OF DISCONTENT

Most of what has been written about citizen negativity stays pretty close to the surface: It details the feelings that citizens express, but fails to explore the deeper roots of such feelings. Whether government wastes money, after all, is never a question that can be answered in a way that ends all argument. One person's waste is another's useful service, just as what looks like red tape to one is another's anticorruption measure. What is more important is why citizens feel the way they do: Why do they accept at face value the anti-government rhetoric in which self-serving politicians indulge? Why is it so easy for citizens to seize on government as the target of their wrath, while other possible explanations are ignored? We address these questions in the balance of Part I, digging deeper into anti-government feelings and their effects on both citizens and public workers. Although citizen discontent can be attributed to latent anti-government attitudes, which are enduring features of the American landscape that are awakened during times of stress, the discontent of contemporary times differs from that of previous eras because of the political-economic context of late 20th-century capitalism, the limitations of representative government, and pervasive understandings of the respective roles of citizens and administrators. The following three chapters examine these root causes of citizen discontent with government. Chapter 2, written with Renee Nank, examines current political-economic conditions, the often ignored but extremely important causes of citizen discontent. In Chapter 3, Ralph Hummel and Camilla Stivers argue that the roots go even deeper, reaching the very structure of the U.S. government and the way in which it reflects a fundamental gap between what government knows and what citizens know. Chapter 4 sets forth some of the areas of impact of this many-layered situation on citizens and on bureaucrats, focusing particularly on the respective roles and relationships of and between citizens and administrators in the U.S. political and administrative system.

From the Conversation[2]

Meg: "It's hard to demonize someone that you have met and worked with over a period of months and years."

Getting beyond the rhetoric to the sources of citizen malaise is important. Even more important, however, is where to go from here. How can the gap between citizens and their government be bridged? Can public workers and ordinary citizens find ways to reconnect? The central argument of this book is that, although the wellspring of citizens' negativity is situated deep in the American political economy and structure of government, much can be done to bridge the gulf that yawns between citizens and their government. Many books have been written to give advice to citizens and grassroots groups about how to get the government's attention. Very little has been written that presents practical suggestions to public administrators about how to involve citizens productively in government work. We believe that tangible steps in this direction are possible, steps that, if taken, would do much to restore citizens' trust in government by offering opportunities for direct connection and collaboration.

In Part II, we present a half-dozen case examples that explore how bureaucrats and citizens can work together. Not all are unmitigated success stories, but all offer lessons to be learned and promising avenues to take. We offer them as food for thought and as catalysts to creative practice. Believing that most government workers want to do the right thing, we hope to facilitate their search for better ways to serve members of the public, beginning by collaborating with them. As de Tocqueville once said,

> When I am told that the laws are weak and the people are turbulent, that passions are excited and the authority of virtue is paralyzed, and therefore no measures must be taken to increase the rights of the democracy, I reply that for these very reasons some measures of the kind ought to be taken; and I believe that governments are still more interested in taking them than society at large, for governments may perish, but society cannot die. (1830/1945, Vol. I, p. 255)

NOTES

1. Compare the following history of American attitudes toward government with the history of the definition of citizenship in Chapter 3.

2. As indicated in the Preface, excerpts from an e-mail conversation among the collaborators are interspersed throughout the book.

Chapter 2

CITIZENSHIP AND ITS DISCONTENTS

The Political and Economic Context

*Camilla Stivers, Cheryl Simrell King,
and Renee Nank*

Our purpose in this chapter is to place declining citizen attitudes toward government into their political-economic context. We suggest the possibility that, spurred on by political and economic rhetoric, Americans have found in "guv-mint" (as President Ronald Reagan was wont to call it) an all too easy explanation for what is actually a much more complex and far-reaching sea change in conditions affecting their lives. Faced with stagnating household incomes and widening disparities between the very rich and everyone else, assaulted almost daily by news accounts of the latest government scandal, and encouraged to focus on the problems government has apparently failed to solve rather than ones with which it quietly copes, many Americans have turned from ongoing, but relatively low-level, skepticism about government to outright distrust or hostility.

The brief history of American attitudes toward government presented in the Introduction shows neither unmitigated citizen confidence nor unrelieved citizen mistrust. We suggest that beneath the surface of the decreasing confidence and trust in government lie factors that extend beyond interest group politics to more basic political-economic arrangements. Our premise is that, as in earlier times, it is not possible to understand the quality of Americans' current feelings toward government without looking into other factors affecting their lives. In this chapter, we focus in particular on the state of the U.S. economy, its impact on ordinary individuals and

families, and the sense of vulnerability and lowered expectations that current economic conditions have engendered.

THE ECONOMIC CONTEXT OF CITIZEN DISCONTENT

After World War II, many white Americans experienced unprecedented
growth in their standard of living. The GI Bill and federally insured home
loans helped millions of families attain a middle-class lifestyle, and an expanding postwar industrial economy generated decent-paying jobs for
most people who could work. True, minorities and the very poor did not
benefit to the same degree, but the overall trend in terms of economic
well-being for Americans was upward. As a result, Americans, including
the poor and minorities, tended to share a common faith in the 20th century version of the "American dream": The economy would continue to
provide for an ever-improving quality of life and their children would enjoy
an even better standard of living than they themselves had.

The American dream no longer applies in the 1990s. From 1947 to
1973, the annual growth rate in household income was at least 2.5% for
all households. In fact, during this period of time, the lowest incomes grew
slightly more than the highest incomes and overall income inequality declined. In contrast, from 1973 to 1993, annual household incomes for the
poorest 40% of households declined slightly, while incomes for the wealthi-
est 20% of all households rose by about 1.3% annually. The average weekly
earnings of rank-and-file workers, adjusted for inflation, fell by 18% between 1973 and 1995. In contrast, between 1979 and 1989, the annual
pay of corporate chief executives rose by 19%, or 66% after taxes. In 1979,
the median weekly income was $498, or $25,896 a year. In 1995, median
income had stagnated at $475 a week, or $24,700 annually. In other words,
over this period of time, the average person had suffered a wage cut of
about $100 a month in constant dollars, or 4.6%. Meanwhile, the typical
full-time worker in the top third of the income distribution had seen an
income increase of 7.9%, the top 5% of families experienced a 29.1%
growth, and the top 1% a spectacular 78% growth. (Cassidy, 1995; Rose,
1992).

These changes mean that income distribution in the United States has
grown increasingly skewed, with big gains for those at the very top and
stagnating incomes in the lower to middle range. In particular, average
family incomes have remained steady or declined slightly despite greatly
increased numbers of working mothers. In other words, it now takes two
earners per family to stay even. Meanwhile, the average price of houses

---

Getting the Shaft

In his account of the closing of the British Petroleum refinery in Lima, Ohio, Marc Cooper (1997) observes,

> What's happening here is a stinging lesson in the logic of the new world economy. This rock-ribbed Republican bastion, . . . a showcase of the Middle American work ethic, is learning the hard way [about] the growing power of multinational corporations at the expense of local, state, and national sovereignty. "When you come down to it," says Ken Belcher, manager of the local electric company, "it really hurts to see how powerless we are as a community." Indeed, Lima's sleepy Main Street . . . , its quiet, semi-rural pace and its plaid-shirt and work-boot sensibility all belie the central fact that this town's main intersection is with global capitalism and decisions taken thousands of miles away. . . . [T]he people of Lima feel that their world has been turned upside down, and that they are on the receiving end of the shaft while faceless others are doing the drilling.

---

across the country increased more than threefold between 1975 and 1995, pricing many families out of the housing market, while the consumer price index more than doubled (Cassidy, 1995). Nearly 2,400 highest income individuals paid no federal income taxes at all in 1993, up from just 85 in 1977 (Johnston, 1997). Felix Rohatyn, investment banker and policy observer, commented, "[W]hat is occurring is a huge transfer of wealth from lower skilled, middle-class American workers to the owners of capital assets and to a new technological aristocracy with a large element of compensation tied to stock values" (quoted in Head, 1996, p. 47).

The economy has been further affected by the globalism that has led to changes in the industrial sectors of the U.S. economy. The need for corporations to compete globally by reducing labor costs has led to dramatic downsizing of the American industrial workforce, particularly lower-income and blue-collar workers. Many low-skilled jobs have migrated to other countries where labor is cheaper. This trend shows every sign of continuing. Well-paying jobs for those without a college degree, still some 75% of the workforce, are becoming increasingly scarce. Meanwhile, family incomes for college graduates have continued to rise (21% between 1979 and 1992; Rose, 1992). Robert Reich (1991) predicts a 21st-century economy dominated by a restricted cadre of knowledge workers, such as those with scientific and computer skills, with the overwhelming majority of workers stuck in low-paying, menial service jobs.

As Simon Head (1996) describes, two trends in contemporary industry are reshaping the average American worker's life chances. One is the advent of lean production techniques applied to mass production of automobiles, machine tools, and similar products. Lean production essentially works on the theory that increased productivity depends on reducing skill specialization among workers, depending instead on hiring people who can "fit into the team." Reduced skills translate into lower wages. The second trend, this time in service industries, is reengineering, which uses information technology to streamline routine functions, getting rid of whole hosts of specialized workers in favor of one employee who relies on specially developed software to coordinate and consolidate a variety of tasks. Reengineering places highly technical knowledge at the service of reengineering "czars" at the top of the corporate hierarchy who control decision making. Although reengineers recognize the impact of such moves on rank-and-file members of the workforce, their tolerance for ordinary employees' reactions is limited. One expert comments that "slapping people's wrists instead of breaking their legs" is a sign of weakness, whereas "making it clear that termination is the consequence of their behavior is a very valid technique" (Head, 1996, p. 50). Head comments that although technological skills will remain in demand among corporations, commanding high pay because they are in relatively short supply, demand for less-skilled workers will remain stagnant and will increasingly be filled by turning to part-time and temporary help.

Many economists look at macroeconomic statistics to determine how well the economy is doing. Overall, these numbers are positive. By 1996, the unemployment rate had fallen below 6%. The deficit has been reduced by more than $100 billion, inflation is low, and millions of jobs have been created. But, as Susan Tolchin (1996) notes, macroeconomic indicators mask the reality that a relative few are doing well and the majority much more poorly. Layoffs are no longer confined to blue-collar workers. Many mid-level managers find themselves dismissed after years of service to the same firm. Many who have been terminated, or downsized, do get new jobs, but have to take sizable pay and benefit cuts and lose most or all of their pensions (Tolchin, 1996). Some are rehired as "consultants" by the same company that laid them off, but with reduced pay and no benefits. In other words, what used to be a temporary reaction to recessions has now become a permanent restructuring of the labor force. Permanent "temporary" jobs, 12-hour shifts, part-time jobs, moonlighting, and more than one earner per family—all are now ongoing features of life in America, despite a consistently strong economy (Lasch, 1994). According to one man who retrains aircraft workers laid off by Lockheed Martin, "The difference between today's economy and a recession is [today] anyone can get a job who wants one; it just depends on what you call a job" (Kilbourn, 1995, p. A1).

Downsizing has become a widespread management tactic for reducing costs. The effects, however, extend beyond the immediate economic impact on individual companies and their employees. Interestingly, roughly 50% more people every year (about three million) are affected by layoffs than by violent crimes (about two million; Uchitelle & Kleinfield, 1996). No longer does job loyalty, an advanced education, or experience guarantee improved economic well-being (Tolchin, 1996).

In the first two decades of the century, many employers, pressed by the demands of active unions, began to offer employees what often amounted to job tenure for life and what were then known as "welfare" services: health benefits, sometimes modest pensions, limited compensation for on-the-job injuries, and human relations efforts like company picnics, aimed at keeping morale high. These measures conveyed the sense that companies cared about their workers and that, barring major economic downturns, employees could expect to keep their jobs. In return, workers were supposed to work hard, remain loyal, and not cause trouble (Berkowitz & McQuaid, 1992).

This bargain, limited as it was (companies always had the freedom to lay off workers), is no longer in place. As *Newsweek* declared, "It used to be a mark of shame to fire workers *en masse*. Today Wall Street loves it" (Sloan, 1996, p. 44). Few, if any, Americans employed in the private sector believe that they can count on keeping their jobs or that having held a job for 30 years is any guarantee of continuing to hold it until retirement. For example, Matt Hoffman of Chase Manhattan maintains, "I can't imagine any corporate entity owes anyone a career" (Kleinfield, 1996, p. A13).

The economy seems to no longer respond in a way that coincides with middle-class ideals. This constitutes a deep failure in the American dream, one of the nation's most sustaining myths. This failure is no secret to many Americans (Hochschild, 1995). Although success has always been influenced by factors other than ability, it is the *belief* that in hard work lies the promise of opportunity, virtue, and greater wealth, regardless of economic class, race, or sex, that has nourished our market system. This belief has weakened dramatically: We have awakened from the American dream. As income inequality has grown, the decline in relative standing has made lower- and middle-income people feel worse, even though their absolute standard of living has remained the same or declined only a little (Rose, 1992).

The flip side of alienation on the part of lower- and middle-income people, according to Christopher Lasch (1994), is disaffection on the part of the elite. He notes,

> To an alarming extent, the privileged classes . . . have made themselves independent not only of crumbling industrial cities but of public services in general.

They send their children to private schools, insure themselves against medical emergencies by enrolling in company-supported plans, and hire private security guards to protect themselves against the mounting violence. (p. 47)

Oddly, as government entitlements have increased over time, so has dissatisfaction. One part of the answer lies with perceptions about what other people are getting from government and why. As we noted in the Introduction, in recent history, government programs have been increasingly geared away from universal benefits for all people and toward groups of people who fit particular criteria. The perception that certain groups of people are benefiting from government services, while not contributing to their provision, has divided Americans. For example, 68% of Americans polled believe that most current welfare recipients are just taking advantage of the system (Morin & Balz, 1996). Jane Haddam (1996), describing what it's like for her and her family to live without health insurance, argues that the problem most middle-class Americans have with the welfare state "isn't that it supports the 'underclass'. It's that it doesn't support anyone else." Haddam maintains that no matter how frantically people are struggling to stay afloat, virtually no employed person's problems are viewed by the welfare establishment as "real need." Most Americans don't qualify for government-subsidized health services, for job training, for Head Start, for subsidized child care, or for mental health services, and they resent those who do qualify. However, Social Security, for which most Americans do (or will) qualify, is "politically sacrosanct" (Haddam, 1996, pp. 18-19).

Given economic uncertainty and perceptions that government programs are not available to help those who are both in need and working hard to stay afloat, it makes sense that citizen anger and resentment are directed at government. The feelings that arise from the incongruities between what we experience in our daily lives and the stories that government and the corporate world tell us about our economic existence lead to anger and resentment targeted at government. Instead of blaming business, for example, 73% of U.S. citizens surveyed in 1993 blamed government for their stagnant incomes; 61% blamed high taxes in particular (Harris Poll cited in Tolchin, 1996, p. 53). As Tolchin states,

Today, when middle managers and blue-collar workers lose their jobs they blame government even though, when pressed, they cannot think of what specific role government played in influencing decisions by Xerox or Mobil or IBM to downsize their workforces or move factories to Mexico. (1996, p. 52)

Jürgen Habermas (1975) gives us a way of understanding the displacement of anger and resentment from the owners of capital to the government. He argues that class-based tensions, which were characteristic of the times within which Karl Marx theorized and which led to worker revolution during the late 19th century, were no longer an appropriate basis for understanding late 20th-century society. Because of the advent of the welfare state and the relative prosperity of workers in much of the Western world, the tensions that Marx believed would manifest themselves in class consciousness and the overthrow of capitalism would instead be displaced in new forms of oppositional movements, particularly opposition against government. Instead of getting angry at the corporations that are taking jobs and economic prosperity for workers offshore, citizens or workers are angry at governments for permitting this to happen (anger that is well placed given the tight relationships between government and business) and for allowing further erosion of the landscape through liberal social programs. As explained by Anthony Giddens (1985) in a review of Habermas,

> Because economic life is today in considerable degree administered by government, in conjunction with the larger corporations, economic crises rapidly tend to become political ones. These are more threatening because the technocratic character of modern politics cannot generate deep and abiding loyalty to the political order. The mass of the population feels no commitment to the political system and readily becomes alienated from it if that system fails to maintain its narrow brief—i.e., to guide sustained economic growth. In such circumstances, the political system faces what Habermas terms a crisis of legitimation. Because of its confined, technocratic character, the political system lacks the legitimate authority which it needs to govern. The tendency for legitimation crisis is the most deep-lying contradiction of modern capitalism. (p. 136)

THE PRIVATIZATION RESPONSE

Ironically, in response to this legitimation crisis and to charges that government—especially the federal government—is inefficient and wasteful, recent years have witnessed a turn toward making government functions and services more business-like, further strengthening the connections between business and government and the disconnections between government and its citizens. Whether by contracting out or outright divestiture, governments at all levels are seeking what are known as public-private partnerships in an effort to convince skeptical citizens that government can be reinvented—that is, run more like a business. While tentative steps in this direction were being taken during the 1980s, privatization achieved something like the status of a civil religion with the publication of *Reinventing Government* (Osborne & Gaebler, 1992). After Bill Clinton was

elected president, he appointed Vice-President Al Gore to spearhead a reinventing effort at the federal level, the so-called National Performance
Review (Office of the President, 1993). The states entered into similar
efforts.

Basing itself on the presumption that the problem with government
today is not what government does but how it works, the reinventing government movement has emphasized entrepreneurialism on the part of
bureaucrats, aimed at achieving results that cost less and work better. The
movement takes aim at red tape as a waste of the public's money and a drag
on creativity. It assumes that what people want is not big policy changes or
active involvement but results, an idea that is as old as Alexander Hamilton's
argument in the Federalist Papers (Cooke, 1961). In much the way that
early 20th-century reformers advocated scientific management in the name
of governmental efficiency, today's reformers tout making government run
more like a business in the name of getting things done.

As recent progress reports have suggested, the National Performance
Review has suffered because of its emphasis on downsizing the federal
bureaucracy, promising to cut 250,000 federal jobs within the first five
years. Yet Nasar (1995) notes that despite all the rhetoric, not counting the
military, federal jobs are a smaller share of all jobs than at any time since
World War II. Since the end of the 1980s, while the private economy was
growing by 8 million jobs, the federal civil service shrank from 3 million
to 2.8 million. As a result of the downsizing rhetoric, morale among federal
workers plummeted as they recognized that getting rid of red tape meant
getting rid of people.

Nevertheless, privatization of government responsibilities is an idea
that has won wide support and resulted in a variety of experimental efforts,
with varying success. Private firms now run state and federal prisons, de-
liver government-subsidized health services, and are currently bidding to
administer state welfare systems under the new welfare reform law. Cities
are selling their logos to the highest bidder, as when Atlanta sold its impri-
matur to Visa USA before the 1996 Olympics. A town in Indiana put ad-
vertising on the backs of police cars to raise money for lights and sirens.
San Diego and Chicago have opened stores to sell leftover parking meters
and manhole covers. New York City is selling ad space on litter baskets and
garbage trucks (Myers, 1995).

Besides questions of appropriateness that such efforts raise, the possibility of outright corruption is ever present. A five-year investigation of
New York's garbage collection revealed that a Mafia-dominated cartel had
controlled collections for more than 50 years, "forcing virtually every business, university, and hospital . . . to pay up to 40% more for trash collection

than they would have in a free market" (McKinley, 1995, p. B16). Nor are privatization efforts necessarily guaranteed to produce more effective government. A recent study of the federal Environmental Protection Agency revealed that control of private contractors over the agency's management information systems was so complete that the agency was dependent on the outsiders for information about itself (Schneider, 1992).

Perhaps, given the level of Americans' apparent distaste for government, governments can't be blamed for hoping that some of business's apparently solid legitimacy might rub off if they try to become more business-like. Such efforts, however, raise troubling questions of how governments that divest themselves of central responsibilities are to hold themselves accountable to an ever-skeptical public. In addition, these patchwork efforts fail to address the deeper sources of American citizens' discontent with government and, in some cases, may serve to intensify the disconnection between government and its citizens.

As this volume is intended to show, changes in the attitudes of Americans toward their government have deeper roots than can be reached by downsizing the federal government, moving welfare to the state level, or turning over trash pick-up to private firms. In the next two chapters, we examine the situation from additional angles before turning to the collaborators' chapters, which suggest that the change needed is not one that intensifies the relationship between business and government, but rather, one that involves a different relationship between American citizens and their government.

Chapter 3

GOVERNMENT ISN'T US

The Possibility of Democratic Knowledge in Representative Government

Ralph P. Hummel and Camilla Stivers

Beginning in the 1960s and 1970s, people in poor urban neighborhoods and rural communities came together to organize their own basic health services. Their work was sparked by the Community and Migrant Health Center grant program. This program gave community boards the responsibility for carrying out locally the intent of a federal law: to provide health care in areas that otherwise had little such care.

The law and regulations set many conditions on the use of the funds. Each center had a federal bureaucrat, a project officer, who oversaw what the community people did. The project officer was the front-line person in a much larger bureaucracy set up to administer the program. His or her job was to ensure that the community people obeyed all the laws and regulations and spent the grant money wisely and effectively. According to the law, the people living in the community were the users of the services, and a majority of the governing board of each community health center had to be users.

Each governing board was responsible for establishing general policies by which their center was run, including the particular mix of services to be offered and a schedule of hours during which the services were provided. They also approved the center's annual budget and hired its executive director.

From the federal government's point of view, the challenge was making sure that the boards of users followed the rules. From the perspective of the communities, the program was a chance to realize some of the dreams they had long had about improving living and working conditions in their areas. This was one of those rare times when ordinary people could exercise authority over public funds, when they could say, and mean, that *Government is us*. Accustomed to being rather passive spectators of the workings of government and politics, they wanted to make the most of this opportunity to shape government actions affecting their lives and the lives of their friends and neighbors. For once, they weren't just onlookers, but participants. They would use the knowledge they had gained from living to make things better for themselves and their communities.

* * *

In American politics, can people be who they are? That is, can they, through the practice of citizenship, become fully human (Aristotle, 1981)? If they could, people and government would be one, which is clearly not the case. Examples of ordinary people directly involved in governing are few and far between. Instead, people believe that government is not a part of their lives. Not only are there occasional outbreaks of aggressive anti-government action, but the feeling that *Government isn't us* is widespread. People perceive a gap between their own sense of their experience and what they see happening in government. Although it is ever present, government seems abstract and remote. Its authority is external, without a foundation in people's lives as they live them. This feeling, we will argue, has deep roots in the knowledge structure of the political system.

Those in government do not know us directly, only in representation. We appear to them as abstract citizens, as voters, as bearers of certain rights, or as statistics in an opinion poll or policy study, not as complete human beings. Legislators make laws for us based on such representations and administrators manage policies over us as *if* we were these representations.

Here lies the dark side of representative government: the effort to make us formally present in the halls of legislation and in agency offices without our physically and substantively being there. Yet, no matter how serious this effort, the fact remains that we are not directly there. We are literally *re*-presented. Laws are crafted and policies administered to fit all, or the average; they therefore fit none of us. Universal categories and instrumental reason overwhelm the sense ordinary people have of the substance of life: what is entailed in taking care of themselves and one another. Government becomes a specialized enterprise increasingly devoted to the exercise of technical rules and procedures, whether or not these take care of real-life problems. Reason, especially instrumental reason, overwhelms care.

Can the splitting of reason and care continue unnoticed? How serious are present-day antagonisms between citizens and their government? Can people be fully known to their legislative and administrative representatives? These questions, when they are addressed at all, are usually answered in terms of interests (e.g., Pitkin, 1967). This approach avoids a prior question: the question of knowledge. How can we speak of each others' interests unless we first know what it is that people are interested in?

Once knowledge differences are moved to the foreground of our attention, the question of representative government ceases to be a matter of how fully people's interests are represented. Instead it becomes one of whether interests can be represented at all. How can what people are and what they want be known, much less re-presented in the processes of legislation and administration?

In opening the question of the linkage between form of government and form of knowledge, however, we are also opening again the question of publicness, or the nature of the political. In an understanding of the political long obliterated by the focus on conflicting interests, Aristotle spoke of the human being as a *zoon politikon* (a political being). This political being constituted not only policy and politics, but itself in political life, as citizens deliberated together about questions affecting them all. In this concept of the political, categories of understanding would come from below, constantly emerging out of public and direct encounters among the citizens.

In contrast, today's categories of government are determined from above, by specialists detached from people's lives: representatives and administrators. The word *politics* has become so degraded that it takes an effort to recollect the neglected, positive meaning of the term. In this forgotten sense, people can fully "be who they are" only if they participate directly in public life, as the community health center board members did. Without the opportunity for such participation, citizens lose the sense that *Government is us,* because it is, literally, not us.

Consider two propositions:

1. In a representative democracy, an originary knowledge gap between the lives of the represented and the reasoning processes of their representatives unavoidably widens over time until human experience becomes detached from the politics necessary for processing it. Laws based only on abstractions and logic are increasingly emptied of the concerns arising from real-life practices. Concepts become divorced from content. The solution would seem to be to move from representative to direct democracy, but the magnitude of such a transformation is beyond the bounds of this chapter. Once we become aware, however, of the gap between people and government *as a*

From the Conversation: Beyond Re-Presentation?

Lisa: What about elected officials? Do we assume that elections fairly represent the citizens' preferences, or not? I can think of a couple of takes on this. First there is Fox and Miller's (1995) argument—the democratic feedback loop is a comfortable fiction. This is interestingly buttressed, I think, by theorists such as William Riker who also argue that the voting system is flawed, but who side with minimalist government. His argument is essentially that voting is so susceptible to cycling and strategic behavior that outcomes cannot be understood as expressing the voters' values.

Cam: [In our chapter,] Ralph and I are addressing the very question you bring up, by saying that representation is fundamentally undemocratic in the sense that it is necessarily an abstraction from the lived experience of citizens. We realize that we aren't going to get rid of representation but we argue that creating opportunities for direct interaction between citizens and bureaucrats at least has the possibility of tempering some of the worse excesses and side effects of representation.

Ralph: Camilla and I argue that as abstraction increases in those who write laws, the experience of people living ordinary lives increasingly becomes only distantly re-presented, RE-presented, which leads to the feeling (judgment) that government ain't us: the laws do not correspond to the experience of our lives, or: in order to live our lives and not get hurt by the laws we must distort our lives. What will be interesting in the second part of our chapter will be how and whether we can extricate ourselves from this quandary.

Lisa: I really like the argument that you and Cam are developing, that legislators are so far removed from the everyday experiences of ordinary people that they are incapable of "representing" their constituents. I also think it's an argument that's nicely buttressed by Riker's work—that the voting systems are hopelessly flawed, and cannot represent true public preferences—and by Steven Lukes's 1974 *Power: A Radical View*, where he takes the pluralism-elitism debate a step further and argues that the dominant interests prevent many issues from even emerging onto the public agenda.

Richard: The question of whether elected officials are connected with the people is complex at the local level, where most of the elected officials are to be found. It is dangerous to generalize about their knowledge at this level, especially in small communities or larger ones with well-developed neighborhood political structures. I think the issue of whether representatives do what the people want has to be seen in the broader context of community power structures and elite groups (thus, Molotch's "growth machine" theory). There is also the problem of false consciousness, that is, would people want what they want now if they had a clear idea of what is going on and what the alternatives might be?

problem of knowledge, we can consider how this gap might be reduced in policy implementation and public administration. This leads us to a second proposition.

2. In public administration as conceived and practiced in modern U.S. government, there is opportunity for narrowing the gap between people and government by opening up the process of implementation. Contentless concepts cannot lead directly to actions. Implementation of legislation and policy requires, on theory of knowledge grounds, the exercise of interpretation by someone. Existing theories of public administration have emphasized the importance of the administrator's role in this interpretative process (see Wamsley et al., 1990). But we will argue that *collaborative* knowledge is possible in administrative contexts: Bureaucrats and citizens, this time not abstractions, but real participants in public life, can join in dialogue out of which arise concepts grounded in real life rather than logic—in care rather than pure reason. These collaborative processes can provide opportunities for people to reconnect government with the realities of their lives, encouraging them to see themselves as active citizens rather than passive critics and clients (or as citizens first, as Gray & Chapin argue in Chapter 11).

The critique of representative knowledge reveals the alienated mode of public life to which representation appears inevitably to restrict us. Opposing such alienation is the possibility of a more active form of citizenship, one grounded in a reopened understanding of public knowledge. The following two sections explore, first, the limits representative knowledge places on public life and then, the possibilities for reconstituting public life through implementation processes based on democratic knowledge. The community health center program will stand as a concrete example of how democratic knowledge is possible. It will show how what people have to say about their lives brings into being public space and public thinking.

REPRESENTING LIVED KNOWLEDGE

We began by asking, "In politics, can people be who they are?" To this question, American representative politics gives a resounding "No!" Embedded in their own experience, from the nation's beginning people were found to care too deeply, that is, to pursue life, liberty, and property too passionately. The founders saw the common people as theoretically creatures of reason, but in practice driven by selfish interests, and therefore in need of representation. So they planted deep in American politics an alienated self-understanding of citizenship. If each of us were permitted to be who we are, that is, to participate fully and directly in politics, the result would be a war of all against all. Prudence dictated otherwise. Against this Hobbesian condition, which would destroy all possibility of a commonwealth, the founders counterposed the notion of representation. Those representing the best in us would moderate the wishes and will of the worst among us (cf. Hobbes, 1651/n.d.; Roelofs, 1976, 1992).

The consequences of representation have frequently been examined in terms of passions and interests. Representation has been defended on the basis that if representatives were like the people, they would think like them, as in theories of representative bureaucracy (Krislov, 1974; for a test of such theories, see Selden, 1997). But is not the real question whether people's needs and wishes *can* be represented? How can representatives *know* their people?

Representatives' knowledge must inevitably be distinct and apart from their constituents' direct experience. In knowledge terms, to represent fully would require knowing what people go through: the actual problems they experience and their resulting self-knowledge. But how can those who do not share our lives know them? When the original question is asked in this way, it becomes clear that American representative government does not require representatives to know their people, only to decide for them.

Where will the philosophy of knowledge take us, in our quest for the role of knowledge in governance? Our exploration will try to support the following propositions:

1. *American government is not a democracy of direct knowledge.* It is a republic constituted by secondary knowledge. Representation is guided by technical-logical operations of reason, not by actual experience. In fact, *knowledge* is confined by definition to whatever can be fitted into the Procrustean bed of reason. Representative politics negate the original, direct, or immediate experience of ordinary folk. Only that experience is considered which can be raised to a universalized conceptual level. As in science, a correspondence theory of knowledge prevails: Only that which fits the categories provided by science or logic is real. This specifically excludes people's original lived experience; objectivity requires representatives to even try to exclude their own experience from the reasoning process.

2. *Law giving aimed at "citizens" excludes us as individuals.* Under the logic of reason, governance prides itself not on expressing who we are as individual human beings but on designing universal laws that make us all abstract citizens. Thus, citizenship includes only that part of us that can be represented under universal categories. So, for example, a citizen is considered equal to every other citizen. Personal identity disappears, wiped out by equality. The citizen is the human being in its re-presented role. In this citizenship, the particular human being is strangely absent.

3. *Administration works not with individuals, but with cases.* Administrative governance prides itself on applying role definitions without fear or favor to all comers. Here the citizen is further reduced to a case. Again, we find very little of the whole human being.

4. *Representation produces alienation.* Representative democracy already estranges legislators from the direct experience of whole human beings. The gap between citizenship and full humanity, so much in the forefront of people's disillusionment with government, was already there at the founding.

> Direct knowledge of life experience cannot be apprehended under the cate-
> gories of abstract reason without loss of what people's lives have brought
> them to care about. Reason ultimately rules without care, that is, without
> respect for people's orientation toward their own situations. Represented
> knowledge leaves real people out.

How are we to understand the carelessness of pure reason? Why are abstractions made possible by reason inadequate to the experience of life? It helps to turn to the history of philosophy and consider the foremost attempts to define the relation between reason and experience in modern knowledge.

The American founders lived in the Age of Reason, which sought not what was peculiar to any individual's life but what was valid for the lives of all those considered citizens. Once people were persuaded that universal laws of human nature existed, they could accept political laws derived from them. Thus the passions of the mob would be controlled. But what else is lost when reason dominates passions?

The exploration proceeds as follows: For an understanding of the historical move toward legislative reason, we turn first to the fullest investigation of reason's representation of experience: Immanuel Kant's *Critique of Pure Reason* (1781, 1787). Then, for an understanding of what was lost when the dominance of reason was accepted, we turn to a philosopher most concerned with life as lived, phenomenologist Martin Heidegger.

The Emptiness of Reason and the Neglect of Sensibility

It is possible to read all human behavior before the advent of the Age of Reason as "nothing but a process of merely random groping." So writes Kant (1787), as he sets forth how reason frees us from dependence on nature. With the coming of the experiment, he says, "A light broke upon all students of nature":

> They learned that reason has insight only into that which it produces after a
> plan of its own, and that it must not allow itself to be kept, as it were, on nature's
> leash, but must itself show the way with principles of judgment based upon
> fixed laws, constraining nature to give answer to questions of reason's own
> determining. (pp. xiii-xiv)

Founders of republics of reason like our own saw the relation between citizens and rational law in just such terms. If universal categories and laws of reason could be discovered, and at least temporarily imposed, then the people, though they were not angels, could be made to strive toward rationality. And because human nature contained a portion of rationality by definition, the founders were not hoping for too much. But their skepticism about the passionate side of human nature, at least as it expressed itself among the common people, led them to count on the fullest operation of reason only among leaders like themselves.

Yet Kant's inquiry into the nature of knowledge warns us that knowledge is possible only when both reason and organized perception have operated. We ought therefore to be suspicious of any structure of government that separates, as the founders tried to do, reason from experience: that is, to expect legislators to operate on the basis of concepts in isolation from the life experience that gives them their content. To understand this insight, it is helpful to review briefly Kant's theory of knowledge acquisition.

Nature gives humans a multitude of perceptions. Perception would be overwhelmed except for a function of the mind that prevents such an overflow, which Kant called *intuition*. He meant not what we think of today—a sort of hunch—but rather an organizing function of the mind, which takes manifold sense perceptions and puts them together into *objects,* organizing what is given in terms of where, when, and how much. Because intuition puts each object together, the operation is called *synthesis.*

Reason then operates on the objects thus cast up, taking them apart (*analysis*) and redefining them in terms of reason's own categories: quality, quantity, relation, and modality. Examining a thing by reference to these categories, reason ultimately gives us a rational (i.e., logical) understanding of what we are confronting. That which stood over and against us is now re-presented in our minds, not in its original perceptual form but as the *concept* of an object. Note that the categories by which analysis is driven are derived from logic alone, not from experience.

Though he says understanding is possible only under the guidance of the categories of reason (logic), Kant (1787) emphasizes that the concepts we make of things in this way must, of course, have a content. Human understanding of nature has two aspects: first, the acquisition of content through *sensibility* (perception) and only secondarily, the shaping of things under the categories of logic. We must therefore, he says, "distinguish the science of the rules of sensibility in general, that is, aesthetic, from the science of the rules of the understanding in general, that is, logic" (p. 77). Both, however, are necessary for knowledge.

Finally, Kant gives us a warning on the relation between pure reason (i.e., thinking as the arrangement and rearrangement of concepts) and sensibility to things (intuition, or the organization of perception). "Thoughts without content are empty, intuitions without concepts are blind" (pp. 75-76). It follows that knowledge acquisition is empty if it emphasizes merely the logical manipulation of concepts without repeated contact with the function of intuition. We can see, however, that this is precisely the tendency in re-presentative government. Let us therefore carry the Kantian scheme of understanding over into the realm of political representation.

Political Sensibility

We see immediately: Legislators are forced to operate with re-presentations of people's lived experience, because immersion in the direct experience of others is denied them. Legislators think, they do not know. The result must be laws in which people can recognize their own experience only insofar as they themselves can think of such experience in abstract terms. In laws based on re-presented knowledge, people cannot recognize the fullness of their own experiences. Instead, laws become empty concepts with the binding authority of reason rather than of lived experience.

Thus, Kant's argument gives us some insight into the dangers of exaggerating the rule of reason in politics. The more rationalistic laws become ("thoughts without content"), the more sterile they seem, and the farther removed from people's lives. This estrangement is all the more acute when we recall that people are quite capable of applying in their daily experiences a sensible logic of their own, one just good enough for the immediate problems at hand (Husserl, 1937/1970, p. 125). Therefore, unless people can be totally persuaded that their own experience counts for nothing, or counts only as a statistic, increasing rationalization of laws produces an everwidening gap between political representation and human experience.

The problem of lost sensibility, however, is actually worse than a purely Kantian analysis suggests. Despite his emphasis on the empirical content of abstract concepts and his demand for sensibility, Kant denigrated the fact that there are aspects of experience that do not lend themselves to being subsumed under universal categories of reason. Re-presentative science, like representative government, is a knowledge system that lends itself to generalities rather than particulars. But it is in the particulars of people's lives that care, rather than reason, arises.

Toward a Politics of Care

Although Kant, by emphasizing the role of sensibility in imparting content to concepts, tried to forestall reason's tendency to dominate experience, his effort applied only to physical things, whose extension in time and space can be measured. He did not aim to deal with aspects of experience that are not material. What are these aspects, and what is their relevance to the problem of political representation?

Here another philosophical inquiry comes to our aid. Martin Heidegger points out that there are life experiences that do not lend themselves to the kind of re-presentation, that is, conceptualization, necessary for scientific study, and yet are experienced. For example, there is the experience of love for another human being and our care for things (Heidegger, 1962). This implies that some of the most important things in our lives are difficult if not impossible to represent, whether in science or government thinking. They cannot withstand the tests of location in time and space and of intensity, and are only poorly understood by means of logical analysis. For example, the *dis*-ease we feel when we are ill is poorly captured in health policy thinking under categories like *diagnosis-related groups* or, even more telling, *managed care*. Similarly, human well-being becomes the abstraction *welfare*, a term narrowly applied to vulnerable people. At one point in our history, our longing for peace was translated by the "Defense" Department into *permanent prehostility*, with its own set of objective indicators, measuring readiness for war.

Kant would advise us that, where abstract reasoning has produced decisions empty of content, we should reemphasize the empirical (e.g., test weapons in the field instead of just on a computer; figure out ways for clinical experience to breathe life into objectifications like managed care). But the empirical itself is limited to what can be placed into dimensions of time, space, and magnitude.

What if we try to turn from overreliance on reason to care? Concepts determined by pure reason must always be abstract: Rational categories shape sensibility to immediate experience, and are not themselves capable of being shaped in turn, because they are based on reason alone. In contrast, care, as we will soon see, is a way of approaching life that shapes and is shaped by immediate experience. When we contrast reason and care, we begin to understand why it is inevitable that a government based increasingly on reason can dictate terms of civil order that appear to citizens, immersed in their daily lives, as essentially remote from that about which they care most.

Turning to Heidegger, we find that, in the interaction between human beings and things, the conditions that make experience possible show themselves. In other words, we exist, and know we exist, only in actual relation to other people and things, not in the abstract. In contrast to René Descartes's "I think therefore I am," which depends on a conceptual split between objects and human thought, Heidegger would assert that "I am, therefore I [can] think." Existence—"being-in-the-world" in specific circumstances—comes before knowing. Unless we have already shown an interest in a thing, unless we have already connected with it, we cannot analyze it through reason. For Heidegger, *care* is what makes possible that connection, that being-in-relationship to something or someone.

Care, as Heidegger used the term, is a difficult notion to grasp, because it is already functioning before we can begin to think about it. By care, he did not mean just the actual cares of life or the care we feel for the people we love (although these are aspects of the broader term), but something more basic: our situated living itself, our always finding ourselves in actual situations, enmeshed in relationships with things and other people. These we already care about, defining our world before we are able to analyze it. Heidegger intended us to become aware that the existence of each one of us is not an abstract concept but a "being-in-the-world." Care is that attentiveness or concern that enables us to orient ourselves toward and connect with things and people in our world and to be aware of those connections. In this scheme, through care, not only does the world become meaningful, but the world is brought into being. Conceptual understanding or thought is only possible because of our experience of life's web of connections: Concepts arise out of life.

Therefore, the basis of American politics—interest—is a derivative of care, of our orientation toward original real-life connections. To understand what people want from politics, then, it is necessary to understand politics in terms of people's care (their attentiveness to their world) and cares (the concerns that arise for them from that world). These have their roots in the most fundamental level of human existence: people's relationships to other people and things, in actual situations.

Here we can begin to see the possibility and structure of democratic knowledge. Within the sweep of care with which people construct their world, all people—all of us—are united. Care, the attentiveness that connects us to others and things, unites us democratically as human beings; differentiations are secondary. One answer, then, to the problem of knowledge in government is as follows: Where governance emphasizes reason to the detriment of care, people need to find and protect spaces in which attention to care, to the interactive fabric of life, can produce both natural connections and oppositions among them, thereby grounding politics in reasonability rather than abstract reason.

How might we move toward this alternative? Consider democratic knowledge. Such knowledge is rooted in participation, disclosed in the course of shared experience. Such direct experience includes talking together about public things (see Foley's discussion in Chapter 9). In democratic knowledge, concepts as ways of talking about things or states of affairs arise out of *care*-ful relationship. In this mode of knowledge, the truth of the situation is uncovered by a political community in the openness of politics. There, what emerges is a letting-come-into-being that reveals the truth of the situation and discloses possibilities. There, a noninstrumental relationship is entered into for its own sake and not simply to accomplish an objective. In contrast to problem solving, which closes off definitions, discussions, and debate in order to move on, democratic knowledge involves grounded understanding, living in the situation further, trying things out, and learning from what happens. Problem solving tries to make a final statement, letting-be remains open. Truth, never final, emerges from the courage to let be. In this context, citizen participation can be seen not as an instrument of bureaucratic action, but a way of living political life concretely.

The phenomenologist Eugene Gendlin (1973) says, "Experience has its own kind of order" (p. 319). Citizen participation lets that order emerge, partly but never totally inventing it. It entails deliberation on practical questions, rather than the discovery of scientific knowledge.

CONSTRUCTING DEMOCRATIC KNOWLEDGE

So pervasive in American political life is our dependence on the idea of representation that proposed alternatives face a tough battle even to gain a hearing. In particular, notions that ordinary people have useful knowledge and that their involvement in governing is not only desirable but feasible tend to be dismissed as, at best, romantic pipe dreams, and at worst, dangerous threats to public order (see Schmidt, 1993). Critics charge that human nature is either too passionate and selfish or too passive and apathetic. Knowledge that comes from daily living is decried as subjective and self-interested, not objective, detached, and scientific. Modern-day government is said to be too big and complex to make room for ordinary people and too dependent on the expertise of professional politicians and bureaucrats. Life will be safer, more stable, and more productive, say the critics, if experts handle the governing while people pursue their private concerns, occasionally donning the role of citizen to visit the voting booth to choose their leaders (for a summary of these arguments, see Pennock, 1979; Stivers, 1990b).

People's distaste for big government and their increasing disaffection for public life has some leaders worried. But the solutions they pose tend to divert people from true participation. "Restoring community" and volunteering are side tracks that keep people from participating in governance.

People are encouraged to become Big Brothers or Big Sisters to disadvantaged youngsters, or to organize their neighbors for block cleanups. Examples include President George Bush's "thousand points of light" or the 1997 Presidents' Summit on Citizen Service, where President Bill Clinton declared that the age of big government was over, calling instead for "big citizenship," that is, voluntarism. Worthy as such private efforts are, they neglect important differences between volunteering and being an active citizen.

In the previous section, we reviewed how the elevation of abstract concepts over the knowledge that comes from daily life has supported a governmental system set up to filter out the passions and interests of the many and restrict the exercise of power to the few on the grounds of superior—rational—knowledge. Now we want to explore how the turn from reason to care, from re-presented to experience-based knowledge, reshapes the idea of politics, that is, of public life. "The public" is an intersubjective phenomenon: Public life is, simply, the talk that goes on in public about public concerns. As long as public life is restricted to abstractions and special interests, representative government will continue to be in large part a poor substitute for democracy. On the other hand, even within representative government lie many spaces of opportunity for the exercise of a different kind of publicness, one constituted by the care-ful connections among people—in other words, spaces for the growth and exercise of democratic knowledge. Democratic knowledge entails both a groundedness in daily life and the exercise of a kind of judgment that takes into account the needs and views of others, that is, by reference to the real, or what is a common issue for them, not in terms of abstractions.

Reopening the Public

In much of Western political thought, a sharp line has been drawn between the public and private realms. This is particularly true of the classical liberal philosophy on which the founders' theory of representative government was based. In this framework, the most important task is to limit the scope of government and keep it from encroaching on people's private lives. The justification for this approach is this: Freedom requires limited government, hence a drastically constrained public space.

This hard and fast line between public and private bars from public debate most of the lived experience of ordinary people, which occurs in all its variety mostly in private. Only those ideas that can be abstracted from experience, smoothed out and universalized in terms of interests, rights,

---

From the Conversation: The Public-Private Split

(A conversation that ensued as a result of Cheryl sending a personal message, intended only for Lisa, to all the members on the listserv.)

Cheryl: Friends and colleagues: Part of my ability to recover from my mortification over accidentally sending the personal message to all arises from your affirming and supportive responses to my "accidental message." I feel comforted. Thanks. Cam wrote to me: "I can imagine you are feeling chagrined by having sent that message by mistake. When I read it I knew it must have been sent in error, but for a moment, I had a flash of—wow, wouldn't it be great if our community of voices were a real community and we could share these kinds of things with one another! So, although I guess you're right to consider it a 'mistake,' it's one I wish we were all capable of making (another instance of the public-private split, no?)."

Cam: I think you may be right, that some reference to your accidental message might be quite appropriate at some point in the book. One thing that comes to mind—when I was working as a sort of community organizer I found that if I was serious I had to engage with people where they were rather than around what I saw as the agenda. So people had a way, when I said I was there to help, of asking me stuff like whether I could help them get a baby-sitter. In other words, they didn't see a line between public problems and personal problems. If I wanted to connect, I couldn't ignore any way in which they reached out.

Richard: I felt as Cam did when I wrote to Cheryl about her "mistake." Cheryl has opened issues that face many of us, and that in one way or another influence the ways we see our work and the field as a whole. It would be healthy for us to able to talk about these things (more "undiscussables"?) . . .

Lisa: On the public-private split: I think this strand of the conversation, evolving as it has from Cheryl's "mistake" message, is really interesting. Liberalism, of course, has deliberately separated the public and the private domains. For women, this separation has had the effect of removing them, their perspectives, and their interests from most of the discussion of politics and philosophy. Before Cheryl's "mistake," our interactions were at the level of our public personas; even though most of us were at least acquainted, our correspondences were not personal. After Cheryl's message, the tone of our missives changed; they became more reflective of friendship, sympathy, solidarity, and care—even as we continued to discuss questions of the "public" sphere.

---

and voting patterns, are admitted to the public arena. If this is the case, then creating a place in public life for lived experience involves not getting rid of the public-private divide, but *opening up* our idea of the public. Such an opening would admit into the public space the knowing and thinking of ordinary people. It would enable meaningful concepts (meaningful because based in daily life) to arise out of conversation in public on public issues.

The political philosopher Hannah Arendt addressed the idea of expanding the public space. She argued that reason should not be the grounding for politics, because political action would become an instrument for implementing "the truth" determined elsewhere, that is, in the minds of powerful experts. People will inevitably have differing views about important questions affecting their lives together. If we approach those questions with the idea that what we are trying to do is resolve differences in order to reach absolute truth, then there is really no point in having a debate. Instead, we could do an experiment or some other analysis that leads to proven conclusions (Arendt, 1968).

But political questions, Arendt argued, are not factual. There are no conceptual "yardsticks" by which to measure them, nor "banisters" of accepted values to cling to as we argue about them (Villa, 1996, pp. 162-163). Reliance on such props thins out public life by giving us the idea that the debate can be settled once and for all by reference to some external standard. But Arendt was insistent that public life is possible only where human beings, different yet equal, listen to one another as they speak about that which is of concern for them. The public space is constructed out of this shared expression of care, not on the basis of consensus.

We see in Arendt's argument the connection between the kind of knowledge we depend on in public debate and the kind of governing processes we get as a result. Arendt believed that reliance on reason-based scientific knowledge would shut down public discussion: Who can argue with the results of the scientific method? Public questions are different from scientific or technical questions: They are questions we have to face without yardsticks or banisters. They are questions to which reasonable answers emerge in the course of argument. Therefore the public space is not a definitively closed space, but a fundamentally open one: open precisely because of the lack of external truth standards. In this openness, Arendt argued, lies our freedom. Otherwise, we must bow to "The Truth" determined elsewhere.

But what about the public decisions that have to be made? Governing is not just talk; it is having to deliberate, then act. This brings us to the question of judgment: On what basis do we weigh what to do next? If we are not guided by yardsticks and banisters, how do we move forward?

Political Judgment and Representativeness

Arendt believed that even though there are no absolute standards, such as reason or the scientific method or transcendental values, by which public questions can be definitively resolved, this does not necessarily mean that anything goes. The coherence of public space depends on the exercise of judgment. Judgment enables differing individuals to deliberate together. Even though people argue, judgment keeps public space intact, neither closing it off nor allowing it to degenerate into a Hobbesian war of all against all.

Hannah Arendt died before she could write the full treatment of her views on judging that would have formed the third section of *The Life of the Mind* (1978). But we can see the outlines of her thinking in her *Lectures on Kant's Political Philosophy* (1982). She based her own ideas about judging on Kant's argument that the very faculty of thinking depends on public use, on putting thoughts to the test of examination by others. Reason, so understood, is made "to get into community with others" (p. 40). Arendt argued, as had Kant, that this testing that arises from contact with other people's thoughts, from taking the viewpoints of others into account, leads to an enlargement of one's own mind. The process she envisioned was something she called "training one's imagination to go visiting" (p. 43; see also Kant, 1790/1987). This is a process by which we use the imagination to put ourselves in another's place, not in order to empathize with them but simply to understand how the world looks from another viewpoint.

Arendt held that people only judge as members of the human community, not as gods. My judgment takes the possible judgment of others into account. The standard that governs judgment, then, is what Kant called the *sensus communis*: common sense, or better, sense of the common. Kant referred here not merely to the aggregate of all views, but to a sense of the between: the *inter-esse*, or understanding of the public interest that emerges from interaction. We judge by putting ourselves in the place of others, comparing our possible judgment with theirs. Judgment therefore liberates us from the privacy and particularity of our own situations, but without discarding them. Instead, judgment makes it possible for us to see both the connections and differences between our situation and that of others. Arendt said that judgment is a faculty that "mysteriously" combines the particular and the general, subjectivity and objectivity. It is a faculty that is acquired only through practicing it, not by following a set of abstract rules.

Arendt (1968) said, "I form an opinion by considering a given issue from different viewpoints, by making present to my mind the standpoints of those who are absent, that is, I represent them" (p. 241). The more standpoints I can imagine, the more valid—in the sense of true to the situation—my judgment will be. Yet I still must persuade others. By deliberating in public, offering my views and listening to those of others, together we discover what we have in common even as we state our differences. And what we have in common is not *purpose,* but a *world.* If politics is animated by the space itself, by the relationship, rather than by shared objectives, two things follow: First, the point of political life is debate, not consensus; second, political discourse brings the public space into being. It is sharing this space, rather than sharing opinions or values, that binds us together. The space does not depend on consensus; instead the space makes these possible (although it neither guarantees nor imposes them).

We can bring the public world into being through our talk because we all share the human condition: We all "find ourselves," through careful attentiveness, in an actual world, in a network of relationships to things and people, presented with many, though not limitless, possibilities. In these encounters, both conflictual and harmonious, we make possible the disclosure of meaningful content. The categories by which we understand the situation emerge from that situation, in the course of our interaction. As we understand, and as we judge and act, our acting is grounded not in the abstract operations of pure reason, but in the very interaction itself. The lack of external grounding is the basis of our freedom: It is what makes possible life, politics, our being who we are. If there were external standards (yardsticks) by which to measure our talk, there would be no need to deliberate. When we expand our imaginations to go visiting in order to understand other viewpoints, we employ a different kind of representativeness than the one we have criticized in this chapter. First, this representativeness is not abstract, but based on the ability to connect the conditions of one's life with the conditions of others, not in order to agree but to get a sense of the situations of others. Second, this representativeness is not a substitute for public debate, but an enabling feature of it. It is what makes it possible for a group of people engaged in public talk to know that their talk is indeed public, because it reaches beyond themselves. The understanding they reach is not a closing off, a solution, but a reflective practice, a living further in the situation while applying their interpretation. In this mode of public life, citizenship becomes not an instrument of correct action, but a way of living political life concretely, of constructing democratic knowledge.

Public Talk in Public Agencies

Our venture into philosophy has given us a sense of the difference between the reason-dominated abstract knowledge on which our system of representative government is based, and the kind of open, interactive, concrete knowledge that we call *democratic.* The first has given us a public sphere constrained by the search for quasi-scientific truth and for right answers. The second offers the possibility of repoliticizing the public sphere by accepting the lack of final answers, the differing opinions, and the ongoing debate that constitute politics. We turn, here, away from the old understanding of politics as power struggles over who gets what, when, and how, toward encounters, often adversarial, about the nature of the political community itself. The point of politics is not the answers it gives, but the process, connections, and arguments it makes possible. This does not mean that real issues cannot be dealt with, only that as long as we put the rationalist search for final answers in the driver's seat, we ensure that the process is on track to a dead end—to the obliteration of public life.

* * *

To return to the communities introduced at the beginning of this chapter: Can they be seen as engaging in the kind of practice described here? Can their work be seen as grounded in something that qualifies as democratic knowledge?

Consider what one community board member says about working with people in her community:

> We'd take a jar of instant coffee and donuts and knock on people's doors . . . find out who the spokesperson was in the building and ask if we could use their living room. It wasn't hard to find them. When you asked who talks a lot about health around here, people could always tell you. (Stivers, 1988, p. 159)

Board members, themselves residents of the communities served by their centers, developed their "sense of the common" through actual conversations with neighbors. Because they literally "went visiting," their judging was grounded in tangible contact with the lives of others. Through such networking, they spread the word about the services offered and found out what people's needs and opinions were. When it came time to deliberate, they had broadened their own sense of what was at stake and how their actions would affect people's lives. Community people, for their part, came to see the center as part of the community, run by people they knew and knew how to find if they had a problem or complaint.

In their conversations with each other at meetings, board members "debated and discussed issues, but the whole board would support the final decision" (Stivers, 1988, p. 161). One board member commented, "We found that a big problem was housing. I fought to get that across to the other board members. Over time, I got them to see it" (p. 156). Gradually, participation in these conversations gives members a sense of the situation

From the Conversation: Making Public Spaces

Ralph and Cam: Lisa, we would like to contrast our theory of public spaces with your theory of the transformational admininistrator (see Chapter 7). The transformational administrator theory, in contrast to the theory of knowledge we present here, thinks it can produce or make conditions under which human beings can come into their own, specifically conditions for liberation and change. This suggests a correct answer can be found, within a system of communicative harmony, to what is wrong with our world: People will expose for all to see the prevailing inequities in power and the distribution of values.

Our theory suggests, not the opposite (which would be to conserve conditions that bind us to the status quo), but a third possibility: Wherever general rules confront particular experience, not only are incompatibilities seen, but opportunities for inventing new human realities open up. These are the public spaces formed where logic and experience, law and life, administrator and citizen, meet.

Instead of leaving the reading of the situation up to an administrator, the suggestion is to bring in the people involved. In the confrontation between what is rational (logical and generalizable) and what is reasonable (particular and meaningful to people), all those attending will have an opportunity to see what is going on and imagine alternative ways of living and working together (cf. Follett, 1918).

The task is not to make conditions, which people must then live up to (to force them to be free), but to recognize the times when one finds oneself in situations where one can operate fundamental levers of constructing one's own life. Before any such construction can take place, however, the attitude required is one not of "making" but of "letting emerge."

Lisa: Ralph and Cam, I believe you are overstating the differences between your "public spaces" and the transformative practice of public administration. The purpose of transformative practice is NOT to force people to be free, but to provide a safe space where citizens can bring their concerns to be fairly considered (in the normative, not the procedural, sense). In a way, it provides the therapeutic setting in which Gramsci's "catharsis" takes place (Zanetti & Carr, 1997).

Both approaches, it seems to me, value and encourage an "emergent" approach to finding solutions in the space—the nexus—where administrator and citizen, state and society, meet. It seems to me that a transformative practice of public administration meshes with your idea of a "politics of care." Transformative practice refers to the accomplishment of a reflective, self-aware manner of human interaction with the world. Such a practice calls for "practical-critical" activity, in which individuals become capable of recognizing that society is open to transformation into one that permits the full attainment of human potential. Like Gramsci's "philosophy of praxis," transformative practice is both philosophical and political, and does not tolerate a separation between "elite" intellectuals and everyday citizens. Transformation cannot occur of its own accord, but must be built through purposive human action.

All theoretical systems and approaches have values. A key difference is that the values of a transformative practice are stated up front and made clear to all—placed on the table, so to speak. Where the transformative practice of public administration—and critical approaches generally—have greater promise, I suggest, is precisely in their refusal to abandon the normative foundation of substantive equality and democracy. We should not be satisfied with "democratic" outcomes of power-skewed political systems. We can do better than that, and we should.

Ralph and Cam: As you say, Lisa, there are some areas of commonality between your idea of transformative public administration and our idea of public spaces. Both are emergent, for example. One difference, though, is that we don't seek a "safe" space, but simply a space for people to talk to one another, with all the risks for everyone that go along with that. We believe that citizens come into such conversations a lot more equal than you say. Their knowledge of their lives has as much weight as the critical (or any other) administrator's theoretical perspectives and values. The dialogue in that space is not between enlightened administrators, who have the "right" (transformative) values, and citizens who need to have their understandings of their lives transformed, but among a group of people, all of whom know things and all of whom have things to learn. What emerges from their interaction can't be constrained up front by a set of values, even transformative ones. That's the kind of interaction we think is truly transformative.

Lisa: I agree that the dialogue must be among a "group of people, all of whom know things and all of whom have things to learn." But aren't you also putting forward a set of values—a more substantive democracy, for example, or a richer theory of knowledge—that will shape the outcome of the dialogue? The absence of a defining set of values will result in nothing but nihilism or chaos. The administrator in a transformative practice is not the agenda setter, ultimately the citizens are. But I must disagree and argue that it is tremendously necessary to provide the "safe space" for people to speak. People who do not feel safe will NOT speak; they will not offer their experiences, they will not offer solutions, they will continue to feel removed and "out of the loop" as they currently feel. By providing the safe space, the administrator committed to transformative practice draws citizens in, earns their trust, and encourages them to find the voice that had been silenced or ignored for so long. Isn't that what a "politics of care" should be all about?

they share, so that when a big issue arises, they are equipped to deal with it and to envision possibilities. As one member said, "When moves are necessary, it's something we've already talked about" (p. 156). Another put it this way: "The board is cohesive; they may see the issues differently but they are of one purpose," namely, "to be of service . . . to advocate, struggle and fight" for "people who need us" (p. 153).

Interactions between federal officials and community members are not always harmonious, nor is harmony the goal. Community members want as much leeway as possible in their use of the funds; they want their own interpretations of the regulations to guide them. Federal officials, who feel their own responsibility to make sure the money is spent legally and wisely, seek both to enable and to constrain citizen actions—one project officer referred to himself as part "cop" and part "consultant" (Stivers, 1988, p. 164). But even so, one can observe how in conversations between them, shared understanding of the meaning of key terms links both public administrators and citizens together into a public space. Even as they argue about technical terms like *group practice, clinical effectiveness,* or *administrative cost ratio,* through their shared attentiveness to the situation they weave together a public space. Citizens bring to bear the knowledge they have developed out of living in the communities being served, and public administrators find themselves not imposing abstract definitions, but negotiating with citizens until they find an understanding both can live with. They do this not by applying external yardsticks or banisters, but on the basis of their care, out of which comes a felt sense of what the situation requires.

Whereas it is true that the federal government has the upper hand in the sense that it can withdraw the funds, it is also true that in this case the agency cannot do its work without citizens, either legally or practically—as one project officer said, "The community representatives [are] the pulse of the people" (Stivers, 1988, p. 170). Public administrators must find ways to work with community members, and this means acknowledging that the community has significant authority over the conduct of project affairs: not just legal authority, but the authoritative judgment that comes from being grounded in real life. Here, public administrators must trust citizens to understand program implementation and to carry it out in their own communities. Only citizens have the direct knowledge that makes it possible to connect the abstractions of the law with the real needs of people. What is at stake in such situations is the underlying knowledge about the state of the community—actual and potential—against which judgments about policy can be made. Democratic knowledge is the condition of sound policy judgment. Here, where democratic knowledge is constructed in conversations between public officials and citizens about matters of public policy, representativeness loosens its hold on the public space, and citizens become able to say, through experience, that *Government is us.*

Chapter 4

CITIZENS AND ADMINISTRATORS

Roles and Relationships

Cheryl Simrell King and Camilla Stivers

Thus far in our attempts to understand the American people's anti-government feelings, we have looked at the history of popular attitudes toward government, the current political economy and its impact on citizens' lives, and the knowledge gap that lies at the heart of representative government. To fill out the picture, one more element is important: the respective ways in which citizenship and administration have been understood and practiced in the United States. It is safe to say that, in general, neither citizens nor administrators are happy with their roles and relationships in the late 20th century, nor are they happy with each other. For every citizen cry against the bureaucracy, there is a matching administrative response that disparages a lazy, apathetic, and uncommitted citizenry. As a Harwood Group study for the Kettering Foundation (1991) states, although Americans have always been distrustful and cynical about government, never before have officials and citizens been so disconnected from each other.

As we will see, throughout our history, ideas about citizenship have given it a constricted and instrumental role, one borne out in the rather limited and distanced part citizens actually play in government today. On the other hand, ideas about the proper role of administration and its actual part in U.S. governance have expanded during the past 200 years. After reviewing the development of these respective roles and how they appear today, this chapter concludes with a discussion of their implications for public administrators and their sense of their working lives, drawing on research conducted especially for this book.

49

CHANGING IDEAS OF CITIZENSHIP AND ADMINISTRATION

The citizen role in U.S. governance has been defined narrowly since the founding. As the *Federalist Papers* made clear, the founders believed that the extended geographic scope and social complexity of the new American state made direct participation by citizens unworkable. James Madison argued that popular governance could only work in "a small spot" (Cooke, 1961, p. 84). More important, however, in Madison's view, was the propensity of popular governments to the "violence of faction" and their tendency to produce decisions based on "the superior force of an interested and overbearing majority" (p. 57). Representation would not only make it possible to extend government over a large area but, by restricting citizen involvement to the selection of representatives, would "refine and enlarge the public views, by passing them through the medium of a chosen body of citizens, whose wisdom may best discern the true interest of their country" (pp. 62-63). Thus, the founders' faith in the will of the people was tempered by acute awareness of the potentially negative effects of citizen power, particularly citizens who were not of the "chosen body."

The Federalists held that, by and large, ordinary people were neither qualified for nor interested in participating directly in governance. A well-run government would win the continuing allegiance of citizens and make their involvement, other than as voters, unnecessary. Alexander Hamilton argued that as people grew accustomed to national authority "in the common occurrences of their political life," familiarity would "put in motion the most active springs of the human heart" and win for the national government "the respect and attachment of the community" (Cooke, 1961, p. 173). This argument, grounded in a view of the people as the legitimate source of legitimacy but in need of protection against their own errors and delusions, sounds a theme that persists throughout subsequent thinking about the relation between citizenship and administration. Instead of a democracy "of the people, by the people, and for the people," the founders' democracy would be an "elite republic of elected representatives who would deliberate together and speak *for* the people" (Fishkin, 1995, p. 21).

The founders' skepticism about the governing abilities of ordinary people made them confine the citizen role to that of voter. Voting is, in fact, the only guaranteed citizenship activity in the United States. If you are of a certain age, were born in the United States or have been naturalized, and have not lost your citizenship rights, you can participate in the voting process. Although, as we have seen, electoral turnouts have varied over the course of U.S. history, voting remains the defining feature of citizenship. In this context, being a citizen means exercising the right to choose political leaders, nothing more. Citizenship is much more a status than a practice.

Perhaps because voting is such a restricted role, less that half of eligible voters today cast ballots in presidential elections; turnouts in state and local races are generally even lower. A 1992 national election study showed that 78% of white, 67% of black, and 61% of Hispanic registered voters actually cast ballots (Flanigan & Zingale, 1994). Registration rates are lower for blacks and Hispanics than for whites, making these voting rates even more problematic. College graduates are more likely to vote than are those with a high school diploma. Those who do not complete high school are least likely to vote. Thus, in practice, there is a class and race bias to the electorate. And those who do vote may be more likely than in the past to feel disaffected, as was seen in 1992 and 1994, "Years of the Angry Voter."

During the early years of the United States, while the public role of ordinary people was restricted to voting, governing was left safely in the hands of wise leaders. From the time of George Washington through the presidency of John Quincy Adams, what Frederick C. Mosher (1982) called "government by gentlemen" prevailed. Although government during this period was generally small and weak, the ambiguity of the Constitution about the proper role of administration planted the seeds of what would become a continuing struggle between the executive and Congress for control of administrative agencies, one that created a space in which agencies "set about developing power resources of their own" (Nelson, 1982, p. 755). During this period, however, the federal government mostly delivered mail, fought wars, secured new territories, and collected customs and excise taxes. Administrative agencies were organized in a semi-aristocratic rather than a bureaucratic fashion, one based on the sense that administration was a "mystery . . . [therefore] a fitting vocation for men who were supposed to carry the knack for governance in their blood and breeding" (Matthew Crenson, quoted in Nelson, 1982, p. 756). Kinship and class shaped membership in the early administrative echelons.

Not until the presidency of Andrew Jackson did thinking about the capacities and proper role of citizens and administrators change. Jacksonian thinking closed the gap between the two, in theory and practice, at least for a time. Jackson asserted, "The duties of all public officers are, or at least admit of being made, so plain and simple that men of intelligence may readily qualify themselves for their performance" (quoted in Nelson, 1982, p. 759). This philosophy greatly expanded the pool of fit candidates for administrative office, from the well-born to any citizen who had demonstrated his loyalty to the political party in power (still confined, during this period, to anyone white and male). Government jobs became, in Senator

William Marcy's famous words, "the spoils" of electoral victory (Nelson, 1982, p. 759). The door to direct involvement in governmental processes was opened to a great many ordinary citizens. Throughout the balance of the 19th century, citizens were not only voters, they could also see themselves as, potentially, occupants of administrative jobs; in other words, as participants in governance.

As we saw in the Introduction, this new view of citizenship led to an upwelling of public activity: meetings, rallies, parades, and the like. For those who qualified, the citizen role was not just a legal status but a performance. In small towns, citizens and their officials worked closely together to govern their communities, although only a select group of citizens was actually involved (Skowronek, 1982; Wiebe, 1967). In rural areas, citizen involvement was paternalistic, populist, and moralistic: "Daily life among the conflicts and inequalities in these intimate communities was eased by community values emphasizing neighborly morality as well as a nonconfrontational norm for public demeanor of exhibiting friendliness and egalitarianism" (Tauxe, 1995, p. 473). In urban areas, participation was engendered through political machines, where party loyalty for the ordinary man or money and influence for the rich could buy participation in politics and administration. Yet for every person in a town, city, or rural area who felt a part of their government, there were handfuls more who were on the outside: slaves or those one step from slavery, women, immigrants, and other marginal people.

The administrative role, still limited by the restricted scope of government responsibilities, was defined largely by ties to political parties. Jackson, however, sought to systematize agency processes somewhat in order to make good on his statement that anyone could do government work (Morone, 1990), thus beginning the slow march toward bureaucratization. Government jobs functioned as a career ladder for immigrants and other men of modest means who had proven their worth to party leaders. When one party was swept out of office at election time, all the workers who had gotten their jobs through that party disappeared, to be replaced by loyalists of the rival party.

The extent to which this broadly democratic approach to administration produced governments riddled with corruption and incapable of efficient execution of the laws is a matter of debate. Today our view of the Jacksonian approach and the machine governments it produced is colored by the aspersions of turn-of-the-century Progressive reformers who sought to dislodge party loyalists and install themselves, or people like them, in the halls of administration. In any event, in the late 19th and early 20th centuries another sea change occurred in views of citizenship and administration, one that reversed the emphasis on direct involvement of ordinary citizens and the simplicity of government work, arguing instead the need for administrative expertise.

Woodrow Wilson's (1887) famous essay, "The Study of Administration," is emblematic of the shift. Arguing that administration was the prime governmental challenge, Wilson asserted the need for business-like and expert methods. Echoing Hamilton, he believed that administrators should be given considerable latitude in the execution of their duties, a freedom that was defensible because, he argued, administration was not political. Administrators carried out the laws, holding themselves accountable to the citizenry at large, whose role was to serve as ultimate source of legitimacy and not to become meddlesome. Citizens became the source of something called public opinion, a factor in political life that ever since has been the object of keen interest, if not outright manipulation, on the part of governmental leaders, as ubiquitous opinion polls today on every conceivable topic and candidate for office attest.

Progressive reformers, concerned with rescuing governments, especially city governments, from what they saw as the ill effects of machine politics, called for administrative practice based on scientific knowledge. In their view, the proper role of citizens in the reform process was to inform themselves about issues and rally around the quest for efficient, expert government methods. Progressives sought, then, to improve public opinion by making it judicious rather than meddlesome. Citizens were assured that the experts and professional administrators were more capable of handling public problems and situations and were better able to make decisions than common folk. The public service, growing rapidly due to the need for infrastructure and services, particularly in cities, was developing into a government "of the technocrats, by the technocrats, and for the technocrats" (Kearny & Sinha, 1988, p. 571).

Whereas the reformers saw the dissemination of technical knowledge as a means of improving the relationship between citizens and their government by informing citizens, which would lead to citizen understanding and support for government, over time, as Dwight Waldo (1948) observed, "research and facts have come to be regarded less and less as devices of citizen cooperation and control and more and more as instruments of executive management" (p. 43n). The advent of scientific management and efforts to professionalize the public service transmuted facts from ammunition for what had been called "efficient citizenship" to the basis of increasingly specialized modes of public administration.

Vast increases in the size and scope of governments at all levels during the first half of the 20th century seemed to justify the continuing call for expert, professional administration. In this environment, citizens relied on policy makers and administrators to make decisions that "enhance[d] the greater good of the community" (Parr & Gates, 1989, p. 55). The administrator was charged with implementing programs that met the policy directives of elected officials. Citizens, busy with the demands of an increasingly complex world and recovering from wars and economic depressions tended to trust, or at least to tolerate, decisions made by administrators. Trust in a knowledgeable elite grew out of increasing reliance on science, and on those who could practice it or apply it, to address difficult issues of industrialization and technological progress. Demands for an active citizen role were muted during this period.

In the 1960s, however, the dialogue about citizenship and administration shifted once again. Growing public distrust of governmental institutions, engendered by events such as Watergate and the war in Vietnam, drove many citizens to challenge the legitimacy of administrative as well as political decisions (Parr & Gates, 1989). This distrust, coupled with federal mandates requiring more public participation, opened the door for citizens to become more involved in administrative processes. The Economic Opportunity Act of 1964, which launched the War on Poverty, called for "maximum feasible participation" by the poor in governmental programs aimed at solving their problems. It authorized a determinative role for citizens in deciding about sizable expenditures and the design and execution of significant programs, a role that met with vigorous resistance by established city governments. After only three years, the Green Amendment put poverty programs back under municipal control. Thus, the federal government flirtation with "power to the people" was extremely short-lived. Meaningful citizen involvement lived on here and there, for example, in the community health center program (see Hummel & Stivers, Chapter 3) and in a plethora of administrative regulations aimed at getting citizen input. In practice, however, many of these regulations were interpreted in a fashion that turned citizen participation into an instrument for the achievement of administrative objectives rather than genuine collaboration or the sharing of authority with citizens.

Generally speaking, citizens came to be seen as clients or consumers, whose needs and demands, although legitimate, tended to compromise the rational allocation of resources and the impartiality of standardized procedures. Citizens were viewed as passive recipients of governmental services rather than active agents who could work with administrators to deal meaningfully with their predicaments. Requirements for citizen participation were generally treated in administrative agencies as a cost of doing business instead of as an asset to effectiveness or a responsibility worth carrying out for its own sake (Jones, 1981; Mladenka, 1981; Thomas, 1995). At best, citizens were viewed as a constituency, the source of important political support (MacNair, Caldwell, & Pollane, 1983) or of important values to guide policy decisions (Stewart, Dennis, & Ely, 1984). Only in the notion of *co-production* (Sharp, 1980) could an active citizen role be glimpsed. Coproduction was based on the idea that citizens could play an active part in the production and delivery of services; yet the idea faced uphill sledding in the context of widespread skepticism among administrators and politicians about the skills and wisdom of ordinary people. As a result, by the late 1970s, public participation began to be perceived as detracting from administrative expertise. Increasingly, administrators came to see citizen participation as a cost of doing public business. This attitude combined with a decreased level of community activism led to a decline in the practice of public participation.

In 1984, about 50 leading scholars and practitioners of public administration took part in a conference on citizenship and public administration held in New York City. Most of the participants were strongly committed to active citizenship but skeptical about its feasibility. Again and again throughout the discussions, speakers urged public administrators to broaden their base by encouraging members of the public to become active in agency work. A central part of the administrative role in these arguments was the education of citizens and their integration into administrative decision making and implementation. Yet many at the conference found it difficult to specify the particular forms and mechanisms through which such relationships could be nourished. "Cudgling my mind as I may," said Dwight Waldo (1984), "I cannot imagine what . . . it would look like in practice" (p. 108).

In fact, few documented models exist of successful citizen participation in governmental agency activities. Most discussions of it focus on theoretical pros or cons rather than showing how it works. Yet, as Dennis Thompson (1970) said, "Ideals have to be grounded in reality" (p. 30). The importance of living examples of active citizenship has been recognized at least since Phillip Selznick's classic case study, *TVA and the Grass Roots* (1949). Selznick argued that a commitment to democracy requires wrestling with the question of the concrete circumstances under which it can occur. Although Selznick's study is often cited as proof that citizens are inevitably co-opted by administrative agencies, his research in fact also lends strong support to the idea that the success of collaborative efforts to work with citizens depends on the nature of organizational arrangements:

> The tendency of democratic participation to break down into administrative involvement requires constant attention. This must be seen as part of the organizational problem of democracy and not as a matter of the morals or good will of administrative agents. . . . For the things which are important in the analysis of democracy are those which bind the hands of good men. We then learn that something more than virtue is necessary in the realm of circumstances and power. (p. 266)

The study by Berry, Portney, and Thomson (1993) of citizen involvement systems in five U.S. cities not only offers one of the few available detailed descriptions of such systems, but echoes Selznick in its emphasis on bringing to light organizational and other factors that contribute to success (see Foley, Chapter 11, this volume).

In the 1990s, environmental activism, new class social movements, neighborhood action in response to crime and other urban problems, and political organization around ideological issues led to a resurgence in public participation activity (Thomas, 1995; Timney, 1996) and to changes in the citizen-administrator relationship. Ironically, although participation in voting is at an all-time low (less than 25% of the eligible voting population elected President Clinton in 1996), and observers are decrying a general lack of civic involvement (e.g., Putnam, 1995), some citizens are demanding a place at the table in administrative decision making. According to a Kettering Foundation study (1991), citizens are not apathetic, as many claim, but rather, feel "impotent" (p. 4). Apathy implies a voluntary, intentional choice. Impotence is involuntary; citizens believe their lack of participation has been thrust on them, against their wishes.

In the current political economy, citizenship tends to be equated with paying taxes and consuming benefits. From this perspective, government uses up people's money and gives them back certain goods and services, a view that restricts possible relationships between citizens and officials. As long as citizens see themselves as taxpayers first and members of a civil collective second (if at all), consumption, or the purchase and use of goods and services, becomes the main connection between citizens and government. Citizens judge government by whether they feel satisfied with the results of their consumption.

Politicians and administrators play to these citizen perceptions. For example, in 1996, Camden County, New Jersey, opened a "county store" in a local mall. In addition to offering county services, the store also makes it possible for people to pay utility bills, register for school, attend small-business classes, register to vote, return library books, secure a photo ID, or get various health-related tests. The county has endeared itself to its residents and won awards for the concept. But, a recent *PA Times* article

The Spritual Condition of Citizenship

"Today, of course, many people who are disengaged from prevailing allegiances have not acquired new ones, and so are inattentive to political concerns of any kind. They are neither radical nor reactionary. They are inactionary. If we accept the Greek's definition of the idiot as an altogether private man, then we must conclude that many citizens of many societies are indeed idiots. This—and I use the word with care—this spiritual condition seems to me the key to much modern malaise among political intellectuals, as well as the key to much political bewilderment in modern society." (C. Wright Mills, 1959, p. 41)

referring to county citizens as "consumers" or "taxpayers" points out that the store was created to meet "taxpayer" demand for "value." For the store, success is measured by whether citizens feel they are getting their "money's worth" (Bezich, 1997, p. 1). Thus, the citizen role is couched in terms of purchasing decisions rather than in terms of a share in the authority and dignity of public life. In such cases, administrators seem to have swallowed whole the assumption that the entire point of public administration is keeping the customer happy.

Seeing citizens as consumers, taxpayers, and customers, and encouraging them to see themselves that way, leads people to evaluate government according to what each individual receives rather than what the community as a whole receives. It also obscures aspects of public life that extend beyond who gets what—such as who decides, who participates, and the quality of relationships among citizens and between citizens and government. When one's only yardstick for assessing government is how long one had to wait in line or the size of one's own stock of government goodies in comparison to those of others, it is easy to turn individual events and allocations into a sense of isolation and discontent. Political philosophers like John Stuart Mill and Alexis de Tocqueville argued that one of the chief benefits of direct citizen involvement in government was that ordinary people would come to see how their own lives were interwoven with the lives and fortunes of others and be able to raise their sights from what they themselves received from government to the overall good of the community. When people think of themselves as consumers or taxpayers and have no say in how things are decided, there is little prompting for them to take the high road and put the public interest ahead of their own private wants. At the same time, administrators see the ideal citizen as one who understands citizenship as being a follower, supporter, and ratifier of government action, conforming to the administratively defined mandate and climate.

The Progressive Legacy: Neutral Competence, Expertise, and Managerialism

Lisa Zanetti

For all its emphasis on technical expertise and political neutrality, the field of public administration was also born out of a desire for reform and some version of social justice. The Pendleton Act had instituted the beginnings of a competitive civil service to combat patronage and corruption in government (Van Riper, 1958). This reform set the stage for the social programs of the Progressive Era (Adams, 1992; Stever, 1986). "Adventurous pragmatists" such as Walter Lippman, Herbert Croly, Thorstein Veblen, John Dewey, and, to some extent, Mary Parker Follett saw in the philosophy of progressivism a means for setting into motion a reform agenda that would rehabilitate political liberalism, using a combination of organic idealism and pragmatism to justify placing the administrator as an important, and legitimate, agent of reform (Stever, 1986, 1990).

Organic idealism was most influential as an intellectual force in America in the northeast, particularly among the educated upper class. As a political philosophy, idealism originated in early 19th-century Europe, first among German philosophers such as Johann Fichte, Friedrich Schelling, and G. W. Friedrich Hegel, and later among the British idealists T. H. Green and his students, Bernard Bosanquet and L. T. Hobhouse. Whereas both the German and the British schools viewed the state as the visible, tangible expression of the achievement of abstract reason in a given nation, the British believed that the state could be constructed and administered democratically. The Germans tended to relinquish the construction and administration of the state to a strong central ruler and a dominant civil service class (Hollinger & Capper, 1989; Sabine & Thorson, 1973; Stever, 1986, 1990).

Green was particularly influential in revising the view of liberalism to one that recognized the mutual relationship between the individual and the social community. This independence was an ethical, not simply a legal, conception. Although the state could not compel individuals to be moral, it could create the conditions necessary to develop a responsible moral character—access to education, reduction of poverty, and regulation of the market, portrayed as a social institution rather than a natural condition. Liberalism, and liberal policies, ought to be an effort to provide a humane way of living to the largest number of persons (Sabine & Thorson, 1973).

Among public administrationists, the influence of idealism was most pronounced in the work of Wilson, Goodnow, and Follett.[1] Wilson and Follett were both exposed to the traditions of German idealism in their studies, but all proponents of an organic approach, in various ways, stressed the need for an evolutionary development of American liberal democracy and argued that the administrator could contribute to this evolution without being a disruptive influence. The vision was that of a nonthreatening administrator who could exercise the necessary technical competence within the democratic political framework (Stever, 1986, 1990).

The organic administrator stressed the need for social change to fit within the native tradition. Professional administrators could contribute to the stable evolution of the American social and political system, but the future would necessarily have to be constrained by the past. The concept of planning was incompatible with such a perception of the administrative role. When administrators did formulate and offer policy recommendations, these would be the carefully cultivated products of consensus (Stever, 1990).

Other Progressive thinkers were more influenced by the philosophy of pragmatism, however, and took very different approaches to the problem of administration. Pragmatism emerged from the late 19th-century preoccupation with the advances of science and the connection with social progress to become the most original and well-known contemporary American philosophy, particularly as it was expressed through the political theories of Dewey. The core of the philosophy was the belief that individuals must act continuously in an experimental fashion, testing beliefs and concepts against existence. Pragmatists rejected transcendent, absolute ideas that could not be confirmed by experience and action. Propositions could only be judged by the results produced when put into practice[2] (Adams, 1992; Lustig, 1982; Skowronek, 1982; Weinstein, 1968).

One of the foremost articulators of the pragmatic method was Charles Sanders Peirce. Peirce contended that any reliable approach to knowledge must meet two requirements: empirical, rule-bound methodology, and public, agreement-bound verification. He sought both continuity and communication. To avoid complete intellectual fragmentation on one side, and tyranny of opinion on the other, he proposed applying scientific methodology to the "community of inquirers" whose collective judgment would control and validate the belief, in line with a "critical common-sensism" (Buchler, 1955; Diggins, 1994).[3] Peirce had great faith in the redemptive power of science and the scientific method, believing that individuals would subsume their differences of opinion in the cause of truth, likening the power of science to both religious faith and romantic love.[4] He believed that the rigorous methods of science were intrinsically moral—that the cooperative ethos characteristic of scientific inquiry would provide an antidote to the ruthless individualism of capitalism (Buchler, 1955; Diggins, 1994).

Rather than viewing history and social change as a smooth, seamless, and evolutionary process, pragmatists partitioned history into periods of stability interspersed with rapid, dramatic, and sometimes revolutionary change. Sudden, sometimes disruptive, adjustments of social structure, law, custom, and interaction often became necessary during these periods. Progressive pragmatists contended that their own time was one such revolutionary era, with industrialization, urbanization, and rapid technological innovation requiring challenges to the social, political, and economic status quo. Pragmatist administrative theory pointed to the administrator as the agent capable of engineering and directing these changes. Such administrators, professionally trained in their areas of technical competence and unconstrained by partisan political considerations, grounded their framework in analytical and scientific reason and the dictates of logic (Stever, 1986, 1990).

The attitudes of the pragmatic progressives eventually prevailed and left the most definitive imprint on the practice of public administration. In particular, Dewey's public-oriented philosophy aimed to bring reflective analysis to the problems of society, defining ends and identifying means by which to achieve them. But pragmatism was also inherently utilitarian. Peirce observed that pragmatism was less about solving problems than about showing that supposed problems were not problems after all (cited in Diggins, 1994). The reformist impulses of men like Dewey came less from the philosophical impulse of pragmatism than from the fact that they were fundamentally decent individuals (Bronner, 1994).

In such a climate, it is not surprising that some citizens get fed up with following, accepting, and receiving what administrators think they should have. Many believe that their concerns will only be heard if they organize into protest groups and vocalize angrily about administrative policy decisions (Timney, 1996). Citizens involved in NIMBY (Not In My Backyard) actions believe they must turn to confrontation because administrators operate on the basis of their own (or their agency's) interests and aren't really concerned with the impact of agency actions on citizens (Kettering Foundation, 1991). In this context, citizens become dissenters, moving from what might have been collaboration with administrators to confrontation that pits them against administrators.

Many citizens perceive the information they receive from agencies as managed, controlled, and manipulated in order to limit their capacity to participate. They see the techniques of participation (public hearings, surveys, focus groups) as designed, at best, to generate input but to keep citizens on the outside of the governance process. They are particularly sensitive to vacuous or false participation efforts that ask for and then discount public input. Such inauthentic processes simply lead to greater tension between administrators and citizens. It is better not to work with citizens at all than to work with them under false, purely instrumental pretenses (King, Feltey, & Susel, 1998).

THE PUBLIC ADMINISTRATOR'S ROLE

As we saw previously, since early in the 20th century, the administrator's role has shifted from party loyalist, ensuring government's responsiveness to the needs of supporters, to neutral bureaucrat and professional expert. In conventional administrative situations, the administrator is the agent of the government, working in the in-between of systems and structures that link their profession, the government, and the citizenry. For many public servants, the first duty is to the profession and to norms of autonomy, hierarchy, and brotherhood (Stivers, 1993); the second duty is to the state or the agency; the third is to the citizenry. This framework, ironically, limits the administrator's exercise of authority by restricting the range of possible relationships between citizens and administration (Forester, 1989).

In the minds of citizen-taxpayers, there is a simple linear relationship between elected officials and civil servants. If they distinguish at all between the politician and the career government worker, it is to see the latter as simply carrying out orders determined politically. When government is viewed as the enemy, as it frequently is these days, administrators and street-level workers become the enemy's foot soldiers. As Tolchin (1996) states,

> No wonder the public now believes the worst about government; why shouldn't it, since it's been lied to so much in the recent past? But the public has gotten the facts mixed up. The lies have come more often from political leaders than from the bureaucracy, for whom the public has reserved most of its contempt. Alas, however, the bureaucrats have all too often served as handmaidens to leaders. (p. 35)

Front-line government workers, those who have most frequent and direct contact with ordinary citizens, are most likely to be the target of citizen wrath. For example, in the western United States, park rangers and foresters have begun traveling in teams and not wearing official uniforms for fear of attack. In the infamous bombing of the Alfred P. Murrah Building in Oklahoma City, street-level workers and their children bore the brunt of brutal violence against government. Because angry citizens can neither see nor get near those in command who craft the policies they disagree with, they vent their feelings on the infantry.

For their own part, practitioners have sought to couch their role in professional terms: to see themselves not as foot soldiers simply following orders, but as experts with a certain level of autonomy, who, in the context of vague statutes and conflicting mandates, have to make tough decisions about how to get things done. In this line of thinking, the administrator is the agent of the government, working in the in-between that links legislative initiatives and citizen recipients. Much of the recent theoretical work in public administration focuses on this "discretionary" role, seeking to justify the power it allocates to tenured, unelected bureaucrats (see Rohr, 1986; Wamsley et al., 1990). Although this professionalized view imparts dignity to what administrators do, it does little to encourage collaboration with citizens. In fact, when administrators think of themselves as professionals, their relationships with citizens tend to be instrumental, if not inauthentic and conflictual, with participation taking place too late in the process to make any real difference—that is, after issues have already been framed and most decisions made. Administrators become territorial and parochial, guarding information closely and relying on their technical and professional expertise to see them through the challenges of their work. The power that citizens exert, in response, is aimed at blocking or redirecting administrative efforts rather than at working as partners to establish parameters, set agendas, develop methods of investigation, and select approaches and techniques.

From the Conversation: Becoming an Expert

Mary: The reason I went to graduate school in the first place was a public decision which affected the neighborhood in which I lived. The community planner, working in concert with a property interest, approved building a fire substation at the entrance to our subdivision. There was ample land for this facility directly across the road from the subdivision, but the deputy fire chief happened to own the land selected. Two hundred residents attended a borough council meeting to protest, not because of NIMBY but because of genuine concern for the safety of our children. The firehouse would have been located beside the school bus stop. The borough manager and the mayor listened to our concerns and then informed us that we didn't have any standing because the planner was an expert and he had assured the council there was no problem. I decided to go to graduate school so I could be an expert too.

As many of the stories in the second part of this volume attest, sometimes administrators are able to see their own roles and their relationships with citizens more creatively, to forge ahead to build tangible partnerships with citizens, either working within existing organizational structures and processes or revamping them as they are able to. Building partnerships requires resigning exclusive reliance on professional expertise as the ground of administrative action, a difficult thing to do given the tenacity of the systems and structures in place and their tendency to reify relationships. In fact, building partnerships with citizens requires *redefining* expertise: seeing what citizens know as useful and relevant (see Chapter 3). Such dissenting from administration-as-usual in fact requires that one swim against the stream. Unfortunately, dissenters are likely to burn out, make promises to the citizenry that can't be kept, or end up having to "whistle-blow," or quit on principle (e.g., the recent high-level resignations in the federal Department of Health and Human Services over the terms of the new welfare-reform measures). These reactions, laudable as some are, do little to improve the administrator-citizen relationship.

HOW ADMINISTRATORS FEEL ABOUT THEIR WORK

Whereas much has been written, in this book and elsewhere, about how citizens feel about government and their relationship to it, little attempt has been made elsewhere to discover how administrators feel about practicing in such an anti-government climate and in what ways this climate has affected their work. Symptoms of a "debilitated public service" are said to be ubiquitous (Ban & Riccuci, 1991, p. 8), but there have been few studies

Experts and Expertise

(From the acceptance speech of Terri Swearingen, winner of the Goldman Environmental Prize, April 14, 1997.)

We have to reappraise what expertise is and who qualifies as an expert. There are two kinds of experts. There are the experts who are working in the corporate interest, who often serve to obscure the obvious and challenge common sense; and there are experts and nonexperts who are working in the public interest. From my experience, I am distrusting more and more the professional experts, not because they are not clever, but because they do not ask the right questions. And that's the difference between being clever and being wise. Einstein said, "A clever person solves a problem; a wise person avoids it." This lesson is extremely relevant to the nation, and to other countries as well, especially in developing economies. We have learned that the difference between being clever and being wise is the difference between working at the front end of the problem or working at the back end. Government that truly represents the best interests of its people must not be seduced by corporations that work at the back end of the problem—with chemicals, pesticides, incinerators, air pollution control equipment, etc. The corporate value system is threatening our health, our planet, and our very existence.

. . . We have become the real experts, not because of our title or the university we attended, but because we have been threatened and we have a different way of seeing the world. We know what is at stake. We have been forced to educate ourselves, and the final exam represents our children's future. WE know we have to ace the test because when it comes to our children, we cannot afford to fail. Because of this, we approach the problem with common sense and with passion. We don't buy into the notion that all it takes is better regulations and standards, better air pollution control devices and more bells and whistles. We don't believe that technology will solve all our problems. We know that we must get the front end of the problems, and that prevention is what it needed. We are leading the way to survival in the 21st century.

. . . Even after seeing so much abuse of the system that I have believed in, I still hold on to the slender hope that my government could once again return to representing citizens like me rather than rapacious corporate interests. If they do, then perhaps there is a future for our species; if they don't, we are doomed.

to find out exactly how demoralized government workers actually are and how they are coping in what they might well feel is a hostile environment.

One exception is the National Commission on the Public Service, popularly known as the Volcker Commission (Volcker, 1989). The Commission was convened to recommend action to the President and Congress on what was called "the quiet crisis," that is, the erosion of the public service at all levels, as the result of public attitudes, political leadership (or lack thereof), and internal management systems.

When the Commission turned its attention to the impact of bureaucracy bashing on the morale of public employees, not only did it discover low morale and declining self-respect, but also that (a) an increasing majority of upper-level public employees said that they would not recommend government service as a career to young people, particularly their own children; (b) bureaucracy bashing appeared to be taking its toll on the ability to recruit new talent into the ranks of the civil service; and (c) public employees expressed frustration over their inability to meet productivity and efficiency standards because so many factors were out of their control, such as shrinking budgets and regulations governing procurement and hiring.

The Volcker Commission recommended three major areas of focus for improving the situation in public agencies: (1) improving leadership, including reforming the federal Senior Executive Service (SES) and limiting the practice of replacing SES positions with political appointments; (2) working to attract and retrain talented people; and (3) focusing on improving performance and productivity (Nigro & Nigro, 1994).

Unfortunately, little has been accomplished, to date, in any of these areas for a variety of reasons. On the contrary, instead of building government service, current political leaders at all levels are reducing the ranks through downsizing and "reinvention." In the last four years, 1 in every 10 jobs in the executive branch of the federal government was eliminated. In a 17-year period, mostly within the last four years, the Office of Personnel Management and the General Services Administration both experienced 42% reductions in force (Causey, 1997).

In preparation for this book, we asked a small group of colleagues around the country to distribute an open-ended survey to students in their MPA programs, the bulk of whom were practitioners. Although we are not claiming that our 120 respondents are statistically representative of public administrators, they do come from programs in six widely scattered states (Colorado, Florida, Hawaii, Ohio, Oklahoma, and Washington). The majority are currently working in a variety of local and state government positions, are almost evenly split between males and females, and closely match proportions of the various racial and ethnic groups in the country. Whereas it is not possible to generalize their responses to all public workers, they do give food for thought with regard to how the current anti-government climate is affecting people who work in government agencies.

One would expect anti-government rhetoric to be affecting public administrators in a negative way, and indeed our respondents showed some signs of this. Having come to public sector work with, as many of them said, the desire to make things better, many are not only aware of the criticisms about unresponsiveness and red tape, but they tended to agree with them. Instead of being energized by the criticism, they tended to feel alienated, ineffective, cynical, and even frightened—and with reason, because workplace violence is a significant threat to government workers (Nigro & Waugh, 1996). Anti-government attacks, then, have a tendency to become,

> a self-fulfilling prophecy, for not very many of the best people in the public services are likely to want to stay there when they are paid far below their peers in the private sector and are the butt of repeated charges of incompetence, dishonesty, and laziness by their neighbors, the media, and indeed their own bosses. (Mosher, 1982, p. xii)

Beneath the surface of these negative reactions, however, were some interesting positive attitudes. Beneath the gloom about the anti-government climate was a continuing commitment to service. In addition to recognizing the extent to which anti-government feelings constitute a dilemma and a threat, our respondents also saw them as a challenge.

Some were quite worried over what one called "near constant harassment from malcontents and political wannabees," found their working conditions "frustrating," or declared, "I resent it. I work hard and the people I work with work hard." Another commented, "It is scary—it makes me want to stay out of the limelight and not make waves."

Some seemed to have internalized public views about bureaucracy, agreeing that government is the problem. For example, one said, "Having been part of the process, I can relate to the public's attitudes." Another commented, "The negative attitude is deserved. There is a lot of waste." Many others, however, looked beyond the immediacy of the criticism, seeing an opportunity to improve public service, as the following sample of quotes illustrate:

- "It can be depressing, but employees who take a positive approach often find that the public is not as negative as one is led to expect, particularly on a one-to-one basis."
- "My understanding of the animus toward government is that this is an extension of non-directed anger and anxiety in the public that they are manipulated by powerful elites who do not have their interests in mind. I wouldn't take it personally."
- "It tends to decrease morale but repeated contacts with the same 'customers' help both of us feel better about what I do."
- "It is challenging/empowering—I'm proud to have the opportunity to turn negatives into positives."

- "I feel like a rebel for the public good."
- "I am a good bureaucrat doing good things for the public."

When we asked how the anti-government environment affected their organizations, respondents cited reduced funding, lowered morale, limits on risk taking, delays, pay freezes, and an excessive focus on accountability, which perversely leads to even more red tape. They also felt that criticism makes working with the public more difficult, reducing public involvement, and creating a challenging need for partnerships with the community and a focus on "customer service." As funds are cut, administrators find themselves having to do more with less, and creativity and risk taking are strangled by the need to maintain or increase visible accountability. It becomes difficult to do one's job, maintain high morale, and recruit and retain the best and brightest. As our respondents' comments suggested, however, the silver lining is that criticism points up the necessity of improving relationships between government agencies and the public. As we argued earlier, whether customer service or other market-modeled strategies improve relationships is questionable, and our respondents agree. Certainly customer service soothes some of the irritation citizens feel at long lines and cumbersome processes, but it does little to engender collaborative efforts by citizens and government workers or to raise the sights of citizens beyond their own immediate needs and wants and give them a sense of connection to government.

When we asked what respondents were doing to counteract anti-government feelings, most mentioned improving interactions with the public, one person at a time. They did not couch these efforts in terms of customer service but rather in terms of one-to-one relationships and bringing citizens into administrative processes. They do "simple things that allow you to get to know people as people," as one person said, like being accessible, responding, educating people about what government does, disseminating information, developing interpersonal skills, listening, and showing genuine concern and empathy.

These comments fall roughly in two interrelated areas: improving one-on-one interactions with citizens, and working to break down barriers inherent in the bureaucratic apparatus. Hannah Arendt argues that bureaucratic management paralyzes action by turning people into "behaving citizens" (cited in Ventriss, 1995, p. 576)—by extension, one could say "behaving public employees" as well. Ralph Hummel (1994) agrees that bureaucratization acts to conceal, deny, and shape the political experience; he warns of two dangers when bureaucratic structures prevail in public life:

The bureaucracy converts public problems into administrative and technical issues, and it constrains possibilities for "full, human politics" (p. 241). As Tauxe (1995) states, public organizations must "not only democratize formal institutions and procedures, but also make room for nonbureaucratic discourse and organizational forms" (p. 489). Clearly, as we move to address problems raised by trying to do public work in an anti-government climate, both relational and organizational strategies are needed, especially given the extent to which the two are intertwined.

NOTES

1. Stever contends that Follett began as an organic idealist but later adopted the pragmatic position when it became more prominent (Stever, 1986).
2. Several good sources on pragmatism and its political influences include Stever (1986), Murphy (1990), Diggins (1994), and Kettner (1995).
3. See, in particular, the essays "The Fixation of Belief" and "Critical Common-sensism" in Buchler (1955).
4. "The Fixation of Belief" (Buchler, 1955).

PART II

STRATEGIES FOR COLLABORATION

Chapter 5

INTRODUCTION

Strategies for Collaboration

Cheryl Simrell King and Camilla Stivers

In Part I of this book, we described citizen discontent with government and situated it in several ways by addressing the following issues: How do citizens currently feel about government? How do their feelings manifest themselves? Are current citizen attitudes toward government similar to or different from those of earlier eras in America's history? What are the political-economic roots of these attitudes? How have American ideas about citizenship and the role of administration changed? How have fundamental notions about representative government and the re-presented knowledge on which it is based shaped the current situation?

In Part II, we present a number of stories from academics and practitioners grounded in real-life examples of relationships between citizens and administrative agencies and processes. In a variety of situations, the authors confront and deal with the opportunities and challenges involved in democratizing public administration by working collaboratively with citizens.

The relation between democracy and bureaucracy is enacted in the daily lives of bureaucrats and citizens and in their interactions with one another. The question of whether the United States is, or can become, a democracy is practically defined by the way that citizens and administrators view one another, work or don't work together, trust or don't trust one another, and share or argue about what makes up the kind of society they would want to live in together. Although administrators are citizens too (Cooper, 1991), that alone isn't enough to construct an *us* that encompasses administrators and lay citizens alike, especially in the context of a bureaucracy. It seems

---

From the Conversation: Connections

Cam: Relationship is not "idealistic" in the sense that committing yourself to it makes you a cockeyed optimist. In a way we have no choice but to start there, because that's what it is to be human. Relationship is therefore better or worse, depending on whether we see other humans as our fundamental commitment or whether we see them as means to some other end. I worry less and less about whether people have "wrong" ideas and more and more about how to connect—really connect.

Cheryl: Our work in this book seems, to me, to be about connections and the essential necessity of connections (in all forms, in all manners, in all situations). Cam and I talked yesterday about a recent *New York Times* article on the origins of language in which the author argued that language happened because we had to make connections that were not based upon bodily actions or touching one another (e.g., primates make connections by touching, grooming, etc.). The essential necessity of connections we are arguing is central to the relationship between administrators and citizens forces us to connect our theory with some action.

---

to us that the time is ripe for rethinking the relationships between administration (bureaucracy), administrators, and citizens:

> If the public service is debased in the eyes of citizens and presidents alike, if the notion of the public interest is empty of any content save compromise, if citizens and bureaucrats no longer trust one another . . . perhaps these are reasons enough to refocus the American dialogue so that citizens are included in the conversation. (Stivers, 1990a, p. 253)

As we have seen, engendering a more active citizenry and administration requires rethinking how we define the citizen and administrator roles in both politics and administration. As evidence of voter and citizen apathy suggests, electoral politics has its limits. Perhaps it is time to try something else—something that doesn't revolve around, and depend on, the "essential passivity of almost all the citizens, almost all the time" (Pollitt, 1996, p. 9). Wolin (1996) echoes this, in reflecting on the lack of citizen response to the government shutdown of December, 1995:

> [When] democracy's government was nearly paralyzed, there was no mass-protest, no million-citizen march on Washington, no demand to reclaim what is guaranteed by the Constitution. . . . The lack of response testifies to the truly terrifying pace at which depoliticization is being promoted and the depths of the alienation separating citizens from their government. (p. 23)

From the Conversation: Being an Idealist

Lisa: I will admit to being an idealist, in the respect that we all have our laundry list of "shoulds" and "ought to be's," if we're honest enough to recognize them as such. Yes, I have my list of normative preferences, but no, I don't view them as fixed or absolute—they are subject to change as my experiences shift my perceptions. In a previous life, for example, I was a staunch supporter of liberalism, free trade, and maquiladoras on the border. But I had led a relatively sheltered and privileged life and did not appreciate the impact such policies had on the lives of the powerless UNTIL my experiences shifted my views—a shift that I will gratefully attribute to the "radical hillbilly" traditions of the hills of East Tennessee (who'd believe one could move to Tennessee and become radicalized?), and a shift that also came about as a result of experiencing societal reactions to a woman's "role" in the institutions of marriage and parenthood.

All of the contributors to Part II believe that citizens want the possibility of becoming more than passive observers, consumers, or customers of public services. And we believe government workers, both those on the firing line and those in management jobs more removed from direct service, want to take active steps to help remedy citizen discontent, not by papering it over with public relations efforts, but by opening government to the participation of concerned citizens. Many of the stories told in this collection suggest that such possibilities are far from remote. And every so often come quiet indications that not all Americans are mindlessly turned off about public life. A newspaper story about the town of Mexico, Missouri, says that citizens there,

> remain quietly confident about their country . . . They may be disgruntled with the Federal Government that they consider far too big, too expensive and too intrusive, but they do not see it as their enemy . . . They feel isolated and powerless to influence national and international events, but they seem ready . . . to bear their share of the pain that they know Federal spending cuts will bring. (Apple, 1995, p. A1)

Perhaps, as well, citizens are ready to bear some of the responsibility for joining with government workers and managers in weighing what particular government agencies ought to be doing, and how. Perhaps they ought to be given the chance to try.

The case examples that follow illuminate both the factors that get in the way of successful collaboration as well as those that help to generate it. Each contributor has his or her own individual tale to tell, but there are a number of important themes that run throughout. All the stories deal in one way or another with administrative agencies' reliance on technical expertise to help frame and decide issues and the extent to which this privileging of expert, professional knowledge blocks or devalues the experience-based knowledge of citizens. The chapters all offer examples that display the tension between abstract knowledge and the democratic knowledge that emerges from people's lives and from their public interactions with each other. The authors all, in one way or another, recognize the threat that scientific, professional, rationalized knowledge poses for democratic citizenship. This is not to say that scientific knowledge is not useful, but science, on its face, can never give a correct answer to any public question. Such questions have no correct answers, only reasonable approaches that have emerged from deliberation in which the lived experiences of the citizens are taken seriously and the citizens themselves are directly involved. All contributors, therefore, advocate that participatory processes are the way to connect citizen or experiential knowledge with administrative, managerial, and scientific knowledge.

The stories raise the question of how far citizen participation processes can and should go in turning authority over to citizens. Issues of accountability, practicability, and the appropriate distribution of power surround this question. It is naive to assume that one can simply turn over administrative control and power to citizens, that all the problems will be solved by simply inviting citizens into current administrative processes. Individual resistance to sharing power gets in the way, particularly when administrators are socialized to be the experts. In addition, public agencies are legally charged with performing activities in the public interest and must work within their respective administrative, legal, political, and budgetary constraints to do so. Finally, administrative systems and processes are currently organized not to include citizens; bringing citizens in requires the willingness and opportunity to make important organizational changes.

The stories also all engage the issue of whether collaboration with citizens can be thought of as important in its own right or whether it has to remain instrumental to the achievement of organizational or policy goals. Each of the stories points to the tension between administrative goals and collaboration with citizens. Collaboration with citizens is not efficient, as least in terms of how efficiency has been traditionally measured. Working with citizens is messy, complicated, and takes longer than it does to make decisions on one's own. Therefore, do we "let the citizens in" only when it fits within the agency standards of efficiency, as Thomas (1995) argues in his book, or do we work toward democratic administration as an end in itself? All of the contributors argue that working with citizens is worth doing for itself, even if it complicates current administrative systems and processes. Efficiency is an administrative, not a political or relational, goal. The authors also agree that even with the extra effort involved, working with citizens usually contributes to the successful completion of agency work.

All the chapters, either explicitly or implicitly, deal with how a political economy skewed in the direction of established interests shapes the context and structures of governance. Practicing full participation or collaboration in the current context requires one to be aware of how established interests, either economic or political, work against participation efforts. Any genuine effort to increase participation, therefore, must address not only administrative power, or the power of expertise, but must also take into account political and economic power in a political economy organized around consumption, a one-world economy, and the growing gap between the haves and have-nots.

This raises an important question woven implicitly throughout the chapters: Can participation efforts be successful in the face of strongly established interests? Or, is it only possible to collaborate with citizens who have traditionally been neglected by government, in communities where there is little organized resistance to citizen involvement? The Orange County story, the Dudley Street Initiative discussed by Foley (Chapter 9), and the EPA's social justice communities all raise this issue. Is it possible to have collaborative efforts when there are strong, vested interests that discourage citizen involvement? Some of the authors believe it is possible, but not risk-free.

Finally, as briefly noted earlier, all the stories raise the question of the extent to which changes in administrative attitudes and practices necessary to support collaborative work with citizens must be undergirded with organizational and systems modifications. Democratizing public administration is not just about changing the way we practice administration; we must also think about how we change the organizations and public systems within which we practice. Without these structural changes, as Phillip Selznick (1949) observed, participation efforts risk remaining dependent on the good will or energies of individual administrators and citizens and may not be perpetuated when these individuals move on. At the same time, however, one must be careful to not overinstitutionalize processes such that citizens become co-opted and bureaucratized, as Gray and Chapin's story teaches us.

These questions and themes emerge from the stories and case examples that follow. Each of the narrators also draws lessons from the experiences they describe and makes suggestions about how to approach collaboration with citizens in a way that improves the chances for a productive

From the Conversation: A Passion for Democracy

Joe: Believe me, involving citizens in a meaningful manner is a complex process with obstacles and mine fields on both sides. The most difficult task is achieving the necessary trust and confidence from both parties to even begin the collaborative governance process. Bureaucrats, by nature, have little confidence in civilian competence and judgment, and citizens have little trust in bureaucrats and they trust politicians even less. However, we [in Orange County, Florida] are happy to report that there is hope.

Ralph: Joe, I'd be interested to know whether you have anything on what it is that citizens actually say about bureaucrats, legislators, and their own needs. Also: when you compare how bureaucrats, legislators, and citizens talk—the vocabulary of what they say—are there patterns of differences? Not only differences in the substance of what citizens want and what government officials are able to give, but whether there is a difference in the level of abstraction? I'm thinking of a *Reader's Digest* article reporting that when five workers died in one meat-packing plant, OSHA issued a nationwide rule that required atmospheric testing across the board even though most work sites had had no problems. I read this as a tendency to react with abstract rules that may make no sense in local conditions and which don't necessarily fix the local conditions that led to the deaths to begin with.

Cheryl: It seems as if Joe has really given us something to chew on. If the only thing we can do is to place our energy and passion in the relationships between citizens and administrators (we can't change the political economy), then what do we do? We find out how to engage, how to achieve the necessary trust and confidence. Trust and confidence come as a result of, or emerge from, the relationships.

Walt: Regarding the discussions about how we interact with citizens, we, of course, cite EPA's efforts to continue to parse up interest groups finer and finer to represent sub-groups of larger groups. We do the same with industry. . . . Then we try to both educate on the issues and engage on the decisions. Some of the chapters argue that this work is narrow, manipulative, devoted to organizational preservation. [But] the information transmission-education function with citizens deserves separation and discussion from the methods of "contactful" engagement for decision-making.

Meg: Much of what I read in the draft chapters resonated with my recent experience with a diversified group of people from different interests that EPA was trying to bring to consensus on strategic environmental issues. For the first time EPA was extending a hand to locally-affected communities—environmental justice interests and grassroots activist networks—to include them in early up-front planning along with the more usual stable of industry reps, national environmental organizations, and state regulators. Talk about an eye-opener! It confirmed that citizens affected by pollution from local industry do not trust EPA much more than they trust corporations. This came across loud and clear, and prevented the group from having dispassionate conversations or reaching consensus on meaningful issues.

Richard: I sensed in Meg and Walt's comments an important message about the intent of people in agencies. Practitioners, or entire agencies, can be doing the best they can in terms of incorporating citizen will, but will still be lumped in with bureaucracy as a whole as a negative public image.

Cam: Incidentally, Walt and Meg, educating citizens also fosters citizenship if it is done in a way that encourages them to be active instead of passive recipients.

Dolores: I agree with Joe's comments and Cheryl's response that since we can't change the political economy we need to place our energy and passion into relationships between citizens and administrators. It seems to me that the structures that inhibit participation and the cultures that promote the citizen are mutually reinforcing. I'm also coming out of some processes where I've become increasingly convinced that many citizens want public administrators to be more efficient, they are not advocating more involvement.

Lisa: Do you (or others) think that citizens want public servants to have passion? Or would citizens rather that public servants be efficient—with the impersonality and objectivity that efficiency implies?

Richard: In most cases, I suspect that a citizen would prefer an efficient and impersonal public practitioner. But there are clearly other times when people respect and listen to the practitioner because s/he obviously cares about the situation and the people. Citizens will always take an interest in a NIMBY situation. But in certain times and places, a significant portion of the population will care deeply about the fate of the community and will participate in self-governance despite the multiple jobs, problems with child care, etc.

Mary: The question before us is "do the citizens want efficient or passionate public administrators?" I'm uncomfortable with both choices. What is usually forgotten is that democracy is not very efficient nor is it meant to be. If we want to uphold efficiency as a primary value then we must also face the consequences in terms of less democracy. But Heaven protect us from the passionate administrator; that individual would more surely determine the direction of policy than the merely efficient one. The passion I want to see in a public administrator is a passion for democracy—listening to and responding to all concerns and being willing to let go of the process for the sake of a better collective outcome.

relationship. We offer no magic formulas or guarantees. But the experiences reinforce each other in interesting ways that suggest that, although a bit of good luck helps, democratizing public administration is not just a matter of happenstance and the idiosyncrasies of peculiar situations. There are approaches that experience suggests are more likely to work than others.

Mary Timney's chapter is our first story. She argues that only by giving up top-down control and turning power over to citizens will agencies be

able to reach effective decisions. Using a case study that documents energy
policy development in three state governments, Timney argues that participation can take one of three forms. The traditional processes where
citizens are relatively uninvolved or only involved from a "buy-in" or "input" perspective are passive processes, as illustrated in the state of Ohio.
Alluding to Lincoln's famous tripartite scheme, Timney calls this kind of
citizen participation "government *for* the people." Active participation is
when citizens control the processes and decisions and citizen expertise
reigns, or "government *by* the people," as shown in the Missouri example.
A hybrid model is one where citizens and government work together to
share control, processes, and decisions, as illustrated in the state of Indiana:
"government *with* the people." The aura of administrative expertise and
control is maintained in both the passive and hybrid models; only in the
active model is control relinquished to the citizens and the final product
"shaped by the public's expertise, not the administrators." In the passive
model, administrative expertise and standing is privileged over citizen expertise and standing. In the active model, citizen expertise and standing is
privileged over administrative. In the hybrid model, citizens are "let in"
and allowed to share the processes, but administrative expertise and standing retains its privilege.

  Timney shows us that most participation efforts to date have been of
the passive type; she suggests that participation has historically been constrained by rule making and the legal concept of *standing*. When they do
not have standing or some other rule-based grounds to open up governmental processes, citizens are locked out of decision making; in effect,
citizens are not allowed to participate. Showing how managerial efficiency
is an administrative goal that works at cross-purposes with participation,
Timney argues that achieving active participation processes requires addressing fundamental questions of democracy, "invit[ing] the public into
the processes and giv[ing] government back to its rightful owners." The
role of the administrator, in an active process, is to facilitate the transfer
of authority to citizens and to attend to the administrative details.

  The next two chapters by Lisa Zanetti and by Walter Kovalick and
Margaret Kelly are both examples of Timney's hybrid models of citizen
participation. Zanetti directs our attention to the thorny issue of expertise
and the role that expert knowledge typically plays in shaping participation.
Zanetti argues that expertise subordinates common sense and ordinary
knowledge and, by extension, disempowers common people. By visualizing
public administration as standing at the nexus of the state and civil society,
Zanetti shows how the "transformative administrator's" role is to reconnect the knowledge of expertise with the knowledge of experience.

Although Zanetti advocates a more active role for the citizen, her transformative administrator serves as the guide to help citizens achieve their goals and to assist citizens in transforming their own lives, which are constrained by the current political economy. In this model, administrators retain the privilege of control because they have the capacity to assist the citizens in their own transformation away from substantiating the status quo and toward new ways of thinking.

Kovalick and Kelly, writing from their vantage point as EPA administrators, advocate a kind of "government with the people" in which the administrator acts as a "task-oriented but inclusive and balanced convener." They write from a perspective that incorporates the realities of operating an agency when the nature of its work has become more complex, more controversial, and less obvious. The public has become more "differentiated," and new mandates have caused the EPA to adapt both program implementation and efforts to engage the public. Kovalick and Kelly show how the EPA has evolved over time in order to cope. Their task-oriented administrator, in the role of convener, is focused on efficiency (balancing the costs and benefits of meeting citizen needs), being inclusive (engaging all factions of the community and not leaving anyone out), balancing all of the competing interests, and making the space (building the table around which all will gather) for participation. In addition, this administrator is committed to making the requisite organizational and structural changes needed to get more closely in touch with people.

Kovalick and Kelly's administrator is one who is looking for the right answer in the process of bringing all the competing interests to the table and moderating the debate. The right answer no longer rests solely in authority, expertise, or science, but in a respectful balancing of these and the participation process. From their perspective, the administrator both facilitates the process and retains final control, not out of capriciousness or self-interest but because of agency realities.

The next two chapters, by Dolores Foley and by Richard Box and Deborah Sagen, are examples of what Timney calls "government by the people." Foley advocates letting communities develop their own structures of governance and highlights some of the struggles implicit in doing so through an HIV prevention planning project organized by the state of Hawai'i for the Centers for Disease Control (CDC). Foley brings to our attention some of the important questions surrounding how community is defined: What is community? Who decides? Are participants in the policy processes chosen with regard to representativeness or relationships? Foley brings to our conversation the idea that community is defined both in terms of place (e.g., geographically) and in terms of space: the table or arena

From the Conversation: Dilemma/Paradox

Cheryl: There are many dilemmas embedded in public administration that keep us from doing our work in the way that Mary so eloquently stated, "generating light as well as heat which can lead to more successful and fairer decisions." In dilemma, paralysis often emerges—no change occurs, often leading to fatal outcomes. Hamlet is a prime example of dilemma. Exposing the dilemmas (which can't be lived with) in public administration and reframing or working with them such that they become paradoxes (which can be lived with as long as the opposing elements are kept in balance; see Harmon, 1995) seems a worthy mission.

Dilemma 1: What does government do?

1. Provide services
2. Set agendas and make decisions for the public good

Dilemma 2: How should government do these things?

1. Efficiently, accountably, within the rule of law
2. With passion, ethical responsibility, a recognition of all interests especially those who are marginalized in the conversation

Dilemma 3: What is the role of public administrators?

1. Manage and administer
2. Govern

Dilemma 4: How do administrators work with citizens?

1. Protect interests of state, profession, and other parts of iron triangle (expert, rational, technicist)
2. Promote democracy, inclusion, etc. (facilitator, partner, collaborator)

Dilemma 5: What is community?

1. A place in which people come together to serve common and individual interests
2. A place where individuals are destroyed, oppressed, tyrannized out of their individual rights

Dilemma 6: What is the role of the citizen?

1. Active (involved, engaged, attends to process)
2. Passive (couch potato; nonvoter; nonparticipant)

Dilemma 7: What drives people's behavior?

1. Self-interest (how are my tax dollars being spent? Better be efficiently!)
2. Collective interest (how does this benefit my community? The people I love?)

Dilemma 8: Why don't citizens get more involved?

1. Selfish reasons (too busy, don't care, etc.)

2. Institutional reasons (recursive practices of administration keep participation to a minimum)

It seems that we are up against these issues that, when framed as dilemmas or dichotomies, paralyze us into *us versus them* or *either or choices*. We also tend to get paralyzed around ideological issues (e.g., public management vs. governance). I'd like to see us completely shift the practices of public administration such that public is in the center rather than administration or management, but this will not happen; administration needs to be both governance and management, both service related and relationship building. Both the place for expertise and the place for relationship. Both efficient and democratic. Citizens are both self-interested and interested in community and in issues that affect them as well as their community. They are both busy and available. They are interested in how their tax dollars are spent and interested in providing service for the poor. Although most of the respondents to the survey we did for this book (see Chapter 4) were gloomy about anti-government sentiment, the majority saw it as a challenge rather than a threat and the things most often cited that they are doing to counteract these sentiments involve improving relationships with the public, one person at a time. Focusing on one-on-one relationships and bringing citizens into their processes. Maybe it will be in these relationships that the dilemmas of governance are transformed into something that we can live with; into paradoxes in which the role of the administrator is to work to maintain a balance between the opposing principles inherent in governing. This means a radical rethinking of what administrators do (as opposed to orthodox notions of administration), but doesn't necessarily require a radical change in government structures and institutions, at least not at the moment. In other words, administrators can change their practices one person at a time until, eventually, if Giddens (1984) is right, institutions will shift with them.

where people can come together to deliberate. As Foley and most of our others contributors note, communities develop geographically and are built by citizens, not government; but administrators can facilitate the development of the space for democracy and deliberation. Foley offers a number of other examples of community governance projects across the nation that further illuminate the lessons learned from the CDC project in Hawai'i.

Box and Sagen provide us with dual perspectives on returning to a smaller, less bureaucratic government. Sagen writes from her experience as both a citizen advocate and local administrator. Box writes both experientially and academically, as a former city administrator and a current teacher-scholar. Together, they offer the notion of a "public service practitioner" who assists citizens in achieving their own goals, instead of agency or administrative goals. Like Timney and Foley, they argue for a fairly limited but important role for the administrator, as one who creates the environment for citizens to govern themselves, building the bridges for citizens back to the governmental systems and structures.

Sagen draws our attention to the barriers to participation in current administrative processes. Drawing on her experience, she cites professional education and socialization, the vacuousness of current methods of "managing" the public, the tensions between efficiency and responsiveness, the pervasiveness of administrative goals, the conflict between technical knowledge and citizen knowledge, and the cults of objectivity and professionalism that separate administrators and citizens into an "us versus them" mentality. Box follows with the hard question: "Whom do we serve and to what end?" He argues that the crux of public administration is to serve the citizens for the purpose of governing themselves, which may require administrators to work against the status quo and to confront established interests. Like Kovalick and Kelly, Box and Sagen advocate finding the right balance between technical efficiency and serving the citizen interest, as well as between responsiveness to the politically and economically powerful and giving ordinary citizens access to the power they need to build and maintain their own governance processes.

Our last story, by Joseph Gray and Linda Chapin, describes a living example of collaborative or integrative participation. Gray is manager of the public affairs office of Orange County, Florida, primarily responsible for overseeing the county's Targeted Community Initiatives (TCI). Linda Chapin is Orange County Chairman, serving her second term in that position. The TCI was developed in order to reach out to communities in the county that had been historically neglected by government. Government officials learned from the experience that their key roles were to spend "lots of time listening";[1] to facilitate opportunities for community members to come together to talk, and make decisions about, community problems; to coordinate services; and to use county resources to build the infrastructure needed to fulfill community needs. The county gave the residents information they needed to make informed decisions, including educating citizens about the legal and resource constraints. They found, however, that their most important activity was to learn from the citizens; to learn how to be better partners with the communities. One citizen said, "They listened, they heard us, and they took action."

Their first effort, in South Apopka, came about at the request of the residents, in response to an incident between a local store owner and a juvenile resident. In Bithlo, Winter Garden, and Taft, the county went to the communities and offered their support. As one county employee said,

"It's hard to change long-held distrust of government. . . . It is a long, on-going process."

In these efforts, Orange County has learned to share governing with the citizens. The officials bring their technical and administrative expertise and knowledge to the table. The citizens bring their lived experiences. Together, they worked to rebuild the communities.

One important lesson this example offers is the crucial role that leadership plays in successful community-administrative partnerships. Without Chairman Chapin's vision, patience, ability to surrender control, and willingness to get down in the trenches, listen to citizens; respond, and learn from mistakes, the program would not be as successful as it is.

Drawing on the Orange County experience, we propose that there is yet another perspective on participation, one that falls somewhere between Timney's hybrid and active models, perhaps a "government *of* the people." Timney's hybrid model is a model of compromise. In it, the administrator remains in control but is willing to "let" the citizens in and to compromise a bit because doing so contributes to already established administrative goals. Mary Parker Follett, among others, believed that compromise is not the best that we can do (Follett, 1924). Compromise assumes that everyone has to give up something in order to reach closure. The best outcome, according to Follett, is what she calls integration, or interaction in which all of the perspectives get into the hopper and what emerges is different from any of the original ideas and better than what would, or could, have emerged in a compromise situation. This is what we call collaboration. In a collaborative model, no point of view is privileged over the others. All come to the table as equals, working together to allow their orders to emerge from the situation. As Follett knew, true integration is not always possible; somehow people are too sharply divided. But we often settle for compromise when, by continuing to work together, a new understanding of the situation might emerge.

* * *

In using stories as a way of evoking what is involved in building collaborative relationships between public servants and citizens, we draw on a property of stories that distinguishes them from science. Stories put the world together, or rather, they are the process by which human beings put the world together. Science, in contrast, takes the world apart. The world can only be taken apart after it has been put together—after humans have done the storytelling that constitutes objects in situations, which then become susceptible to scientific analysis. Science neglects the choices it has made (the stories it has told) in order to see things one way or another—for

From the Conversation: Authority, Responsibility, Discretion

Lisa: I am struck by one of the common themes in our chapters which is relinquishing authority back to the citizens. A question for us to consider: Where does discretion come into play? Are administrators obligated to surrender their discretion altogether? If we do, have we simply inverted the neutral competence model—instead of responding unquestioningly to the elected officials, we respond unquestioningly to the citizens instead?

Cam: My current take on the issue you raise, Lisa, is that my "ideal model" of the relationship between citizens and bureaucrats would entail both sides perceiving it as collaboration rather than a zero-sum deal that involves "relinquishing" and "surrendering." You're probably right that bureaucrats might tend to see it that way, but I'm hoping they can be encouraged to see the knowledge that citizens have as crucial to doing good work. If so, then maybe together with citizens bureaucrats can develop a joint understanding of what's involved in particular situations and end up being more effective than if they sit in their isolated offices and "exercise their discretion."

Ralph: Authority comes from citizens to begin with. It is because citizens no longer grant authority to government that it increasingly is perceived as non-legitimate (not the same as illegitimate).

Lisa: Your point is well taken. . . . Authority does come from citizens first. Still I have questions about how we justify/explain the role of administrators in a more substantively democratic polity. I think that part of our challenge in defining our field, and our expectations of it, is our very name: public administration. To me, that smacks of the business administration ethos—which is amoral at best, and guided by principles that I think many of us in this conversation would reject but which have so colonized the mentality of Americans that even the Democrats are calling for running government like a business.

Cam: The way I think of discretion is that it is not only valuable and necessary but inevitable. In other words, exercise of discretion = what people do by way of interpreting statutes, regulations, etc. as well as what they do by way of interpreting the situations in which the laws, etc., are to be applied. This interpretation is unavoidable. No law can be written specifically enough so that the question of how it applies becomes moot. Interpretation is therefore constitutive of administrative practice. It can't be avoided. Therefore the question is not whether it can occur or should occur. Rather it is, when it occurs, how does it occur and how should it occur—i.e., on what basis? What should administrators take into account? Where critical theory plays into this in my view is that the consciousness of administrators about whom they serve and for what purposes affects how they interpret. They can choose to collaborate with citizens (or not) as they interpret. Or they can fool themselves into thinking that they're just carrying out orders.

Ralph: Looking at this phenomenologically, discretion is the necessary space within which those who apply the law ("bureaucrats") and those who change their own behavior to conform to it ("citizens") treat legal specifications as only one of many factors present in a lived environment, all of which must be taken into account to make anything happen at all. Discretion, in this view, is not optional: it is mandatory if work is to be accomplished and if lives are to be lived. . . . Discretion becomes the ability to make sensible judgments in the site where law and other factors come together.

Richard: Your essential point is that we cannot knock all the discretion out of the role of the public professional. . . . Someone must carry the accumulated knowledge of practice to the citizens who need it. . . . On top of this, I think the practitioner must on occasion consider stepping outside the accepted sphere of discretion in order to accomplish goals that she or he believes to supercede questions of accountability and legitimacy. This could be justice and social equity, honesty and fairness in governance, democratic citizen access, or something else.

Cheryl: As with our colleagues writing about legitimacy, we are also struggling with the essential issues of serving the public in a postmodern era. Forget about what postmodern literature does or does not contribute to our understanding, whether our work is "highmodern," or otherwise. Contextualize the issues in the moment. These issues (authority, responsibility, accountability, discretion, elitism, idealism, roles of actors in the political process) are paramount because we have lost our faith (rightfully so) in modernity. There is no higher authority to which we all can agree we answer. Not the Constitution, not "God," not scientism, not rationality, not agency, not a code of ethics, not the, or a, "profession," not anything. So, with what are we left? What one is left with in these crazy (and wonderful) times when we can no longer believe in something outside of ourselves to "show us the way," are our relationships, as I think we are arguing in this book. Everything happens in relationship.

Where does this lead us? All of these thorny issues that we are throwing about, particularly authority, accountability, responsibility, and therefore discretion, are situated in the relationship between citizens and administrators. This is problematic because of its idealism. As we all know, authentic relationships require that all people involved be engaged, committed, and willing to do the work they need to do on their Self in order to serve the relationship. In a time in which administration is framed as a business or commodity relationship between a "seller" and a "consumer," the possibility of having an authentic relationship is slim to none. The onus for shaping the relationships between citizens and administrators (or between citizens and their government) is on the administrator (Letcher, 1994). What administrators do is to shape things, both intentionally and unintentionally. Our power lies in our positional ability to shape.

Cam: On citizens "seeing themselves": Cheryl, this reminded me of one of my favorite books, Lawrence Goodwyn's *The Populist Moment,* which we used to use at Evergreen a lot. You're right, citizens "see themselves" as consumers, voters, taxpayers, but not as participants. For Goodwyn the significance of the populist movement was that, for a brief moment, ordinary folk came to see themselves as "experimenting in new democratic forms." Goodwyn goes on: "In the world they created, they fulfilled the democratic promise in the only way it can be fulfilled—by people acting in democratic ways in their daily lives."

continued

Lisa: Drawing out my analogy to the citizenship, administration, and government question, it seems to me that, agreeing with Cheryl here, citizens DON'T perceive themselves as such—in other words, they don't have that distinct sense of self as citizen that is necessary for the relationship with government. Except that, rather than being subsumed by the relationship, they are incapable of establishing it in the first place (administrators being the representatives of government—not to be confused with the elected representatives!).

Walt: I was reading the conversations about "victim" and customer and "contactful" engagement (and some other models that yet need to be invented) in the papers as being cast as either revolutionary or as "either/or." I think there are probably a couple (probably not including "victim") of useful kinds of models of relationships that need to be available depending on the work of government we are discussing, whether the citizen is affected at the primary/secondary/tertiary level. Life is complicated enough (aside from relating to government) for one model to do it all. For example, neighborhood AIDS education is at a different level than municipal refuse service or state driver's licensing processes or delayed airplane schedules due to air traffic control shortages or (on our front) whether the U.S. is agreeing to too much (or too little) at the climate change convention (which will affect the air our children breathe as adults). I would also refer us to the polls taken during the Federal government shutdowns and startups for commentary about what functions citizens "do" care about—some were service delivery (getting entitlement checks and passports), i.e., a "customer's reaction," but some were not.

Most of what we collectively have written goes directly to the interpersonal/individual level and a lot of the recent conversations about PA theory seem to relate (if I understand correctly) to the paradigms that these individuals—including public administrators—operate in. Meg and I have suggested, and so does the reference at the end of our article, that it's not neutral arbiter nor our EPA-value laden administrator that is in the future, but the convenor of a diversity of expertise (including the citizen's expertise about his or her own views) that we need to be about. The Agency is being "trusted" to assemble of diverse set of competent views—not be silent about who should be "at the table" nor dismissive of participation.

Richard: Which brings me back to PA and our role as practitioners and academicians. If I feel this sense of being a product of a deep, long, conceptually and emotionally rich and dialectical history, then I feel responsible to transmit it to others so they can take action based on knowledge. Lacking that, they simply do the same thing over and over again and, instead of your Hegelian advancement, they never go anywhere.

Cam: On citizens seeing themselves: There have to be some enabling conditions for the practice of citizenship. This is one thing I think administrators can foster perhaps more than they do. Incidentally, Walt and Meg, educating citizens also fosters citizenship if it is done in a way that encourages them to be active instead of passive recipients. The convenor role you mention is quite close to my notion of what administrators can do to encourage active citizenship.

example, to see particular elements in a situation as "variables" (Hummel, personal communication, June 1997).

A story is "a report about an event, a situation, a little world, as seen through the eyes of the storyteller. . . . The listener is asked to step into the [storyteller's] shoes" (Hummel, 1991, p. 237). The listener thus makes contact with the world of the storyteller and is able to see the ways in which the storyteller's world is like or unlike the listener's own. As a parks and recreation manager put it, when you listen to or read a story about someone else's work situation, "You're looking for somebody that has the, that shares—this is a contradiction in terms—that shares a unique experience" (p. 237). In other words, you are able to see "what's the same in what's different" (Hummel, personal communication, June 1997).

As phenomenologist Eugene Gendlin says, "You can use any experience as a way of patterning another. Thereby commonalities will, as it were, fall out. . . . A common aspect *can be created* in the process of schematizing one experience by the other" (1973, p: 298). Stories enable us to get in touch directly with aspects of our own experiences in order to formulate them in a different, and possibly better, way. We find out whether the new way is better by living further in our situation.

We present the following stories in order for readers to be able to listen to them and make their own connections—by relating them to their own situations, to see in them what's the same in what's different.

NOTE

1. All direct quotes were taken from the videotape *T.C.I.: Targeted Community Initiative* prepared by the Orange County government (Orange County, Florida, 1997).

Chapter 6

OVERCOMING ADMINISTRATIVE BARRIERS TO CITIZEN PARTICIPATION

Citizens as Partners, Not Adversaries

Mary M. Timney

From its earliest days, public administration established administrators as the experts in government or public policy implementation. The primary emphasis in the field has been the search for the "one best way" to do public management, whether in supervising employees, making optimal decisions, or designing programs or regulations in response to legislative mandates. Since the establishment of independent regulatory commissions in the late 19th century, the public administrator has been identified as the primary expert in the political arena—the cool-headed nonpartisan who can make the right decisions using professional criteria untainted by political pressures or ideology.

Guided by the dominant value in the field—efficiency—administrators have developed processes for public review of agency proposals and decisions that achieve both the nominal requirements of democratic deliberation and the administrator's desire for efficiency. The Administrative Procedure Act of 1946 codified the process for public participation in regulatory rule making. This process serves as the model of citizen participation for administrators at all levels of government, particularly when federal laws are being implemented, especially environmental regulations.

This chapter examines the administrative process as a barrier to meaningful citizen participation. I outline three ideal types or models of citizen participation, identified through field research, that constitute a continuum of administrative control over citizen participation. These are assessed against frameworks for citizen participation, drawn from the literature, that guide the development of administrative strategies for managing public input. I assert that extreme cases of dysfunctional citizen participation, for example, NIMBY (Not In My Backyard), can be caused by administrative processes that place limits on public participation, leaving citizens no action choice other than protest. The chapter concludes with a discussion of the necessity for administrators to develop better processes to achieve the kind of relationship described in other chapters of this volume. To do so, administrators will have to relinquish control, seek expertise among the public, and allow citizens to make significant policy decisions.

MODELS OF CITIZEN PARTICIPATION: CASE STUDIES
OF STATE ENERGY POLICY DEVELOPMENT

In a 1992 study of state energy policy development, I found three distinct examples of citizen participation that form a continuum from traditional agency-controlled citizen participation to citizen responsibility for policy development, with the agency taking an advisory role.

The purpose of the study was to document state activity in energy-policy development during the 1980s and early 1990s, in the absence of a strong federal presence in energy policy as had been the case in the 1970s. The study included 17 states roughly comprising the northern Midwest and West, an area from Ohio to Idaho, bordered on the south by Kansas and on the north by Canada.[1] The methodology included both quantitative and qualitative data: A survey was mailed to state energy administrators to gather common data about energy-policy development, followed by a set of face-to-face interviews in selected states and cities. In each state, interviews were conducted with the state energy administrator, a legislative staffer, and an environmental group in order to identify common goals and political conflicts.

Prior to the 1980s, energy policy was a national rather than state focus. In the late 1970s, states were given funding to develop energy offices to help them comply with national policies developed by the Carter administration. States developed energy policy tailored to their differential needs depending on their climate and indigenous energy resource base. In the 1980s, the Reagan administration dismantled much of the Carter energy program, and declining energy prices led to a change in national focus from demand management to supply expansion, leaving energy policy to market forces.

The study investigated the extent to which states adopted energy-policy development independently of the federal government. My hypothesis was that states, particularly those in colder climes with few energy resources, would be vulnerable, economically and socially, to extremes in energy markets and would be likely to develop policy to avoid the kind of dislocations suffered during the 1970s energy crises. The states in the study covered the range of energy producers to energy consumers, outside of oil producing states. For example, Minnesota and Wisconsin have no energy resources and high energy demand due to extremely cold winter temperatures. Wyoming and Colorado are coal-producing states and contain deposits of oil shale, a potential synthetic energy source; Kansas has huge deposits of natural gas; and Indiana and Ohio export electricity generated from their large coal deposits. The states also vary in the extent to which energy industry interests dominate state politics.

I expected to find that formal energy policy was more likely to be developed by states that are energy importers whereas energy exporters would be more likely to support free market policies. This hypothesis was not supported; most of the states in the study had developed some kind of energy policy by 1992.

The three states from which the models were drawn were Indiana, Ohio, and Missouri. Each state had similar goals for articulating state energy policy during a period free of federally mandated energy policy. Although their politics and energy vulnerability are different, the aim in each state was to develop a plan to integrate energy policy with environmental protection and economic development. Each used a different form of citizen participation with predictably different outcomes.

Ohio's Energy Strategy

In Ohio, the governor appointed an ad hoc committee of nine department secretaries who met for 18 months to develop the state energy strategy. During the closed administrative meetings, the committee consulted with other experts, principally representatives of the energy industries and large energy users. Politically, the state can be described as favoring economic development over environmental protection, and it is a major producer and exporter of electricity, as well as a coal producer.[2] The aim of the energy strategy process was to protect state business interests while developing ideas for complying with new environmental protection laws.[3]

Two rounds of public hearings were held across the state. The committee made the final recommendations and developed a policy document that favored industry interests and emphasized economic development. Citizens' comments were included in an appendix to the report. Citizen organizations have continued to fight the recommendations and to work for giving energy conservation a stronger role in state energy policy. A major foundation provided a multiyear grant to the Ohio Environmental Council to carry out the Campaign for an Energy Efficient Ohio, which has intervened in utility rate hearings and published compilations of energy efficiency cases by businesses and residents across the state.

Indiana's Policy Process

The state of Indiana is similar to Ohio in energy resources and politics. The state's utilities export electricity and the state is a major coal producer. It too is dominated by conservative political interests. Thus, the incentives to develop an energy policy to protect business interests were very much the same as Ohio's. In Indiana, however, the process was initiated by the chair of the senate who wanted to develop a consensual decision process for contentious policy issues. Energy was not a politically hot issue at the time and energy industries have considerable power in the Indiana legislature. Indeed, Indiana was the only state where I was unable to meet with a legislative staffer and was referred, instead, to the president of the Indiana Electricity Institute, the primary energy lobby. Nonetheless, environmentalists are perceived to have the power to defeat or delay legislative or economic development efforts.

The focus in this case was as much on the process itself as on the policy. The energy agency, which is housed in the Department of Commerce,[4] was charged with designing a way to maximize citizen participation. The agency identified relevant publics to be involved, drafted discussion documents, and set up task forces by subject emphasis (e.g., transportation, air pollution, etc.) to develop recommendations for the state energy policy. Membership on the task forces was open to anyone willing to participate.

Ultimately, more than 200 people from all economic and social sectors worked on the final product. The task forces were given resources to bring in outside speakers and to develop a library. The final policy document was a compilation of task-force recommendations approved by the agency staff.

All the participants I interviewed expressed great satisfaction with the process, although they did not all agree on the final product. The Hoosier Environmental Council refused to endorse the report because it failed to emphasize transportation as an energy conservation strategy. Both the director of the council and the lobbyist for the electricity industry expressed to me how well the process worked in helping them to understand each other's viewpoints. They had never before had the opportunity to listen to each other's concerns. The typical public hearing format, where they customarily interact, requires them to be adversaries, to discredit each other as a political tactic. The task-force meetings established a collaborative setting and enabled them to move beyond their stereotypes of each other to see issues and interests more clearly. Both expressed an interest in continuing the dialogue, although there were no meetings scheduled at that point. The director of the agency reported that the senate was so pleased with the outcome of the process that they were considering a similar effort on a more politically charged issue such as education.

Missouri's "Citizen's" Energy Policy

The case of Missouri represents the other extreme of the continuum from controlled to open participation and citizen decision making. As in Indiana, the state energy agency was directed by the legislature to develop an energy policy. Missouri does not have powerful energy industries or major pollution problems, so there was no critical political reason for the state to develop an energy policy. It was initiated because of the personal interests of individual legislators.

Following normal procedure, the energy administrators drafted working materials that defined the problems, proposed alternatives, and generally limited the parameters of the discussion—just what managers are trained and expected to do. At this point, however, they departed from tradition: They contracted out the citizen participation element of the process to a citizens' organization, the Kansas City Metropolitan Energy Center.[5] The center identified a set of relevant publics across the state—business, labor, environmental groups, Chambers of Commerce, small businesses, and so forth—much the way an administrator would do. But the similarities ended there. Individuals in these groups were then asked to identify who *they* thought should be involved in the process.

A series of more than 30 focus groups was held throughout the state to review the administrators' recommendations and develop consensus on implementation options. At first, many of the participants felt that the discussion papers were a draft of the final report that they were being asked to approve or modify. However, center personnel structured the meetings to develop comments and input from the participants; facilitators of the discussions focused on hearing, rather than presenting, information.

In the end, the focus groups rejected the priorities of the agency administrators, restructured the study outline, and redirected the presentation of

TABLE 6.1 Characteristics of Citizen Participation Models

Active	Hybrid (Transition)	Passive
Missouri	Indiana	Ohio
Citizen control	Shared control	Agency control
Citizens identify parameters	Agency identifies parameters	Agency identifies parameters
Proactive, open	Broad, open process	Closed process
Consensus decisions	Consensus decisions	Agency decision
Citizen role is dominant	Citizen role advisory	Citizens react to proposals
Citizens articulate policy	Administrators articulate policy	Administrators articulate policy
Agency serves as consultant	Administrators as staff & participants	Agency only as participants
Citizens own the process	Participation as process goal	Participation as a formality
Citizens come in at beginning of process	Citizens come in middle of process	Citizens come in at end of process
Government *by* the people	Government *with* the people	Government *for* the people

the materials. Citizen participation was so powerful in this case that the seven-volume final report was written by the Energy Center, not the energy agency. And because this was a consensual process that developed political support across the state, the legislature quickly enacted most of the recommendations (see the *Missouri Statewide Energy Study,* State of Missouri Department of Natural Resources, 1992).

SUMMARY OF CASES

Table 6.1 summarizes the characteristics of each of these cases. These ideal types show the extent to which administrators can exercise or relinquish control over the policy process.

The passive or traditional model of public participation used in Ohio excludes citizens until the agency has completed its work. Citizens are then asked to approve the draft report or to present opposing testimony. The administrators, however, retain the final say over how that testimony is used and whether the report will be revised as a result. This is government *for* the people, where administrators view their role as hired experts to carry out policy as articulated by political leaders—the pure form of the politics-administration dichotomy. Citizens have a very small role, if any, in this model.

At the other extreme, the active model gives the policy process to the public; the administrators serve as consultants or advisors to the people and also fund the participation effort. Citizens are predominant in this model, which represents the pure form of government by the people. Administrators still have an important role to play as expert consultants and policy advisors, but their primary responsibility will come after implementation of the public's recommendations. This may diminish the parameters of administrator expertise somewhat, but it also makes the job easier because of the high degree of citizen consensus about the goals of the policy.

The aura of expertise is retained in the hybrid model, which represents government with the people. Here, public participation is an administrative goal and the process is designed for building consensus, not merely airing competing views. Administrators develop a partnership with the public and rely on the public to develop agreement on recommendations, which are then used by the administrators to draft the final reports. Although administrators still maintain control over the process, it is much more receptive to and dependent on public input than the passive model.

The critical difference between the hybrid and active models is in the retention of administrative control. In Indiana, administrators retained their authority to reject task-force proposals with which they disagreed (or that they considered politically infeasible). The public was invited in but did not take over the administrative building. In contrast, the Missouri agency relinquished control and the final document was shaped by the public's expertise, not the administrators'.

CITIZENS AND CITIZEN PARTICIPATION

The models reveal that citizen participation can take many forms. The literature identifies several meanings of citizen participation, from the simple act of voting to lobbying to affect political decisions to actual involvement in decision making, as in a town meeting. In this chapter, the term *citizen participation* does not encompass lobbying, but refers primarily to efforts to influence administrative decisions of policy-implementing agencies. Crosby, Kelly, and Schaefer (1986) distinguished the two as follows:

> [Lobbying efforts] are attempts to change public policy by getting large numbers of people to contact the appropriate public officials. The assumption is that a particular view is correct and the aim is to get as many supporters as possible to express this view to the public officials. Citizen participation . . . is an attempt to do the reverse: to start with a diverse group of people, inform them on the

topic, and then get them to recommend that policy option which they find most appropriate. (p. 171)

Lobbyists are generally paid to represent an interest, whereas citizen participation is most often a volunteer activity.

For most citizens, the reality of the public participation process rarely meets the promise of democracy. Public input in administrative decisions is likely to be solicited only after administrators and selected consultants have defined the problem and developed proposed solutions. Public participation is little more than a formality in many cases, designed to allow the public to comment while protecting the agency's interests. Although citizens are given the opportunity to provide input, their suggestions rarely change the outcome of the process because the most critical decisions have usually been made already. As Daniel Kemmis, former mayor of Missoula, Montana, observed, "not much 'public hearing' goes on at the typical public hearing" (cited in Stivers, 1994, p. 368; see "The Listening Bureaucrat" sidebar in Chapter 10).

The process for public hearings was outlined by the Administrative Procedures Act (APA) in 1946 and has been routinely followed by administrators at all levels of government for the past 50 years. The essential steps in the process are (a) the agency develops a proposed regulation, set of rules, implementation plan, and so forth, working either internally or in consultation with other experts in the field, often, and increasingly, including industry representatives; (b) the proposal is published in the *Federal Register* or the state counterpart with request for comments within 30 days; and (c) the agency may choose to schedule one or more public hearings for the purpose of receiving comments on the proposal, in which case the time and location of the meeting(s) are also published. After the hearings and at the end of the 30-day review period, the agency then issues final rules that may or may not reflect the public's comments. There are two types of rule making described by the law: formal and informal. Formal rule making requires that persons making testimony at public hearings be sworn, and allows them to be cross-examined; participants are treated as expert witnesses. Informal rule making allows open hearings with unsworn testimony, thus enabling more citizens to participate. Formal rule making processes are rarely used for environmental regulations.

Another factor critical to citizen input is the legal concept of standing. In lawsuits, only plaintiffs who have standing can bring an action. Standing is defined as having a direct interest in an issue, usually the danger of being harmed physically or economically. Environmentalists who want to preserve wilderness for its own sake, for example, may not have standing to bring action against developers or property owners who want to build a shopping mall or resort. Environmental laws have been designed to overcome this problem by establishing general standing in the laws themselves. Thus, citizens have a much broader avenue for participation in the implementation of environmental policies than in, say, the awarding of military contracts.

Nonetheless, there are significant barriers to citizen participation that act to limit the number of citizens who typically respond to a rule making proposal. The time and location of hearings are of critical importance. If a hearing is scheduled in the state capital on a workday afternoon, the turnout will likely be much smaller than if it were scheduled in the evening in an affected community. The cost in travel and lost workdays is much greater for citizens than for paid lobbyists. Citizens are perceived, by administrators and elected officials, to lack expertise on the issue and to trade on emotionalism rather than "objective fact" (see MacNair et al., 1983). Citizens often feel that the deck is stacked against them, particularly when they observe the often compatible relationships between administrators and industry professionals. Because their concerns are most often ignored or swept away, it should not surprise us that the most likely citizen participants are the ones who are the angriest and the most dedicated to undermining the administrator's careful efforts. The portrayal of citizens as obstructionists, therefore, can be directly linked to their weak assigned role in the process.

ADMINISTRATORS AND CITIZEN PARTICIPATION

Most administrators would probably admit to viewing citizen participation as a necessary evil, at best. It is disruptive of administrative routine and often wasteful, particularly when only a handful of citizens shows up at a public hearing. Twenty years ago, I attended a public meeting in Pittsburgh, sponsored by the Pennsylvania Department of Transportation to report on plans to reduce transportation-related air pollution. Other administrators included representatives from the national Department of Transportation, the EPA, and the National League of Cities whose expenses were borne by the state. Of the six citizens who turned out for the meeting, only one was unfamiliar with the programs discussed. The agency's purpose was to comply with the public participation requirements of the governing legislation. This seemed like a very expensive method for little public benefit.

Sherry Arnstein, in a widely cited 1969 article, described a ladder of citizen participation. As outlined in Crosby et al. (1986), "the lowest end of the scale is manipulation, followed by therapy, informing, consultation, placation, partnership, and delegated power. Actual citizen control resides at the top of the list" (p. 173). Public managers rarely relinquish the control necessary to permit citizens to reach the top of the ladder, nor is even partnership very common. For the most part, public managers view citizen participation as appropriate for informing, consultation, and placation. Elena Van Meter (1975), former president of the League of Women Voters, observed that the major reason for traditional resistance to citizen input "is that citizen briefings *take up too much time* and *delay* urgently needed action" (p. 811; [italics added]). The essential reason for this attitude can be linked directly to the origins of public administration itself and the emphasis on the manager's expertise. The literature of public administration clearly places the responsibility for "managing" citizen participation on the administrators. Such management has many facets—selecting participants, limiting access to the process, convening educational or informational meetings rather than "hearings," staffing advisory committees and controlling their agendas, and limiting the autonomy of advisory boards. The intent is usually to maintain agency stability and protect agency goals.

John Clayton Thomas, in his book *Public Participation in Public Decisions* (1995), provides a comprehensive overview of the public administration literature on citizen participation. He identifies five decision making approaches for public managers that roughly capture the essence of Arnstein's ladder below the top step:

1. *Autonomous managerial decision.* The manager solves the problem or makes the decision alone without public involvement.
2. *Modified autonomous managerial decision.* The manager seeks information from segments of the public, but decides alone in a manner that may or may not reflect group influence.
3. *Segmented public consultation.* The manager shares the problem separately with segments of the public, getting ideas and suggestions, then makes a decision that reflects group influence.
4. *Unitary public consultation.* The manager shares the problem with the public as a single assembled group, getting ideas and suggestions, then makes a decision that reflects group influence.
5. *Public decision.* The manager shares the problem with the assembled public, and together the manager and the public attempt to reach agreement on a solution. (pp. 39-40)

In each of these approaches, the manager maintains control over the process and the substance of the discussion. The public is viewed as isolated from the administrative process until invited in by the manager on the manager's terms. This implies that the decision must reflect administrative and organizational goals; there is no indication that public values or goals should be allowed to overrule agency decisions. In discussing the question of how much decision making authority should be shared with the public, Thomas recommends, "the manager who anticipates public agreement with the agency's goals has reason to share more authority. The manager who anticipates disagreement or who does not know what to anticipate will want to retain more authority to protect *agency* goals" (p. 58; [italics added]).

Applying Thomas's outline to the models, we can see that the Ohio process exemplifies approaches 2 and 4, modified autonomous managerial decision and unitary public consultation. The Indiana process used approach 5, public decision, as the agency shared the problem. Note that Thomas does not show a category to describe the Missouri process.

Citizen participation, therefore, is not designed primarily for citizens but for agencies. Because it almost always fails to approach the top of Arnstein's (1969) ladder, public participation rarely enables citizens to significantly change or influence agency decisions. Citizen participation for many citizens is a hollow exercise with high costs in terms of time and effort and very little return other than a good feeling for having done one's democratic duty.

In many cases, communication is a one-way street from administrators to citizens. The basic assumption of many public administrators is that citizens have, at best, marginal expertise, not essential information, and thus, are best left out of the process until the important decisions have been made and they can do little damage. What is striking is that this approach is most prevalent in situations where protest is anticipated and public agreement most crucial, as in environmentally sensitive decisions such as siting of undesirable facilities or LULUs (Locally Unacceptable Land Uses). Barry Rabe (1994) asserted, in a study of hazardous waste siting in Canada and the United States, that "extensive public education and participation are unlikely to result in siting agreements if they merely set the stage for top-down site selection by private corporations or governmental authorities" (p. 155).

NIMBY is the kind of citizen participation that administrators fear most, a breakdown in public discourse and total resistance on the part of certain publics toward administrative decisions. Administrators anticipating a potential NIMBY situation, however, usually tighten up their controls over the process in an attempt to limit public contention, which leads to further diminishing of public trust in the administrators.

To move beyond NIMBY, according to Rabe, agencies must adopt a new approach that is "broadly inclusive, capable of generating public trust in a sphere of environmental policy that has become synonymous in many states and provinces with corruption and incompetence" (pp. 153-154). Rabe's analysis concluded that successful sitings of waste facilities occurred where (a) communities voluntarily accepted the siting and (b) agencies agreed to give communities equal power over management decisions. The significant element in the successful cases was building trust between the communities and the agencies. Only by relinquishing top-down control and ceding power to local communities were agencies able to reach effective decisions. In these cases, citizen participation occurs at the second highest rung of Arnstein's (1969) ladder (partnership) and may at times reach the top.

A NEW MODEL OF PUBLIC ADMINISTRATION

For most of the history of public administration, the public has been viewed as an unwelcome interference in administrative affairs. Citizen participation is relegated to the legislative process or, perhaps ideally, to voting. Indeed, as Box and Sagen observe in Chapter 10, citizen access is even limited by the actions of powerful political elites. Administrators are isolated from the public and carry out their tasks for their own benefit in the name of public service. There is no room in this picture for active citizen participation in administrative processes.

In both Indiana and Missouri, however, administrators welcomed the new insights and information that citizens can bring to the table. Furthermore, the citizens demonstrated that they are willing to make the time to be involved in the policy process where they perceive that their contributions will receive active consideration. Meaningful public participation is more successful and satisfying for administrators as well as for citizens.

Other cases in this book also demonstrate the emergence of the active and hybrid models. Both Kovalick and Kelly's "task-oriented convener" and Zanetti's "transformative administrator" are examples of the hybrid model—government with the people. Both also inch toward the active model, empowering citizens, but at the same time retaining autonomy over the process. As long as administrative control is primary, the possibilities for government by the people are limited.

If the visions of other authors of this book are to be realized, it will be necessary for public administration as a field to abandon the expectation that the administrator should be the sole expert in the policy implementation process. For administrators to become facilitators and partners with citizens requires a fundamental change in public administration theory and practice. Administrators will have to overcome the tendency to opt for the controlled process merely in the name of efficiency. Any efficiency gained from such a process is short-term at best. In the long run, building consensus on policy goals is far more efficient than the ongoing conflict and dissensus that can result from controlled administrative decisions.[6]

To change the role of administrators from experts to facilitators, we must address some fundamental questions of democracy. In a democracy, should professional administrators have sole control over administrative decisions that affect millions of citizens—government for the people? Or should they use their expertise in the service of the public to enable citizens to develop their own solutions—government by the people? Which of these roles is closer to democratic ideals? Which can bring more satisfaction to public administrators?

I believe that the ultimate goal of public administration is the achievement of government by the people. This does not mean that every decision should be taken through a plebiscite. In practice, administrators must balance governance needs with cost-effectiveness. We do not serve the public well by wasting resources.

The key, in my mind, is to distinguish between administrative routine, where expertise counts, and public policy decisions that affect life. The latter tend to be more potentially explosive. The natural instinct of administrators to control these discussions more closely only makes the situations worse. It is in these cases that administrators must relinquish control, give responsibility to citizens, step aside, and let democracy happen. As risky as that seems, it may be the only way to find agreement on contentious policy issues.

Finally, it may be impossible to overcome public anti-government sentiment without a fundamental change in the basic theory of public administration. The image of the uncaring, incompetent bureaucrat stems directly from practice derived from public administration theory which sets the administrator apart from the public, leading to mistrust on both sides. Government today is seen as an entity separate from the rest of society, not the means by which we achieve collective goals as a democratic people. The only way to overcome this perception is to invite the public into the process and give government back to its rightful owners.

Truly effective long-term solutions to contentious political problems can come only from an open, inclusive process where administrators welcome citizen participation as essential to their work rather than as a challenge to their own expertise. In the end, it is citizens who must live with the consequences of policy decisions, not administrators.

NOTES

1. The states in the study were Ohio, Michigan, Indiana, Illinois, Wisconsin, Minnesota, Iowa, Missouri, Kansas, North Dakota, South Dakota, Nebraska, Colorado, Montana, Wyoming, Idaho, and Utah. The region was drawn by the project's funding agency, the Midwest Center of the National Institute for Global Climate Change.

2. Indeed, Ohio invented acid rain when, in the early 1970s, the state approved the use of tall stacks on coal-burning power plants rather than scrubber technology to comply with the Clean Air Act.

3. The 1990 Clean Air Act Amendments, designed to regulate the acid rain problem; the Inter-Modal Surface Transportation Act (ISTEA); and the 1991 Energy Policy Act, which required that electric utilities incorporate energy conservation into rate increase requests.

4. This administrative placement in itself indicates that the state priority for energy policy is to aid business, not environmental or consumer interests.

5. The Center was originally established by the city of Kansas City during the 1970s to comply with Carter administration regulations. It later became an independent nonprofit organization, funded by contributions, grants, and contracts.

6. When presenting these ideas at conferences, I have been challenged by administrators who tell me there isn't enough time to use consensual citizen-participation methods. It seems odd that there is rarely enough time to do it right, but always enough to do it over.

Chapter 7

AT THE NEXUS OF STATE AND CIVIL SOCIETY

The Transformative Practice of Public Administration

Lisa A. Zanetti

> Each man [sic], finally, outside his professional activity, carries on
> some form of intellectual activity, that is, he is a "philosopher," an
> artist, a man of taste, he participates in a particular conception of
> the world, has a conscious line of moral conduct, and therefore
> contributes to sustain a conception of the world or to modify it,
> that is, to bring into being new modes of thought.
>
> —Antonio Gramsci (1971)

In a fundamental way, the theory and practice of public administration is at the heart of all questions of government and civic life.
Seventy years ago, the Italian theorist and political activist Antonio Gramsci (1971) noted that law was at the intersection of the state and civil
society, possessing the simultaneous potential for both coercion and transformation. In the current age, as government permeates nearly every
aspect of life, Gramsci's observation might well be modified: It is public
administration that is at the nexus of the state and civil society. Public
servants function as the mediators, in many instances, between the citizens
and their elected representatives—and the reverse. They are in a position
to perpetuate the status quo, or maneuver toward change.

It is a powerful position to be in, and an isolating one. Public servants, somehow, are neither fish nor fowl, and are scorned by both the political representatives and the citizens they serve. This bizarre limbo was vividly illustrated for me early in my public career, when I had recently begun to work at the U.S. Department of Commerce. One of the responsibilities of our office was to disseminate information about doing business in the Caribbean Basin. One day a caller inquired about importing and exporting regulations. I could give him general guidelines, but recommended that he consult a customs broker for specific information. It was clear that the caller didn't want to retain a customs specialist, because he continued to push for detailed instructions that I was not qualified to provide. Rather than give him erroneous information, I continued to suggest that he obtain a specialist's advice. Finally, the caller informed me: "I am a U.S. citizen. My taxes pay your salary, so you work for me. I *demand* that you get me this information!"—as if we public servants paid no income taxes ourselves. By his logic, I figured that I was self-employed.

But this anonymous caller's attitude left a profound impression. I had approached his questions in good faith, making my best effort to respond to his needs. I had offered to send information, refer him to others who could better respond to his queries, and had spent a good deal of time with him explaining the general purposes of the program. Why the hostility? Negative attitudes toward public servants proliferate. The stereotype of the clock-watching bureaucrat who leaves promptly at 4:30 or 5:00 is well known. A dear friend of mine who recently left a short stint at a quasi-public agency did so, she said, because she couldn't function in an environment that didn't value the "work ethic." But the civil service was instituted as a meritocracy, a means for ensuring that the best qualified individuals were hired to do the job. Why has the bureaucrat come to symbolize laziness and ineptitude? Why has the phrase "I'm with the government and I'm here to help" become such a laughable proposition?

Part of the explanation can be supplied, I believe, by examining the general attitudes toward knowledge and expertise that have prevailed during this century. Science and analytical techniques have become the benchmarks for establishing the acceptability of various forms of knowledge. Science relies on objectivity to produce results that are statistically significant and therefore valid. With the growing value placed on expertise, however, has come an increasing segregation between experts and nonexperts. Knowledge gained through the subjective experience of everyday people— nonexperts—is not valid, because it is tainted by personal bias. The practice of public administration has wholeheartedly embraced the idea of the neutral expert. But in relying on objectivity, we have been guilty of perpetuating what Yvonna Lincoln (1995) calls the voyeuristic gaze. In building the image of the professional technocrat, we have become separated from our identities as concerned and involved citizens. We have come to appear remote, disinterested, and unconnected with our fellow citizens—hence the attitude of my anonymous caller.[1]

The purpose of this chapter is to describe a transformative practice of public administration that reconnects the knowledge of expertise with the knowledge of experience. It does so by combining technical proficiency with a normative foundation that values the wisdom gained from common sense and personalized observation. Transformative public administration allows the public service professional to function as a critical specialist who recognizes that neutrality and objectivity have a dark and troublesome side. It is a practice of interested science (Alway, 1995) that is conducted with the purpose of furthering a more inclusive, substantively democratic polity.

THE TRIUMPH OF "TRENDS"

In the late 1980s, I was employed at the U.S. International Trade Commission (ITC). The ITC is one of those semi-obscure agencies that proliferate in Washington, D.C., to carry out missions that seem remote to most everyday people. Technically, the ITC is an independent regulatory agency, headed by six commissioners whose political affiliations are to be divided in a manner that gives no party more than three positions. The ITC serves a variety of functions, but one of its most prominent responsibilities is to conduct investigations of product "dumping"—the sale of imported goods at unfairly low prices that constitute damaging competition for domestic companies. These investigations are initiated at the request of U.S. industries that claim to be adversely affected by the imports.

My official position was that of an investigator. In this intimidating-sounding capacity, it was my responsibility to coordinate teams of experts (economists, attorneys, industry specialists) to gather information about the condition of U.S. industries facing import competition within the time frames mandated by statute. As part of the process, we designed and mailed questionnaires, tabulated the responses, conducted hearings, made site visits, talked with industry insiders (trade associations, etc.), read trade press and general news accounts, and generally acted as detectives, ferreting out information that we felt best explained the current condition of an industry and the direction in which it was headed. Then we compiled all the information into a dense, dry report and forwarded our findings to the commissioners, who read them (or had their personal staffs abstract the reports), sometimes requested private briefings to explain the findings, and eventually cast their votes in public hearings.

During the time that I was employed at the ITC, a debate was brewing among the commissioners regarding the most appropriate evaluation of staff findings. The nature of the investigation process involved the accumulation of both quantitative and qualitative data. Staff constructed and mailed surveys to all known members of the industry under investigation, requesting information on production levels, capacity and capacity utilization, shipments, inventories, employment, wages, productivity, and financial health, among other indicators. Compilation of this information was mandated by statute and the information could be subpoenaed from companies that declined to provide it. These data were aggregated to provide a picture of the trends in the industry and used to determine whether import competition was contributing to material injury of the domestic industry.

But the staff also compiled a tremendous amount of qualitative information on the condition of the domestic industry. Interviews, site visits, testimony offered in hearings, responses to queries from staff—all contributed to the formation of gut reactions by investigative staff regarding what was happening in the industry. Sometimes this qualitative information reinforced the quantitative analysis, but in other cases it did not. For the most part, however, it was not given great weight in the commissioners' final vote. In the years I worked there, commissioners either looked at the financial trends in the industry—reaching a finding of injury if domestic manufacturers were in decline while import shares rose and prices fell—or relied on econometric analyses of domestic industry and a sometimes hair-splitting definition of what constituted a market.

In these cases, it is often the investigative staff that has the best understanding of what is transpiring in the industry. After six to eight months of intensive, exclusive focus on a given case[2] and access to a great deal of confidential information, the investigator frequently knew more about the industry than industry members themselves. Much of this understanding was based on an accumulation of anecdotal evidence corroborated by multiple sources. Despite the richness of the qualitative explanations, however, they were rarely relied on to justify a commission vote. At the public hearing where the commissioners cast their votes, investigative staff are called on to provide summaries of their findings. In one investigation I handled, I began my briefing at the vote with an explanation of some of the unusual circumstances that surrounded the case. My summary was cut short by one commissioner who interrupted my statement, requesting that I provide "just the trends, please."

As much as I genuinely enjoyed my work at the ITC, I found the emphasis on quantitative analyses frustrating and confining. When I could not present qualitative evidence to build the legal foundation on which a decision was made, I felt that I had failed in my responsibility to accurately convey the stories people had told me as a part of the investigation.[3] In all fairness, I should point out that individual experiences presented as testimony at hearings or as part of written filings did become part of the legal record, and I do not mean to suggest that such information was never considered. I am certain that there were cases in which it was. However, the investigative findings that were given the preponderance of consideration were those trends backed by the authority of quantitatively verifiable facts.

Given the evolutionary history of the public administration profession, this situation is not surprising. Since the Progressive era (see Chapter 4), public administration has moved in an increasingly instrumental, managerial direction, valuing the application of scientific methodology to the resolution of public issues and building an identity of neutral expertise. This identity was to provide legitimacy for those employed in public service. I suggest, however, that the legacy of neutral competence and expertise has instead contributed, perhaps unwittingly, to the estrangement of public servants from the citizens they are called on to serve.

RECONNECTING THE KNOWLEDGE OF EXPERTISE
WITH THE KNOWLEDGE OF EXPERIENCE

The emergence in this century of the "knowledge society" has had consequences that were unanticipated by the pragmatic Progressives. For them, science was to be the great equalizing force, contributing to the formation of a democratic community. The unexpected result of elevating the scientific method, however, has been the creation of a knowledge elite (Bell, 1974; Gaventa, 1993; Merrifield, 1993). The production of so-called valid knowledge has become increasingly concentrated in the hands of the universities, corporations, and government and correspondingly separated from the experiences of ordinary individuals.

Membership in the knowledge elite is, in a sense, by invitation only—extended through the conferring of degrees, the acquisition of professional credentials, or the securing of other forms of exclusive certification. Certain types of social controls govern the type of knowledge produced and for whom, through the organization of academic disciplines, the promulgation of professional standards, and incentives and reward structures for career advancement. Knowledge is transmitted through the publication of professional journals, participation in conferences, and membership in networks open only to those who are members of the club. Additionally, much of this knowledge is passed along in language that is unfamiliar to the uninitiated—the specialized jargon employed by different fields (Gaventa, 1993; Ricci, 1984).

In this environment, the experts become the power brokers. By choosing to offer or withhold information, experts can manipulate the actions, or inactions, of others, controlling the emergence of issues. When issues do emerge, these experts can exercise tremendous discretion over how the issues are defined (Gaventa, 1980, 1993; Lukes, 1974). The effect is frequently to declare as a "nonissue" many of the problems encountered by everyday citizens. Furthermore, because the knowledge of expertise is segregated into disciplines, little attention is given to the cumulative or interactive effects of related issues. Gaventa (1993) writes,

> Take, for instance, the case of a worker who is employed in a chemical plant, lives in a nearby community, eats and drinks the food and water from the land, and is dying of cancer. To gain a response from the system for action on the cause of the cancer, he or she will have to subdivide the problem into that derived from work, governed by the Occupational Safety and Health Administration or the Department of Labor; that derived from air pollution, governed by the air quality control board; that derived from the water, governed by the Water Quality Control Board; that derived from toxins in the food, regulated by the Department of Agriculture; that derived from eating wildlife obtained through hunting, regulated by the specialists in the Department of Fisheries and Wildlife; that derived from the consumption of other foods, regulated by the Consumer Protection Agency; and that derived from the interactive effects of them all—regulated by no one. (p. 29)

Lived experience is a cumulative undertaking, but only the individual parts are examined by the experts, with no effort made to sum up the whole.

Expertise can be used to manipulate or perpetuate societal power relations. It can be used to delay and defuse an issue, as in doing a study that takes so long and produces such inconclusive results that the issue is abandoned. Expertise can be used to impress and bemuse—marshaling voluminous statistical evidence or sheer numbers of experts to overwhelm opponents. Finally, expertise can be used to gloss and confuse an issue, basing political decisions on somewhat arbitrary standards that are presented as scientifically (read: objectively) valid. An example is the acceptable mercury level for fish, which had been set at 0.5 ppm (parts per million) until 1977, when, after lobbying by the tuna-fishing lobby, the "safe" level for mercury in fish doubled to 1 ppm[4] (Merrifield, 1993, pp. 74-75).

Even more problematic is the fact that, for the most part, knowledge experts are not accountable to those affected by the knowledge. This lack of accountability is rooted in the premise that scientific knowledge is superior because of its objectivity. Sharp distinctions are maintained between expertise—the study of a problem—and experience, or the subjective living of the problem. Experts may study the problems of poverty, homelessness, or inadequate prenatal care, but they must not experience these same problems, or identify with those who do, for fear of jeopardizing their objectivity. Information or knowledge that comes from personal experience is tainted with subjectivity and given little weight in official decision making because it is not scientific. Belief in the authority of expertise subordinates common sense, and in so doing subordinates common people (Gaventa, 1993).

In addition, there is great reluctance on the part of knowledge experts to share information with the public, out of concern that ordinary people will not understand the information or will use it for partisan purposes in a manner that threatens the experts' reputation for objectivity. Experts, like science itself, are supposed to be politically neutral. Having a professional obligation to describe only what is, and not what ought to be, allows the expert to abdicate responsibility for expressing opinions or taking remedial action (Merrifield, 1993).

Public administration has been caught up in this culture of expertise, with detrimental effects. For many of the historical reasons discussed in Part I, public administration has become captivated by managerialism (Ventriss, 1987). The education and practice of public service professionals has become characterized by the mastery of instrumental analysis and technique, elevating process over purpose. The effect is to convince citizens that the substance of their concerns is unimportant.

I experienced (and, I am sure, did my share to contribute to) this culture of expertise as a public service professional, but its negative effects became most evident to me as a doctoral student. I was involved in a year-long interdisciplinary class on collaborative research. As part of the requirements of the class, each student collaborated with a local citizens' group to address an issue of concern to that segment of the community. The group with which I was working was Solutions to Issues of Concern to Knoxvillians (SICK), a grassroots organization with a history of community action and a particular interest in health care issues for indigent populations in Knoxville. SICK is particularly concerned with the lack of adequate prenatal care available to women on public assistance. When Tennessee adopted TennCare in 1993,[5] with little lead time or preparation, confusion was widespread. SICK's interest was in compiling a list of obstetricians and primary care providers who were willing to see TennCare clients for pre-natal care and delivery.

Like many issues that reflect deep structural social, political, and economic inequities, this one appeared deceptively simple. The complexity of the project was quickly revealed when I was unable to obtain such a list from the TennCare office. I tried calling individual Managed Care Organizations (MCOs),[6] but nearly all were unwilling to release lists of participating physicians, despite the fact that Tennessee's own TennCare literature suggested that this information was to be available to potential enrollees. When I pointed this out, several MCO representatives explained that the lists changed frequently and therefore were not widely disseminated so as to avoid confusion. If I wished to ask about specific physicians, however, they could tell me if the physician was a participant in their plan.

To compile the list SICK needed, we decided to conduct a telephone survey of local obstetricians, gynecologists, and primary care physicians to ask several basic questions. We compiled the list based on telephone listings and those few MCO directories we were able to obtain. Advised ahead of time that telephone consent was not legally defensible, we knew that we would be required by the university's Institutional Review Board (IRB)[7] first to send letters to the survey population requesting their consent to be contacted. I completed the necessary request and submitted it to the IRB. We made it clear in the proposed cover letter to be sent to physicians that confidentiality and anonymity would not be protected. Because TennCare was a publicly funded program, it seemed to us that confidentiality and anonymity should not have been a substantial concern, although we recognized the importance of obtaining informed consent from the survey population.

My appearance before the IRB was unexpectedly difficult. As it turned out, several IRB members had a number of ethical concerns regarding my proposed project, specifically because of my collaboration with SICK. In this case, the proposal had been circulated in advance to three members, who reviewed it in detail. Two of the reviewers recommended approval with slight modifications. A third reviewer, however, had vehement objections. This reviewer was an outside member, a physician with a private practice who had been asked to serve on the IRB and who had tremendous personal objections to TennCare. Specifically, he insisted that physicians be notified that I was working in collaboration with SICK, because it was a group with a history of confrontations with the medical community. During the discussion, another member of the IRB asked whether SICK intended to use the results of the project to initiate a class-action lawsuit. Once the word lawsuit was mentioned, faces around the table paled visibly. Although

I had no knowledge of such plans, the damage had been done. It was clear that members had no desire to see the project go forward with the possibility of political controversy it presented.

Eventually, the project was approved, but with a key revision: I was required to declare my affiliation with SICK. The physician who insisted on this change indicated that he expected such a declaration to damage the results of the survey, and he was correct. Only 5 consent forms out of the 45 that I originally mailed were returned, clearly not enough to compile a usable list. Though I cannot know for sure whether the affiliation with SICK was the only reason (the nonconfidential nature of the responses probably contributed, as well), I did receive a letter from one practice specifically denouncing the organization as a "troublemaker" and refusing to participate in the survey because of my collaboration with them. The only practice that willingly participated (and offered additional information, with attribution) was a birthing center, which has its own quarrels with physician dominance and control of the medical profession.

What did this case illustrate? I found it instructive on a number of points addressed in this chapter. First, experts manipulated the definition of the problem. Women in need of prenatal care knew from experience that they were unable to obtain it easily. Because administrative procedures had been put into place, however (never mind that they weren't working), the inaccessibility experienced by many community members was discounted by experts on the grounds that the women were poor, or uneducated, or ignorant, or just too lazy to help themselves. But I was a doctoral student, a former public servant familiar with the essence of bureaucracy and the if-then logic of working my way through bureaucratic channels, and I couldn't complete a simple task, either. Whose problem was it?

Second, experts controlled the availability of information. The state abdicated much of its responsibility for running the program to the MCOs, which, as private organizations, were not obligated to release information regarding their contracts with individual physicians.[8] These same interests, represented on the university's IRB, also sought to control the manner in which I requested information. By dictating the format of the survey request, they effectively guaranteed that we would obtain no usable results. It was a version of the delay and defuse tactic.

Third, this experience again illustrated the preference for "objectivity." At the same time that I was working on this project, SICK was also involved in a second collaborative project with another member of the university. The second project sailed through IRB approval relatively cleanly. Although SICK was a coparticipant, the study was formulated along traditional social science lines: large sample size, confidentiality preserved, results aggregated, reliance on probability theory to determine the validity of the findings. It was acceptable to focus the "voyeuristic gaze" on poor women and their reproductive histories, but not on the professional medical community.

Finally, by working in a collaborative fashion with community members, I was able to experience, disturbingly clearly, their perception that "government is *not* us." As a former public service professional, I was inclined to be sympathetic to the TennCare program. I was confident that the administrative procedures would function as the state advertised, and was willing to grant some leeway and understanding for the difficulties in getting a program up and running. Perhaps I am a hopeless idealist, but I was truly shocked at the extent to which government appeared remote from and unconcerned with the problems of the citizens it purported to serve.

My experiences in the capacities of public service professional, public administration academician, and politically aware citizen have led me to the conclusion that, in order to reconnect with citizens, the study and practice of public administration must leave behind the arrogance of expertise. We must have the courage to step away from the comfortable (and comforting) identity as managers and neutral efficiency experts and be open to the knowledge that ordinary lived experience provides. By combining training in instrumental techniques with a normative foundation that emphasizes the rectification of historical and political conditions of inequality, critically minded public administrators can use their unique position to act as transformative agents of change.

POSSIBILITIES FOR A TRANSFORMATIVE PRACTICE OF PUBLIC ADMINISTRATION

The call for transformative public administration is predicated on the assumption that the bureaucracy does not necessarily equal the state. Those on the left have in the past committed the instrumental reductions of "law equals state" (see Hunt, 1993) and, less explicitly, public bureaucracy equals state—a questionable leap (Ventriss, 1987). The literature on administrative discretion, however, amply illustrates that public servants are not of a singular mind or unified action. In many instances, administrators are required to make judgment calls based on their own interpretation of the proper ends (as well as means) of a given administrative action or policy initiative. Recognition of the legitimacy and acceptability of administrative discretion[9] provides a foundation for transformative action.

The phrasing *transformative administrator* is suggested by Guba and Lincoln's (1994) discussion of critical research approaches (see also Giroux, 1988). In describing the critical perspective, Guba and Lincoln note that it is informed by historical realism, an approach that views reality as shaped by social, political, cultural, economic, ethnic, and gender considerations that have ossified over time and are now, mistakenly, assumed to be fixed. These structures have become a kind of virtual reality, but if uncovered, they can be changed. A critical perspective recognizes the interaction between the investigator and the investigated. All findings are shaped by values brought to the research situation by those involved; therefore, the expert's objectivity cannot exist.

A critical perspective seeks restitution for historical wrongs and emancipation for individuals that are trapped by these ossified societal structures. There is a moral tilt toward revelation and the erosion of ignorance, incorporating values of altruism and empowerment and combining them with a stimulus to action. The critical perspective requires a transformative intellectual to act as advocate and activist, and, interestingly, demands a kind of resocialization—the understanding and mastery of quantitative analytical techniques utilized confrontationally, for transformative purposes (Guba & Lincoln, 1994).[10]

Administrators trained only in instrumental approaches and interpretations do not know to question the effects of their actions on the lives of subordinate groups or give weight to knowledge gained from experience. But administrators who function as critical specialists, who recognize that they are part of a larger system of ideological tensions, and who can provide the mediating function that encourages counterhegemonic change, can serve as agents for transformation.

A transformative administrator is one who accepts certain assumptions about politics and knowledge. First, she or he recognizes that thought and ideas are fundamentally influenced by power relations that are socially and historically constituted. That is, the dominant characteristics of Western culture, which are to privilege certain races, classes, and genders, are human constructions that have been built over centuries of uncritical acceptance. But they are neither revealed truth, nor immutable reality, and they can be challenged and changed. Privileged groups retain that status because they have convinced the less-privileged that inequality is the way of the world, and that it is futile to protest or challenge it.

Second, she or he understands that facts cannot be isolated from values or normative assessments of the world. Because we cannot simply observe the world, but instead continually interact with and influence it, our values and experiences color our observations. When we are aware of these influences, we can act to correct certain tendencies—such as the tendency to accept the superiority of expert knowledge in all instances.

Third, an administrator working from a transformative perspective recognizes the potential for all citizens to be democratic philosophers.[11] This recognition is the essence of the quotation at the beginning of this chapter. Each individual has the choice to draw on his or her experiences either to substantiate the status quo or to recognize the contradictions and work to resolve them by creating new ways of thinking about the world and putting those new modes of thought into being.

Finally, she or he has come to appreciate how mainstream (instrumental) research has the effect (if not always the explicit intention) of reproducing and reinforcing the conditions of the status quo (Kincheloe & McLaren, 1994). Critically enlightened and sympathetic administrators can play a crucial role by providing the administrative access necessary to bring about change based on experience as well as expertise. They can act as interpreters and facilitators, but they can also act as transformative agents by educating citizens about how to articulate concerns, voice needs, and implement community-developed strategies for change.

In this capacity, public administration might learn from recent developments in the practice of law.[12] Supporters of a critical approach to law have recognized a need to become more creative in their strategies for social justice and have constructed "critical lawyering" as a partial solution. These proponents of change suggested that the law might become a means for deepening the political consciousness of subordinated groups (White, 1987-1988). In other words, the legal process can be used, not just to function within the game rules of the liberal framework, but to effect transformational[13] change.

With critical lawyering, critical legal theory is used to provide insight into the nature of client disempowerment and to politicize the legal process toward the goal of substantive equality. But critical lawyering also includes a participatory-educative approach that involves the client group in framing the question, developing strategy for change, learning how to use the system to effect change, and obtaining skills that can be used in the future. Importantly, it also helps dissolve the unequal power relations in the legal arena and joins the knowledge of experts with that of the laity. It is a means for giving the socially marginalized the ability and the right to speak for themselves (Buchanan & Trubek, 1992; Tremblay, 1990; White, 1987-1988).

The example of critical lawyering is particularly applicable to public administration for several reasons. First, both law and public administration face a similar duality of theory and practice. Both fields must ultimately reconcile academic theory with actions by practitioners. Second, law and public administration share the function of serving as legitimizing agents for the state. Both lawyers and public servants take oaths and both professions have shared reformist tendencies at different points in this century. Finally, the genesis of the critical perspective in both fields was similar, involving a rejection of the prevailing combination of philosophical liberalism and instrumentalism. Success in using the legal process to effect transformational change holds promise for using the administrative process in a similar fashion.

As a starting point, a transformative practice of public administration might adapt the tenets of critical lawyering (from Buchanan & Trubek, 1992),

Humanize: Resist the reduction of citizen experiences and "stories" to quantitative trends, administrative categories, and procedural solutions. Frame the issues in human terms. Overcome the "voyeuristic gaze."

Politicize: Employ political theory to understand and provide insight into the nature of citizen disengagement from government, symbolized by the growing expertise-experience gap.

Collaborate: Encourage the participation of citizen groups in the administrative process, on their terms, if possible. This means going beyond panels and surveys, which typically don't allow much citizen input in framing the issues (see Fox & Miller, 1995). Construct academic-practitioner-citizen collaborative efforts, wherever feasible, to overcome the partitioning of kinds of knowledge.

Strategize: Use citizen experiences and perspectives to evaluate the delivery of public services. Encourage citizen feedback as a tool for assessing the size of the expertise-experience gap at any given time.

Organize: Although administrators cannot be openly political, those functioning as "critical specialists" welcome the results of collective efforts by citizen groups, make space for those groups to be heard, and pay particular attention to rectifying procedures or language that is exclusionary.

Current demographic trends in public service may also be conducive to a transformative practice of public administration. Administrators who enter public service at mid-life may bring life experiences and perspectives that help them bridge the gap between the knowledge of expertise and the knowledge of experience. These individuals can build on their own experiences and be more able to appreciate, value, or act on the experiences of others.

The source of the transformation stems from the ability of a critically minded administrator to expose the contradictions of contemporary society—

the appearances and arrangements accepted by the dominant culture as natural and inevitable. Ideologies are directly related to social and institutional practices; therefore, people act *as if* certain cultural and social conditions are true. Individuals choose to misrecognize the relations of power for different reasons. The dominant groups accept existing conditions because these work to their advantage. Subordinate groups accept the existing conditions because they have been convinced that these conditions are the way of the world—fact, nature's plan, inviolable. This acceptance of inevitability and immutability on the part of subordinate groups effectively removes their concerns from the societal agenda. They become disengaged from the political discourse by allowing the rules to be defined by those who stand to gain (or retain) the most (Kincheloe & McLaren, 1994).

A transformative practice goes beyond the empirical re-presentation of the world. An essential element of the process is *reflection*—comparison of the judgments of expertise and those of experience, between "is" and "ought to be"— connected with *action*.

IMPLICATIONS OF A TRANSFORMATIVE PRACTICE OF PUBLIC ADMINISTRATION

The goal of a transformative practice of public administration is to carve out opportunities to achieve fundamental changes in the perception of knowledge, and its reflection in administrative practice, in very localized settings. For example, it is an approach that may initially be more feasible in state or local agencies that deal more directly with citizens on issues that touch their lives directly—delivery of prenatal care services to low income citizens, for example, rather than more macroissues of international trade balances.

The applicability to more localized settings is based on several lines of reasoning. First, Gramsci (1971, 1985) argued that successful societal change could only take place if it moved up from the people in a number of segments of society. The purpose is not to take power and give it to the powerless,[14] but to help the marginalized find their own answers. To do otherwise is paternalistic and undemocratic. This means that the outcome of the process must be respected, even if it may not be in complete accord with the outcome the administrator might have envisioned. Ideally, the synthesis between expertise and experience produces an outcome that is better than what each might have produced alone.

Second, a transformative approach may initially be more feasible in state or local agencies that deal more directly with citizens on issues that

From the Conversation: Is a Transformational Administrator Possible?

Ralph: Lisa, your chapter says that transformational administration must raise to the light of reason previously hidden maldistributions of values and power. Your rule is, rejoin what has been rent asunder: facts and values.

But this requires a method. Antonio Gramsci, cited here, does not develop such a method; but the critical theorist Jürgen Habermas's may serve as an example: Get people to talk in terms that make possible an open communication without hidden agendas. Like any method, this method has standards. People must speak so others can understand them. Their word must show it can be trusted. Their claim to represent others must be legitimate. And they must speak factually. The standards are those of comprehensibility, sincerity, legitimacy and truth (Forester, 1989, p. 151).

The administrator who wants to transform silently taken-for-granted power relationships and values distributions would have to become an expert in getting people to measure up to such standards. Again, just as previously, people living ordinary lives would have to live up to someone else's method. Method, not life, would become the context of what they have to say, the standard both for meaning and validity. One kind of expertise (facilitative administration) would replace another (top-down administration).

Critical theorists want to bring methodically produced "facts" back in contact with human values. But they want to do so according to their own methods. Again expertise dominates experience.

Lisa: Ralph, you have characterized the transformative practice of public administration as simply one more form of "expertise," enacted in accordance with elitist critical theory methods. This characterization, however, does not capture the democratic essence of what is intended by the approach.

Transformative practice is one that begins with people's lived experiences. Its method is to ask citizens to compare the platitudes fed to them by elites—such as "all men (sic) are created equal" and "ours is the land of opportunity"—with the realities of their own lives. Do they feel equal? Is there opportunity to earn a living wage? As individuals begin to recognize the contradictions between their lived experiences and the picture presented to them by elites, they become inspired to resolve these contradictions by demanding change and devising THEIR OWN strategies for the accomplishment of this change.

The role of the administrator in a transformative practice is to provide spaces for the disillusioned to speak and draw on the meanings they derive from their experiences. It is NOT an arrangement in which the administrator presumes to know the final answer. It is NOT the "methodical production of facts," it is the mediation between "is" and "ought." Administrators trained only in technical approaches may recognize tensions and contradictions but do not know how to resolve them.

Administrators who can function as "critical specialists," however, are able not only to listen, reflect, and engage in discourse, but also to make space for action that results from new modes of thought. Gramsci's approach is considerably more democratic than is Habermas' discourse theory. Habermas creates an ideal but does not tell us how to achieve it. He says, in effect, "if the world were perfect this is how we would act," but he cannot tell us how to get there. Gramsci says, more forthrightly, "the world is NOT perfect, we don't have to accept injustices, and this is how we can change it." As one of the marginalized, Gramsci well understood the alienation that results from political exclusion.

Habermas assumes that we are all rational, cerebral, and cooperative. But unlike "Habermasian man," most of us are emotional and passionate, and not even that articulate most of the time. Gramsci's approach allows ALL of us to speak in ways that are the most meaningful to us—music, art, poetry, skits, drama, stories. His appreciation of the everyday is far more genuine and profound. The transformative practice of public administration is a radical proposal, but it is one that takes its sustenance from the spirit of the Constitution. The administrator is just ONE element of society that contributes to change. Operating "at the nexus," the purpose is to draw on the wisdom of the everyday "democratic philosopher" that resides in all of us.

touch their lives directly. Gramsci noted that transformative change must take place throughout all segments of civil society before being put into place at the level of the national governmental structure. Administrators function to keep equilibrium between state and civil society. They represent the state, yet are the living, breathing point of contact between citizen and government. Street level bureaucrats (Lipsky, 1980/1992), in particular, are often called on to make judgmental decisions regarding the intent, purpose, and interpretation of legal statutes. This pivotal positioning means that the administrator can serve an important bridge function between elitist or potentially authoritarian approaches and the fragmentary relativism of radical pluralism (Carroll & Ratner, 1994). More macrolevel applications of this approach, in national agencies such as the U.S. International Trade Commission, for example, would be expected to come later, after critical-transformative collaborations have produced democratic, workable solutions. It is a filter-up, rather than a trickle-down approach.

But as a proposal for building a public administration to help overcome the estrangement many citizens now feel from "their" government, the transformative practice of public administration is an overall approach that can be relevant in a variety of venues. Such a practice of public administration, however, will require administrators (and academicians) to take a very different view of their mission as public servants. Administrators, in particular, will have to walk a fine line in balancing their critical social visions with their legal-political obligations. I suspect, too, that it will be uncomfortable at times.

When I worked with SICK and attended community meetings, I felt ostentatious as an outsider in appearance, dress, speech, background, and life history—a distinction that at times made me deeply uncomfortable. The irony was palpable: Perfectly comfortable walking the corridors of power in Washington, I was brought to adolescent speechlessness (or worse, mindless and overly cheerful chatter) at the prospect of interacting with seemingly ordinary community members. It was a humbling experience that left me profoundly insecure about my ability as a white, upper-middle-class, highly educated, cosmopolitan female to articulate a critical perspective, no matter what my political or intellectual leanings. How could my veneer of academic knowledge and my professional experience in government contribute to their efforts? At one level it would seem that our life experiences provided a common ground—after all, this project involved prenatal care and I knew the experiences of being pregnant and female. But what I know is being *privileged*, pregnant, and female, with access to insurance that pays the fees the doctors are happy to make room for in their appointment books. Schooled in a culture of meritocracy and accreditation, I could not figure out how to earn for myself the credentials possessed by these organic intellectuals.

Although I did not recognize it until later, such painful experience produced a certain epiphany: Perhaps that same insecurity is the source of many an expert's retreat to the comfortable crutch of objective knowledge, although most might be highly unwilling to admit it. Having worked so diligently to acquire our academic and professional accolades, we don't enjoy being challenged by the quiet and powerful voice of experience. After all, when we have followed the prescribed steps to research and consulted all the proper literature, on what grounds can our theory and findings be questioned? Yet such a challenge is precisely what transformative practice requires. If we admit to our discomfort in surrendering the status of expertise, we might be surprised to see what we learn.

Public administration is composed of many tensions and contradictions, as I noted in the beginning of this chapter. These tensions can be a source of destructive tendencies that perpetuate the estrangement of citizens from government. But contradictions can be used constructively, as well. A transformative approach aims for synthesis—of academic and practitioner efforts, of citizen and administrator, of trends and stories, of expertise and experience—taking advantage of public administration's position at the nexus of government and citizen to produce a more integrated, connected, and substantively democratic practice of public administration.

NOTES

1. See Humel and Stivers (Chapter 3, this volume) for a similar argument about knowledge in public administration.

2. Because of the exhaustive demands of compiling a comprehensive study within the statutory time frame, investigators almost never covered more than one case at a time.

3. For discussions on the value of stories, see Hummel (1991), Bailey (1992), and Schmidt (1993).

4. See "The Lost Mercury at Oak Ridge" (1983).

5. TennCare was implemented by the State of Tennessee effective January 1, 1994, as an experimental, state-based alternative to Medicaid. TennCare was envisioned as a program to provide expanded health care services to a broader range of citizens, including those who had previously been uninsurable under Medicaid. .

6. TennCare is structured to provide health care through privately operated Managed Care Organizations (MCOs), which contract with the State of Tennessee to provide services. MCOs negotiate separate contracts with each physician; physicians may choose to participate in several plans, but clients must elect to subscribe to a single MCO and may only see those physicians contracting with the MCO. Because TennCare was so recently implemented, the legal status of the contracts was unclear. The contract between the State of Tennessee and the MCO was considered a public document; however, the contracts that each MCO negotiates with individual physicians were tentatively being considered private instruments. Therefore, MCOs and physicians argued that they had no legal obligation to reveal to the public any information regarding these contracts. This was a legal distinction that was being contested, at least informally, by public interest groups on two points: that MCOs and physicians should have greater accountability for how a publically funded program was administered, and that potential enrollees should have access to full information in order to make an informed decision regarding the selection of an MCO.

7. The role and function of IRBs in most university research processes is a complicated one. Broadly, IRBs are tasked with eight main responsibilities, which revolve around minimizing risks to participants and ensuring that participants are provided adequate background on the risks and benefits of the study to be able to give their informed consent to participate. Many IRBs today have further extended their review process to include evaluation of the methodology to be used in the proposed study as a means for assessing the potential for scientific benefit (Berg, 1995).

Guidelines governing membership on IRBs are broad and allow considerable latitude. Each IRB must have at least five members of varying backgrounds, and membership must be mixed with regard to gender, profession, and race. Additionally, each IRB must contain at least one member whose work does not include the sciences or social sciences (for example, a lawyer, ethicist, or member of the clergy). However, these guidelines do not stipulate how to select or locate IRB members, what research qualifications members should possess, or the length of the term to be served (Berg, 1995).

The evolution of IRBs was spurred by the valid concern for protecting the welfare of participants. In particular, many early advocates had as a goal the protection of powerless populations (children, the mentally ill, prisoners, the underclass). What became institutionalized along with the concern for protection, however, was a scientific-behavioral model of research that accorded greater importance to accumulating knowledge and to preserving a certain "knowledge hegemony" within institutions of higher education than to widening the community of inquirers.

8. At the time of my involvement with the project, there was some legal disagreement over whether contracts were to be available to the public.

9. Indeed, this legitimacy and discretion are inevitable on epistemological grounds (see Hummel & Stivers, Chapter 3, this volume).

10. Inspirations for the transformative administrator can be found within Gramsci's (1971) theory of the intellectual, helpfully explicated by Holub (1992). In Holub's analysis, Gramsci envisioned four primary categories of intellectual. The first, which Holub calls the "traditional intellectual," includes the public figures, academics, doctors, teachers, artists, publishers, professionals, and semiprofessionals that represent the dominant class. This category takes account of the nonneutrality of ideas and knowledge and the political role of certain intellectuals in disseminating and validating the status quo (hegemonic condition). The second category includes Gramsci's "organic intellectual," which Holub separates into "new intellectuals" and "critical specialists." Gramsci spoke of the organic intellectual to represent the bearers of knowledge that emerge from every major social and economic formation. Holub's new intellectual is a specialist, a technocrat who understands his or her role in isolation but not the interconnections between other elements of complex systems. The critical specialist, by contrast, understands that his or her activity is partial and connected to other activities in a larger social, political, and economic system (Holub, 1992).

Gramsci also referred to the ability of every individual to understand and participate in the exchange of societal ideas—what Holub terms the "universal intellectual." Finally, Gramsci discusses the ability of certain groups to mediate between the dominant and subordinate classes. Holub terms this the "structure of feeling," or the "intellectual community." The interaction of this mediating group between the dominant and subordinate classes can reinforce a single world-view and be used to perpetuate hegemony, as in the case of the traditional intellectuals. However, there is also the possibility that dialogic interchange can be a factor in the production of a counterhegemony, where the articulation of alternative views is nurtured, validated, and encouraged (Holub, 1992).

The justification for the administrator as a transformational agent is found in these conceptions of the intellectual. An administrator who functions as a new intellectual will be incapable of recognizing or realizing the possibilities for transformation.

11. Gramsci's (1971) organic intellectual—people whose lived experience combines with their awareness of how political, social, and economic structures contribute to inequality and marginalization. Organic intellectuals are important because they do not simply describe social life from the "outside"; instead, they can use the language of a culture to express feelings and experiences that others find hard to articulate for themselves (Kolakowski, 1978).

12. Traditional public-interest law places faith in the available policy solutions (e.g., the War on Poverty), relies on procedural strategies to attain benefits for the socially marginalized, and maintains the effectiveness of advocacy positions in traditional arenas (such as the litigation strategy that produced the successful outcome in *Brown v. Board of Education*, 1957). Public interest law initially was viewed as a means to correct the deficiencies of the legal "marketplace" and to legitimize the welfare state by providing opportunities for otherwise unrepresented groups to be heard. The emphasis was on process-oriented responses to social inequities (as in the case of *Goldberg v. Kelly*, 1970), and this approach relied on the assumption that advocacy in traditional legal forums, particularly the courts, could bring about change. Challenges were framed in terms of the "rights" of marginalized groups to establish claims to social goods (Buchanan & Trubek, 1992).

In the 1960s and 1970s, impact litigation became a powerful instrument for welfare reform. It focused on changing institutional norms or practices, rather than resolving individual problems. Litigation was typically controlled by specialists working out of centralized locations (usually federally funded public-interest law offices), and often the individuals named as plaintiffs in these cases had little contact with lawyers or involvement in the suit after their complaints were filed and depositions taken. In times when the courts are receptive to claims of distributive justice, impact litigation can result in court orders that transfer funds or coerce institutional changes.

With the public funding cutbacks of the 1980s, however, such sweeping lawsuits became much more difficult to mount (White, 1987-1988). There was also a growing understanding of the paternalistic, dependency-inducing effects of traditional advocacy approaches. In essence, they represented another form of "expertise" based on membership in a particular knowledge class.

13. The word *transformational* here suggests change of an almost quantum nature in the manner Gramsci (1971) envisioned. Gramsci argued that substantive change required constructing a new intellectual and moral order. Repressive institutions must be challenged within the context of a democratically enlightened and politically engaged awareness that is both a precondition for, and a central aspect of, human liberation and substantive equality.

14. For something of a contrast, see Alinsky (1971, p. 3).

Chapter 8

THE EPA SEEKS ITS VOICE AND ROLE WITH CITIZENS

Evolutionary Engagement

Walter W. Kovalick, Jr. and
Margaret M. Kelly[1]

Few federal agencies have had as much direct impact on citizens as the U.S. Environmental Protection Agency (EPA). The air we breathe and water we drink, the insecticides and chemicals we use and are exposed to, the automobiles we drive and the fruits and vegetables we eat, and the gas stations and waste sites that need cleaning up—all are affected by decisions made by the Agency. Reflecting on our experiences as practitioners in a federal regulatory agency, we see several important influences and forces that shape the nature of a public agency's interaction with citizens.

We believe a complex set of factors influence how the Agency has structured and is developing its interactions with individual citizens. Whereas some of these factors may be common to all public institutions, some strike us as unique to the kind of public administration carried out at the EPA. We explore three themes in this chapter as a basis for our characterization of how the EPA engages the public at the most local level. First, the nature of the "work" of public health and environmental protection has become more complex, less obvious in its impact, and more controversial over the last 20 years. Second, the EPA's organizational arrangements to engage citizens have changed and adapted over the same period in order to adjust to the increasing needs for relations with many different subsets of society. Third, the mandates presented to the EPA—largely through legislation, but also from other authoritative sources—have caused it to adapt both its program implementation strategies and, more specifically, its efforts to engage the public in general as well as citizens as individuals.

Using a variety of organizational arrangements and program mechanisms, EPA practitioners have sought "mechanisms" to improve the level of engagement with the citizens impacted by EPA programs. Our label for the currently evolving role that EPA staff is adopting is the "task-oriented, but inclusive and balanced convener." Although this evolution is far from complete, it is some distance from where the Agency started.

ENVIRONMENTAL PROTECTION—THEN AND NOW

Between 1970—when the EPA was established—and 1996, public attitudes toward the Agency evolved from expectation of an advocate in the public interest to a mixture of cautious trust, dissatisfaction, and, at times, suspicion. Perhaps this just reflects a trend toward government in general; however, there are a set of societal developments and changes in our level of understanding of environmental issues that may explain the particular animus that developed toward the federal government's chief environmental watchdog, the EPA.

How was the EPA transformed in the eyes of the public from an agency working in their interest to one that should be viewed with caution? During the 1970s, the start-up years of the EPA, the first administrator, William Ruckelshaus, and his immediate successor, Russell Train, were faced with gross examples of environmental pollution. The Clean Air Act and Clean Water Act were directed at resolution of air and surface water pollution that were visible and understood by the public. Further, Administrator Ruckelshaus believed it was important to establish the serious intent of the EPA's enforcement arm and undertook a series of important, public enforcement actions against corporate and municipal entities (U.S. Environmental Protection Agency, 1993).

Despite an ongoing commitment to regulation and enforcement by the EPA, there are several reasons why public attitudes toward the EPA have changed. Most of these have to do with changes in the "what and how" of the work at the EPA. We would include the emergence of environmental and economic tradeoffs, increasingly opaque approaches to identifying pollution threats to health, an enforcement approach that is based on compliance with prescribed standards as opposed to exposure to pollution, a perception by affected communities that the EPA is unresponsive to immediate citizen concerns, and unintended consequences of certain regulations.

Further, three years of experience with new consensus approaches that include community participants have provided the EPA with additional insights into public attitudes.

Environmental Protection and Economics

The 1970s were a time of significant societal change in the policy environment surrounding the EPA. Along with new worker and consumer protection statutes, several new environmental protection statutes were enacted, including the Clean Air Act, the Toxic Substances Control Act, and the Resource Conservation and Recovery Act administered by the EPA. At the same time, serious inflation and high interest rates made the cost of borrowing money expensive for everyone, including industry. This meant that capital and operating expenditures necessary to comply with many new environmental regulations, including pollution control or treatment technology, had to compete with other investments that corporations wanted to make. Concern was raised about stringent regulations and their resulting costs. In its role as a regulatory agency, the EPA had incorporated cost-benefit considerations in developing many of its rules (although consideration of costs was less explicit in certain environmental statutes). However, during this period, several succeeding administrations placed an emphasis on cost considerations and conducting economic impact analyses. Since that time, the balancing of social and environmental benefits and societal costs has become increasingly important (U.S. Office of Management and Budget [OMB], 1996). Finding the correct balance between costs and benefits is good public policy; however, this added dimension to the EPA's role may have contributed to its diminished image as an "advocate" for the environment.

Increasingly Complicated Approaches

As regulatory programs were implemented and had positive effects, gross pollution problems were brought under control (such as emissions from large industrial sources and automobiles, poor visibility in national parks, toxic and flammable chemical releases to rivers, etc.). Scientists began to develop analytical tools, such as models, which the EPA used to evaluate health and ecological impact resulting from environmental regulations.

The concept of risk assessment was also introduced as a scientifically credible expression of potential harm, along with explicit recognition of the uncertainties in such assessments due to a variety of reasons (e.g., the quality of the data itself, the effects of chemicals on animals as differentiated from humans, and the nature of exposure; National Research Council, 1983; Environmental Protection Agency, 1990). Risk assessment tools and models were used in a prospective sense to identify risks associated with diverse industry practices. The sheer numbers of industrial and municipal facilities also made modeling necessary because it was often impossible for EPA or state regulatory agencies to isolate and assess risk on a source-specific basis.

The change in the environmental protection mission from removing visible assaults on the air and water to risk management using risk assessments with thoughtful consideration of costs and benefits is not widely understood by the general public (National Research Council, 1994). Further, there is disagreement among the experts themselves as to the appropriate characterization of both the health and ecological benefits as well as costs. These complexities have caused some constituencies to view EPA decisions more skeptically.

Better Detection, Smaller Risks

Technology rose to meet the challenge of environmental regulations. New and improved detection devices enabled regulatory agencies and industry to detect the presence of minute amounts of toxic pollutants in air, water, soil, and food. The ability to detect low levels of pollutants led to the feeling on the part of some citizens that any detectable amount was a hazard to public health. The EPA was not always able to explain in an understandable way to the general public the relative significance of exposure to small amounts of chemicals and pollutants, adding to the public feeling that the Agency was not protecting their health.

Industrial Permits and Allowable Pollution

To implement its several statutes, the EPA developed a system of permits aligned with the Agency's media programs (e.g., air, surface water). These permits allow an industrial facility to emit or release a certain amount of pollution, based sometimes on available control and treatment technology and sometimes on calculated risk. For example, the Resource Conservation and Recovery Act required permits for treatment, storage, and disposal methods for hazardous waste. It is important to note that a permit applies to individual facilities, and cumulative effects from other facilities are not considered, although this approach is under review. Thus, if a second facility in a community applies for a permit, the application will not be considered in the context of other facilities and the pollution allowed by their respective permits. Permits do not, therefore, historically consider cumulative risk in a community. Indeed, if an industrial facility manages to reduce emissions of air pollutants through process or other operational changes, it may then increase production volume until subsequent emissions increase again to the levels allowed in their permit. The realization that environmental permits allow industrial facilities to pollute is not acceptable to many communities, who see neither compensating health or economic benefits to themselves nor incentives for facilities to pollute less over time.

Monitoring for Compliance, Not Real-Time Health Effects

One complaint expressed by communities is, "If there are so many regulations, why are we still sick?" Identifying exact causes and effects is difficult; and there are confounding lifestyle factors that may make such connections ultimately impossible. However, this opinion reflects a belief on the part of some citizens that environmental regulations are removed from real-world effects on their health. In fact, monitoring programs established through regulations are generally targeted at measuring not health impacts resulting from industrial operations, but whether the industrial process is in compliance with applicable regulations and permits. An exception to this is the notice given to localities of high ozone levels and subsequent directives to sensitive individuals. Although the Agency has made some progress over the years in measuring "indicators" of environmental improvement, it still enforces compliance with regulations based on a technology standard or risk assessment. Neither of these approaches is necessarily based on real-time health effects in an affected community—primarily because it is not scientifically possible to do so at this time.

Subsurface Pollution

Prior to the 1980s, the institutional arm of the EPA that addressed waste activities focused on disposal of municipal and industrial solid waste. Changes in environmental statutes, however, defined distinctions between solid and hazardous waste and created a new regulated universe of hazardous waste facilities. Today, the EPA is responsible for establishing federal regulations that govern transportation, treatment, storage, and disposal of hazardous waste, including permitting. Further, in the early 1980s, Love Canal in upstate New York alerted the country to the hidden threat to communities and their drinking water from decades of neglect with respect to land disposal of toxic materials. Later in the 1980s, the public was made aware of the environmental impact of tens of thousands of leaking underground tanks at gasoline stations across the country. Water pollution problems from nonpoint source runoff and from thousands of individual, nonindustrial air pollution sources also came to our attention in the last decade.

The environmental programs at the federal and state level have now focused on tens of thousands of individual, nonmanufacturing sources of pollution. Specifically, in the hazardous waste arena, the differences from the EPA's previous regulatory focus were the following: (a) The great proliferation in terms of numbers made it difficult for the Agency and the states to show progress; (b) Contamination of soil and ground water was relatively invisible to the public, and technology and expertise to resolve the problems were in their infancy (National Research Council, 1994); (c) The EPA started prioritizing problems well after they had been identified for the public, causing suspicion about how the EPA developed criteria and its motives for not taking action; and (d) Relatively small numbers of citizens were highly impacted by the individual sources, producing a cost-benefit dilemma for the EPA. How much of society's resources should be spent to remediate contaminated sites that may affect thousands of citizens, when air pollution sources can affect millions? The proliferation of contaminated sites affecting subsurface groundwater and the EPA's learning process about how to technically address them has further complicated citizens' perceptions of the environmental agenda.

Citizen Perceptions of Unresponsiveness

There are several instances of vocal citizen opposition and anger toward federal and state EPA decisions to permit industrial facilities, such as those that treat toxic waste. A recent example of this is the permitting of the Waste Treatment Industry incinerator in East Liverpool, Ohio, located in close proximity to a children's school and a residential neighborhood. This particular situation, and dissatisfaction with environmental authorities, resulted in the emergence of local grassroots activism to oppose the permitting of an incinerator at that site. Further, local activists filed citizen suits to prevent the incinerator from operating (U.S. Government Accounting Office [GAO], 1994).

In another instance, an industrial release in clear violation of environmental permits caused an outcry among neighboring communities in Contra

Costa County, California. Enforcement and response actions by regulatory agencies did not satisfy the citizens. Organized community activism emerged, obtaining a monetary settlement for the citizens and an innovative agreement on the part of the facility to partner with the community to provide access to information, inspections, and independent technical assistance ("Unocal Will Settle Suits," 1997). Affected communities are demanding and obtaining the capacity to appraise on their own the sustainability of industrial facilities, in a manner that goes far beyond what the EPA may (or can) require of a facility under the law.

Unintended Consequences of the "One-Size" Approach to Regulation

There are instances in which the EPA appears to be implementing the law in a way that appears unfair or lacking in common sense to citizens. People expect the EPA to enforce against violators that threaten health and the environment. Violators are generally perceived to be corporate or large organizations (sometimes governmental) that behaved out of a misguided profit motive, ignorance, or blatant neglect. However, at times, laws or their implementing regulations have been written in a way that does not discriminate among types of violators when meting out "punishment." In addition, the independent treatment of each permitted facility and its emissions—irrespective of its location adjacent to other industrial or pollution-control facilities—gave rise to concerns of undue impact of multiple such sources on communities of lower socioeconomic status.

Thus, examples of small businesses bearing disproportionate burdens to comply with regulations designed for an entire industry category have often been cited over the course of the EPA's history. In addition, the insensitivity of the facility siting and permitting processes to multiple exposures became the concern of the environmental justice movement. In both instances, the perceived unfairness and lack of common sense in the regulatory processes further eroded the citizens' faith that the EPA is operating with the proper priorities.

ORGANIZATIONAL LENS

While these changes in the nature of the EPA's work were going on, the institution itself was adjusting and adapting its organizational structure to better recognize and collaborate with its numerous and diverse publics—including the citizen as an individual (USEPA, 1971-1976). In reviewing the changes in this structure, we see some pointers to the EPA's evolving role as the convener of interested parties. Several significant aspects of these organizational changes are the increasing pace of change and adaptation during the last decade, the maturing of the organizational role from public "affairs" to "liaison" with an added educational component, the growing number of named constituencies with an organizational focus, and, recently, the creation of organizational entities tied to underrepresented stakeholder groups. What we will see during this review is that despite numerous adaptations and positive efforts to touch citizens as individuals, a federal agency must primarily use recognized groups or communities to interact on national issues. Recent efforts to define underrepresented populations and then seek to define and respond to their interests are works in progress.

Formed in 1970 through an amalgamation of a number of programs across the federal departments, the EPA's suborganization to engage the public began as a traditional Office of Public Affairs nestled comfortably with numerous other functional offices reporting to the administrator. A Citizen Information Division came (and went) as part of this office between 1972 and 1977, along with the advent of a visitor center and an information center. In these early years, one sees in the organizational structure the "standard" approach used by many federal agencies. The use of the language *public affairs* implies the simple transactions between the agency and citizens. Information is disseminated as necessary and requests are fulfilled when made. Of course, an early, important function included interaction with the press on the EPA's business as well.

In 1978, in the Carter Administration, the Office of Public Awareness became the new moniker, with a specific Media Services organization cited on the organization charts. Again, the choice of the word *awareness* began to imply a different kind of responsibility and relationship than transaction management and information dissemination. Further, in 1980, a separate and coequal Office of Press Services was created. Presumably, this was a signal of equivalent attention to be devoted to raising the sensitivities of the public and to keeping the press up-to-date.

Beginning in 1981, in the Reagan Administration, the public's "office" went back to being the Office of Public Affairs, again subsuming the press functions within it. William Ruckelshaus, returning to lead the EPA for a second time starting in 1983, established a "government in a fishbowl" policy. This was a reaction to the brief tenure of the previous administrative team, which had been accused of holding meetings with corporate representatives behind closed doors. The net result was a more determined effort to make the "public's business" more open through such mechanisms as

making available calendars of senior officials, better documentation of interactions with advocates on any side of rule making, and a more open approach to supplying nonconfidential information requested by the public.

In 1984 came the first elevation of external relations for the Agency,
creating an assistant administrator for external affairs, a presidential appointment confirmed by the Senate. Grouped under this presidentially appointed political official were Offices of Congressional Relations, Federal
Activities, Intergovernmental Relations, Legislation, and Public Affairs. At
this juncture, the Agency was grouping all of its relations management
under a senior political official. In one sense, it meant that relating to these
publics—Congress, federal agencies, states, tribes, and cities, and the press
and the general public—was important enough business to garner the use
of a scarce presidential appointment. From another perspective, the EPA
had begun to parse up the general public into subgroups for more focused
attention—with citizens being one among many. In 1985, some additional
changes were made with an Office of Public and Private Liaison being
substituted for Intergovernmental Relations and a new Community Relations Division being formed. Here we see the first organizational manifes-
tation of a need to relate to the public as citizens in communities—not via
the press or their other surrogates.

In 1986, some further shifts were made to create an Office of Community and Intergovernmental Liaison in parallel with the Office of Public
Affairs. Here we see "community" being linked with cities, elected officials,
and other organized bodies as a set of groups of citizens as opposed to
individual citizen relationships.

In 1989, in the Bush Administration, the assistant administrator's organization was transformed into associate administrators—one for Regional,
State, and Local Relations, one for Communications and Public Affairs,
and one for Congressional and Legislative Affairs. Although the level was
reduced from a Senate-approved appointment, we see the advent of three
senior officials—two of whom specialize in the EPA's transactions with its
own regional offices, other governmental partners, and the Congress, and
one focused now on the press, stakeholders, and communities of citizens
(as distinct from their elected officials). In the early 1990s, we saw the emergence for the first time of an Environmental Education Division—tied to
EPA intentions to be attentive to the educational aspect of its missions as
well as to a law creating an Office of Environmental Education at the EPA.

In 1992, the associate administrator title was broadened to be Communications, Education, and Public Affairs, giving environmental education
its full seat at the organizational table. This work was linked especially to

engaging the education establishment through grants to create educational materials for various levels in the education system.

Two changes in 1993, in the Clinton Administration, were (a) the creation of an Office of Environmental Equity to address the specific problems outlined by both external critics and an internal task force, and (b) formation of a Public Liaison Division under the Associate Administrator for Communication, Education, and Public Affairs. The first office related to the redressing of the apparent disproportionate share of the burdens of environmental pollution from air and water pollution and waste disposal being borne by low-income and otherwise disadvantaged citizens. This office became the Office of Environmental Justice in 1994. The title of the Public Liaison Division suggested a different kind of relationship than the traditional public affairs office as well as a specific avenue for environmental, health, and consumer organizations, labor unions, industry associations, and educational and youth groups, among others, to have a clearer relationship with the Agency.

Finally, two more recent changes show the Agency's intention to develop better links with affected citizens. In 1994, a separate and distinct Tribal Office was established to respond to the unique needs of Native American tribes, which are accorded the status of states in many EPA statutes. The office was placed within the administrative umbrella of one of the Agency's major program-implementation offices—the Office of Water—but was to serve the needs of Native Americans in relating to all EPA programs. Most recently, in 1997, the Agency established an Office of Children's Health Protection, attached directly to the Office of the Administrator (U.S. Environmental Protection Agency, 1997). Its purpose is to influence and directly impact the Agency's programs that affect children.

Although there are numerous reasons for reorganizations including mission, statutory changes, budget redirection, and even personalities, our analysis is directed at the pace and labeling of these organizational changes as it relates to engagement with citizens. What we observe from this review is that the tempo of such changes accelerated in the late 1980s and early 1990s as the Agency sought to establish its "official" mechanisms for public engagement. We observe that the EPA's organizational labels for its entities that relate to citizens were stable during much of the Agency's early existence. Then, external relations rose in importance and the diversity of the publics needing the Agency's attention grew. The general public—citizens per se—seem to be served *through* many others (i.e., the press, elected officials, stakeholder groups) rather than directly, although the EPA does serve individual citizens when they initiate the contact. In addition, the recently created offices focused on environmental equity and children are an indication of outreach and the need to engage special categories of citizens who are underrepresented by traditional stakeholder groups. The difficulty in engaging individuals from the federal level is manifest in these numerous organizational attempts to build more direct, improved connections.

We also note that the language *public affairs* is grounded in a more transaction-based context (as in corporate public affairs departments). The more educationally grounded titles like *public awareness* and the concept of *liaison*, which the dictionary suggests is based on a close relationship rather than a transaction, imply that the EPA's organizational changes were directed at getting more closely in touch with citizens.

STATUTORY AND PROGRAM MANDATES

At the same time as these shifts in the nature of the environmental protection mission and these organizational changes were taking place, there was an increasing demand in EPA statutes and through implementation of associated programs to perfect the Agency's ability to engage the public at the level of the citizen. These experiences are in large measure drawn from the EPA's waste-management-related statutes and programs; thus, they are not a random "sample" from across the EPA. But they are drawn from several of the programs that are typically involved in site-specific actions affecting citizen neighbors (i.e., clean up decisions at Superfund sites, permitting of incinerators, and so on). On the contrary, most of the EPA's programs are conducted at the national level as the federal regulator with delegated state programs. Thus, it is often the state government that is engaged with citizens on the issues of implementation of air and water regulatory programs.

In addition, we should acknowledge that all of the EPA's programs have included organized and dedicated efforts to communicate information about their direction and implementation. By that we mean long-standing efforts in the various programs to develop fact sheets, guidance, handbooks, decision-maker's guides, citizen guides, newsletters, and, of late, home pages on the World Wide Web to better outline, explain, and elaborate on regulatory requirements to numerous audiences. In many cases, these materials were also "rolled up" by the public affairs office into more generic explanatory guides and descriptive materials on the EPA's programs and regulations. Although recognizing these efforts at (primarily) information dissemination and communication about both the process of regulatory development and enhancing understanding and compliance with the requirement, the EPA's experience base is much more limited in terms of engagement and interacting with citizens—largely for the programmatic reasons suggested earlier.

Thus, several mandates from the mid-1980s were targeted at improving the Agency's engagement with persons at the individual level. The first was contained in the 1984 amendments to the Resource Conservation and Recovery Act to appoint an ombudsman on waste-management issues. Here was a statutory message that the existing organizational structures were not sufficient to solve problems raised and that an advocate for resolution was needed within the organization. Although one could argue that the Office of the Ombudsman is equally visible to individual companies with regulatory and compliance questions, it was still a statement of need for easier access and better engagement. More recently, the EPA established ombudsmen for waste programs in each of its 10 regional offices. Again, the Agency is attempting to relate more closely to individuals where they are.

In 1986, a significant change to the Superfund law was the creation of a program for Technical Assistance Grants for communities affected by the EPA's waste cleanup decisions (U.S. Environmental Protection Agency, 1992b). Basically, the EPA would award grants of up to $50,000 to community organizations to allow them to retain expert professional and technical advice about the nature of the proposed solutions to the contamination problems being proposed by industry and to be approved by the EPA. A Superfund Bill introduced in the Senate in 1997 proposes that this amount be increased to $100,000. Without giving an extensive history of the Superfund program, suffice it to say that the mandate was for the EPA to help pay for the information that would allow authentic citizen engagement with the remedy decisions. This was a significant new program area for the EPA, one that required the Agency to more fully empower local citizens to understand and have valid input into the decision-making process that affected their immediate environment.

In 1992, a third major shift in the nature of citizen engagement occurred, one that grew out of the EPA's lack of differentiation among its citizen "clients." Responding to several important critiques and reports on the issue of environmental contamination disproportionately affecting minority and low-income populations, the EPA prepared a report, *Environmental Equity: Reducing Risks for All Communities* (U.S. Environmental Protection Agency, Office of Policy, Planning and Evaluation, 1992a), documenting its views on these criticisms along with a series of findings and recommendations. One of the findings was that these populations have higher than average exposure to certain air pollutants, hazardous waste facilities, and contaminated fish and agricultural pesticides in the workplace. The previously mentioned Office of Environmental Equity (now Justice) was formed at this time as well. Here was one of the first occasions in which the EPA began to differentiate among citizens affected by its actions—other than by using the avenue of traditional constituent organizations.

Another development in the waste-management realm was also the April 1996 *Final Report of the Federal Facilities Environmental Restoration and Dialogue Committee.* Chaired by the EPA, this committee conducted highly inclusive deliberations directed at the processes of stakeholder involvement in the cleanup decisions at and around federal facilities—especially those of the departments of Defense and Energy. Although primarily focused on the overall process of stakeholder interaction at these sites— many of which had been operating under a cloak of national security for decades—what is important for this discussion is to highlight and point to the need to engage individual citizens, people of color, low-income individuals, and local elected officials around such facilities and the elaboration of how communications and, to some extent, engagement needs to be improved.

Outside the realm of specific waste programs, we also draw attention to two other significant initiatives that altered the EPA's institutional "styles" in engaging the public. First, in 1986, new provisions were introduced into the Superfund Amendments and Reauthorization Act, entitled Emergency Planning and Community Right-to-Know (Superfund Amendments and Reauthorization Act, 1986). This legislation caused the Agency to embark on a major information-transfer program at the community level to increase the awareness of individual citizens and others as to the level of routine releases of chemicals into the environment beyond those that may be permitted. Although this program has caused a major rearrangement of the dynamics of individual company pollution prevention and abatement programs, namely, focus on the nature and type of unregulated releases and their volume, it has largely effected change without any EPA or state regulatory action.

Second, the EPA's Common Sense Initiative (CSI) has become a microcosm of more sophisticated levels of interaction between the Agency and citizens —as individuals, members of local communities, and members of national organizations. In 1994, EPA Administrator Carol Browner announced the formation of this new initiative within the EPA. The CSI offers some new approaches to environmental planning and regulatory development; one of the most innovative aspects is the extent to which local community representatives are included at early stages in the development process. CSI is built on a consensus approach whereby community and environmental justice advocates, industry executives, national environmental organizations, labor representatives, and state and local environmental regulatory agencies together formulate and recommend changes to EPA operating programs. The objective is to achieve improvements in environmental protection over what is achieved by current EPA policies and regulations in ways that are "cleaner, cheaper, and smarter" than existing baselines. The CSI approach is also sector based, that is, focused on particular industries, such as petroleum refining, metal finishing, auto assembly, iron and steel, printing, and computers and electronics. A sector-based regulatory approach acknowledges that "one size fits all" regulations may not be the most effective policy in terms of costs, pollution prevention, and emissions reduction.

Two other initiatives being pursued by the Agency—but not treated in this chapter—are also attempting to build stronger bridges between the EPA and states, their regulatory programs, and the direct interests of affected groups of citizens and, to some extent, individuals. The Community Based Environmental Protection (CBEP) initiative seeks to tailor and integrate the multiplicity of regulatory, permitting, and other programs of the Agency around common geographical areas. CBEP is designed to maximize the use of scarce resources, encourage local support, and consider the economic well-being of communities. The recent Brownfields initiative seeks to make environmental protection a building block—not a stumbling block—in the reutilization of underused or abandoned industrial contaminated properties in central cities. The economic redevelopment of such properties is often stymied by concerns over the liability for and cleanup of such contamination.

EVOLUTION OF ROLES

As a preliminary perspective on our argument for the evolving role of the public administrator as a "task-oriented, but inclusive and balanced convener," we cite the study *Public Knowledge and Perceptions of Chemical Risks in Six Communities: Analysis of a Baseline Survey* (U.S. Environmental Protection Agency, Chemical Emergency Planning and Preparedness Office, 1991); it is very instructive on the difficulty for government in establishing an effective interaction with individual citizens. When more than 3,000 persons were surveyed on a variety of questions related to chemical risks, they were asked *where they received most of their information* about chemical risks, *whom they trusted* for this information, and *who they thought was most knowledgeable* about these risks. Regarding the source for their information, news reporters and environmental groups were chosen by 27% and 21% of the respondents, respectively—local, state, and federal government ranked at 5% or below. On the issue of who they most trusted, doctors were chosen by 46%, with governments ranking at 12% or below, and the chemical industry at 8%. Lastly, as to who is most knowledgeable, the respondents named chemical industry officials (58%), followed by environmental groups (53%), and the federal government (36%).

At a minimum, one sees in these data no congruence in information sources, authoritative voices, or technical information providers. In addition, the absence of governments in general and the federal government in particular, except for its scientific assets, gives credence to the kind of role we see evolving.

Although our portrait of developments in the complexity of environmental protection, the EPA's organizational evolution, and programmatic change is abbreviated and incomplete, we think it conveys a sense of development and transition in the roles played by the EPA in carrying out its mission with and through individual citizens. We suggest that there have been at least three major roles that the Agency has played or is playing in its evolutionary engagement with individual citizens.

The first role was that of the authority—which the *American Heritage Dictionary* (Morris, 1971) describes as "an *accepted* [italics added] source of expert information or advice; a claim to be accepted or believed." In exercising its discretion to interpret statutes and write regulations, the EPA was the preeminent authority on solving what were the more obvious and visible problems of the 1970s. Its engagement with the outside world—let alone citizens—was the dissemination of information about its actions, the reasons behind them, and the results. In these times, there were no disagreements about the nature of the problems (i.e., the many large industrial sources of pollution), let alone the apparent solutions. So, the EPA was the trusted purveyor of the "facts and figures" about the problems of the environment and what needed to be done about them. There was less need for individuals to get engaged in decision making, as the Agency was new, making progress on obvious fronts, and appeared to be exercising its discretion on behalf of the public interest.

The second role was that of neutral arbiter. An Agency anecdote in the late 1970s and 1980s was that if the EPA issued a regulation and was immediately sued by both industry and the environmentalists (i.e., national environmental organizations), the EPA must have "gotten it about right." Gone were the days of the trusted public agent. The Agency was responsible for making a regulatory proposal, hearing from all sides and, based on that input (and presumably its expertise), making the decision that met its statutory responsibility to protect public health and the environment. This was a time of increasing complexity of problems with less obvious solutions. The EPA sought heightened public awareness (rather than pure information dissemination) and tried to move beyond the organized interest groups to include the public at large. But as we saw organizationally, the collected publics became further and further differentiated into states, tribes, cities, elected officials, and industry, with the individual citizen not obvious on the regulatory scene. Late in this period came the realization about environmental education—that giving students a background in environmental issues promises more environmentally conscious adults. Thus, the Agency was no longer perceived as principal information purveyor, but began to empower others to learn about these issues as well as to call on the broader science community for information. Then, and now, the call for "good science" began to be heard in order to still debates on regulatory decisions that lacked sufficient anchors in the "truth."

In the meantime, immediate "fixes" were sought through laws requiring an ombudsman and providing grant funds to allow citizens to choose their own mentors on complicated scientific and technical issues. In the Superfund program, for example, the EPA community-relations coordinators became agents for community involvement in the decisionmaking *with* the EPA. Citizen participation—the "act of taking part in" (according to the *American Heritage Dictionary*)—became the watchword for developing solutions at Superfund sites, even though the EPA was still the penultimate decision official about the remedies at these sites.

We believe that the role that the EPA is evolving toward in its regulatory, voluntary, and partnership efforts, and even its site-specific work, is the task-oriented, but inclusive and balanced convener. The Agency retains its statutory responsibility to exercise discretion in the interest of public health and the environment, and it still has its technical and scientific assets to draw on. However, many of its new voluntary and nonregulatory programs deal with problems where the Agency's technical expertise is not unique or comprehensive—especially given the diverse and widespread problems faced by its traditional programs (nonpoint source pollution in water, thousands of leaking underground tanks, etc.) In addition, the answers to complex scientific and risk assessment questions come from numerous sources—some trusted even more than the EPA. So, it follows that the EPA has become the convenor—"one who causes people to assemble, usually for an official or public purpose," in the words of the *American Heritage Dictionary*. The Agency is being trusted to bring all the interests to the table and to be balanced in moderating the debate on the question at hand. In addition, in matters of regulation, the EPA is still driven by its statutory mandates to protect public health and the environment, so its role is beyond the neutral facilitator. It is the explicit final decision maker in regulatory programs, less so in voluntary programs. But in either case, the Agency has an agenda for completion of the project or achievement of the goal—often statutorily driven. Hence, the concept of task orientation: the need to keep the process moving to conclusion, to exercise governance over the "group process," and to persuade, and, if necessary, overrule those who would hold veto power in what might be a consensus process.

It is in this role that the EPA finds itself moving beyond information transmission to the citizen and beyond being the judge of submitted views (especially when citizen views didn't get articulated). The EPA must be trusted to get all the views at the "table"—especially those who need help in understanding the technical issues—to make sure none are drowned out or are too timid to speak, to utilize its own scientific and technical assets, and to operate a transparent decision process for all concerned. So, we add to the role of convenor the responsibilities of task orientation as well as inclusiveness and balanced treatment. The distance from the authoritative role is great, and the journey was not direct, but the resulting engagement moves ever closer to connecting directly to the needs of individual citizens.

Two years of experience with CSI have provided insights into the dynamics among all the CSI stakeholders but especially between community activists and the EPA. In terms of definitions, community activists represent people in at least one of the following three categories: (a) environmental justice advocates, or low-income minorities living adjacent to or near industrial facilities, who believe their health is disproportionately affected by the industrial operations because of their race and income levels; (b) local grassroots citizens, not necessarily minority, who are concerned about neighboring industrial operations; and (c) members of community organizations and other activists who are focused on and energized by preservation of their local environment. The first two types of activism are often based on the belief that the industrial facility is sacrificing community health for operating efficiency or financial gain. Whereas environmental regulation got its start in the United States because of grassroots citizen activism (e.g., Rachel Carson's [1962] book *Silent Spring*), the current slate of activist groups representing community interests, in particular environmental justice communities, is relatively new.

It is inevitable that the EPA will conduct much of its future business through consensus forums consisting of a balanced representation of viewpoints. CSI is the first step in the process of refining our skills as conveners and facilitators in order to successfully include all stakeholders in crafting the national environmental agenda.

THE EPA AND ITS CITIZENS

The public administrator in the late 1990s faces a much more complex environment than his or her predecessor of even 10 years ago. We believe the role to be played in relating to the citizens who are being served is evolving to be much less authoritative and less oriented to the balancing of "interests" to a more collaborative, inclusive role. This role is mindful of the need to seek out underrepresented interests, while at the same time attentive to the need to complete the "public's business" in a timely fashion. Also not forgotten in the background is the administrator's mandate from the legislature or other authoritative sources to exercise discretion in the public's interest—however that is defined in the law. All of these responsibilities are no small task and require a special awareness at multiple levels— personally, organizationally, institutionally, and in the larger society.

NOTE

1. The opinions expressed in this chapter are those of the authors and do not necessarily represent the views of the United States Environmental Protection Agency.

Chapter 9

WE WANT YOUR INPUT

Dilemmas of Citizen Participation

Dolores Foley

Solutions designed to promote citizen participation often focus on the citizen. Whereas many advocate that citizens need to take more responsibility for self-governance, there are increasing calls for those in government to develop new skills and reform structures to promote citizen participation. A self-governing democracy with citizens as active participants and public officials as facilitators will require structural and attitudinal changes. In this chapter, a community planning case is used to highlight some of the issues associated with promoting citizen participation in this way. In many respects this process was a model of how to involve citizens; yet at the same time, this case illustrates some problems and barriers to promoting citizen participation. Both the successes and problems may provide useful insights to other communities.

COMMUNITY PLANNING FOR HIV PREVENTION

In 1994, the Hawai'i State Department of Health (DOH), as part of the HIV Prevention Cooperative Agreement with the federal Centers for Disease Control (CDC), initiated a participatory community planning process for HIV prevention. The community planning process began at the instigation of the CDC. In January, state and local departments receiving HIV-prevention funding were mandated to involve communities in developing comprehensive HIV-prevention plans. These community plans would then form the basis of future cooperative agreements between the localities and the CDC. Each locality was given great latitude on how they would design the community planning process. In some states, only one community planning group was formed, whereas in other states, numerous groups were formed.

In Hawai'i, an ad hoc planning group met in February and March to design the community planning process. The committee was composed of members from the community, the DOH, and HIV and AIDS service organizations. The design included 10 communities and a state planning committee. The state planning committee was composed of representatives from the community planning committees, DOH, representatives from affected groups, and community coordinators.

There was considerable variation in the numbers of members and meetings held by the different community groups. The entire process had a short time frame; the final plans were due in December. The state planning committee met monthly beginning in June, culminating in a retreat in October to draft the state plan. The final report was written by staff and went back to the communities for approval. Final approval by communities was one of the requirements of the CDC to ensure a truly participatory planning process.

Positive Outcomes

The participants, from those with extensive backgrounds in the field to community members without any previous knowledge of HIV and AIDS, generally viewed the community planning process as an important and positive learning experience. Some individuals gained new knowledge about HIV and AIDS. All the participants were positive about what they had learned about the resources in their own community, in other communities, and within their own organizations. Many community networks were developed or expanded.

The identification of resources in the community was one part of the process about which everyone was unequivocally positive. For most groups, this effort successfully identified the resources and made individuals more aware of how existing resources could be utilized. In a number of communities, efforts to inform and educate began as a result of what was initially a data-gathering effort, with HIV-prevention activities being undertaken as a result of involving individuals in the process. Community members repeatedly said that they had benefited from the process and from the knowledge they had gained. Linkages were also developed that will be important in the implementation of HIV-prevention strategies; many participants cited the value of the contacts they made through this process. A number of the members of the West Hawai'i group expressed the intention that some of their plans for HIV-prevention activities would be pursued "regardless of the state plan." Another member stated that "the survey helped create a dialogue; we were taken more seriously." The surveys and interviews provided useful data but, just as important, they created a process to educate and develop networks throughout the community. A number of community members also indicated that they had become more aware of the need for less reliance on the state and a greater reliance on community resources. As one community member stated: "One of the things I have gotten out of this process is that we can't rely on the government. We have to make use of what resources we have. We found out what other agencies have to offer and what they're lacking. We have to have more interagency cooperation."

Many community members felt empowered; they believed that significant efforts to improve community awareness and actions came out of the process and will continue. Although previous experience with governmental efforts at the community level had resulted in skepticism and distrust, many community members developed ownership of HIV-prevention planning. The process was cited as important in the development of linkages and networks within and between communities. The process has also been successful in bringing new people into the HIV and AIDS area. As one community member stated: "It's been important in bringing people together that would not have gotten together otherwise. We had a conservative religious person and a gay man representing opposing views (on condom distribution in schools). We were able to discuss this issue and find some agreement."

As a result of the community planning process, despite a long history of distrust of the DOH, community members indicated that their level of skepticism and cynicism decreased. They believed that the department was really trying to make this a participatory process and appreciated being included in the process. The process was generally viewed as innovative and as potentially catalytic in bringing about changes in DOH funding priorities and community responses.

Problems of Participation

Despite the positive results and the fact that there was strong commitment to community planning within the group that represented CDC, DOH,

> **Community**
>
> "A *community* cannot persist simply because some of its members have a strong conviction that it ought to persist. A community... needs to have something fundamental to do, an organic purpose beyond 'fellowship.'" (Lawrence Goodwyn, 1978, p. 307)

and the private citizens, many participants found it a frustrating experience (Foley, 1994). Among the complaints from the citizen representatives were the process in which communities and participants were selected; under-representation of specific ethnic groups and the community in general; and unclear CDC and DOH expectations and the level of technical reporting required of community groups. Government representatives voiced the difficulty in recruiting and retaining community representatives and the reliability of some of the community reports.

Many of the barriers to participation that were noted by the participants of the Hawai'i HIV-planning process are problems that have been encountered in other states (Academy for Educational Development, 1994). These include insufficient funds for planning, lack of training and technical assistance, the lack of representation by key populations, transportation, and planning-group membership.

In the next two subsections I focus on two issues that have implications for change that will be addressed later in this chapter. One of the issues concerns how to define community and how to insure representation; the other concerns the tension over expertise.

Defining Community

Increasingly in contemporary government practices, some form of community participation—varying from informing the public or actual shared decision making—is mandated by law or required by the funding agency. From the beginning of the HIV project, mechanisms were put in place to ensure community input. The CDC stipulated that community representatives be involved throughout, from the initial ad hoc planning group that designed the process to the final report that required community representatives to sign the document. However, developing the decision protocols for community representation was a more complex task than was originally conceived. The ad hoc planning committee discussed the definition of *community* as well as the identity of the community. The planning committee had extensive discussions on what constituted a community—they wanted to go beyond the usual demarcation of Hawai'i into four counties, recognizing that no one would define the counties as communities. The dilemma was how to divide the state into a workable number of communities that would be representative of geographical and spatial (e.g., ethnic, religious, interest group) communities. The decision was to divide the state into 10 geographic communities and to also have a number of at-large seats on the state planning committee to allow for representation of other groups.

The group was aware of the arbitrary nature of selecting 10 as the number of communities, but thought that too many community representatives would make the process too convoluted. Hawai'i has many suburbs, rural areas, and islands that can be considered as communities but increasingly, with urbanization and new suburban developments, the task of identifying areas as communities has become problematic. In some cases, identifiable communities were grouped together, whereas in others, there was little real sense of community within the artificial designation. The group recognized that generally the term *community* was a useful term only when referring to certain geographic areas. For example, for this process, the urban core of Honolulu was considered *a* community. There are many neighborhoods within this area that residents identify as communities, but overall, residents in this area would not identify this demarcation as their community. Although many criticized the final divisions, all found it difficult to propose a workable alternative.

The term *representation* also became problematic. Members chosen for their ethnic background (Japanese, Filipino, etc.) or interest group (gay, substance abuse, etc.) were uncomfortable with the expectation that they were representing their group. The ad hoc planning committee debated the concepts of representation and diversity. The committee decided that whereas it was impossible to ensure that all views would be represented, they would attempt to ensure that the makeup of the committee would represent the diversity of the community.

The issue of representation in a multiethnic society such as Hawai'i touches sensitive nerves. Traditionally, members of Asian, Pacific Islander, and Hawaiian groups do not volunteer to participate in committees or public processes. Some members said that the design of public processes has a Western cultural bias and that residents of Asian or Hawaiian descent don't feel comfortable speaking up at meetings, especially when there are differences of opinion.

The difficulty is that Hawai'i has numerous diverse ethnic groups without any one group having a majority. With Asian, Pacific Islander, and Hawaiian groups avoiding participation, the potential for excluding groups is compounded. This process was criticized for not making sufficient efforts to include Asian and Pacific Island groups on the state planning group and the community planning committees. The ad hoc planning group expected that these ethnic groups would be represented by the community-level representatives to the state level. However, most community-level committees found it difficult to get volunteers. In retrospect, a number of participants acknowledged that special efforts should have been undertaken, particularly as HIV and AIDS (still a taboo subject) is becoming more prevalent in Pacific Islanders.

In many communities, few people volunteered to serve on the planning groups, many in part because of negative past experiences with state advisory and planning committees. It is a common refrain among active citizens that they are often asked for their input, only to have all of their recommendations ignored. Many of those who agreed to participate did so in spite of their cynicism. A number of the volunteers who did participate were connected to human service delivery agencies and thus were involved at least in part because of their jobs, and not solely out of community spirit.

Technical Expertise and Community Participation

Tensions arose over the data community groups were expected to collect and analyze. The attempt to design a process that promoted community participation based on "a sound scientific basis" created a number of anxieties. The theory underlying this process was that "HIV prevention programs developed without community participation and a sound scientific basis are unlikely to be successful in preventing the spread of HIV infection or to garner the necessary public support" (Academy for Educational Development, 1994, p. 9). Yet, the pressure to produce reliable data necessary for a scientific basis was a strain on most community groups. A community planning process that was inclusive, combining the concerns of the community with the necessity of collecting reliable and valid data, meant that some community groups thought they were getting conflicting messages. The guidelines (Academy for Educational Development, 1994) stated,

Although the priority-setting method described here relies on core decision analytic principles, doing formal, quantitative decision analysis in every community planning group is probably not possible at this time due to inadequate resources to perform all such analyses and difficulties in meeting the data requirement of formal analyses that are custom tailored to particular communities. (p. 9)

From the Conversation: Challenges in Community

Meg: Dolores's description rings true with experiences at the federal EPA. Major problems: (1) The community is unable to meaningfully participate, not because they are uninterested, but because they lack technical assistance to translate the reams of paper and the detailed technical nature of the data they're given. Activist communities are now asking not for an EPA technical expert, but for the cash to go out and purchase technical advice on their own. EPA can be limited by law and funds from doing this. (2) Citizens frequently view the bureaucratic process as unfriendly and inflexible. For example, EPA faces the problem of reimbursing people we invite in for meetings. Regulators try to include people in the process and then get the blame because bureaucratic rules make this difficult. The system so far has resisted 'reinvention' in this area, fearful that flexibility will result in misuse of funds.

One of the problems with this approach was that community members without scientific backgrounds were asked to develop needs assessments of their communities. The groups included teachers, housewives, students, health professionals, hotel workers, and others who were genuinely concerned with HIV and AIDS issues in their community, but unfortunately lacked the technical skills to analyze existing AIDS surveillance and HIV seroprevalence data, let alone gather new data.

In response to group members who voiced the need for more information, DOH planners went through an extensive data-gathering exercise and supplied groups with statewide and community HIV and AIDS data. However, when the reports arrived, many members were overwhelmed. Their eyes glazed over when they saw thick stacks of paper with vast amounts of technical data.

The planning groups also asked for more training on the participatory community planning format and more technical assistance, which the DOH and CDC provided in the form of workshops, manuals, and other assistance. Department personnel provided data analysis, which arrived very late in the process; these reports were often too complicated for the community groups. The CDC and DOH also provided technical assistance through community coordinators hired specifically for this process. The community coordinators, who were hired based on their community organizing experience, had very little background on, or understanding of, how the state bureaucracy worked. They also had minimal technical expertise. They became frustrated with what they saw as fuzzy guidelines. The coordinators and groups repeatedly asked for more guidance on the format for reports. The CDC and DOH officials' explanation for their fuzziness was that they wanted to avoid telling communities how to collect information on their communities.

Some public officials voiced concerns that community members were ignoring the technical data and creating reports and making conclusions that did not take into account the available data. Some participants countered that the technical data provided to them was too complex to be useful. Department officials admitted, in retrospect, that the reports were not presented in a format that was usable by most community representatives.

The fact that community groups varied substantially in expertise was reflected in their final community reports. Some groups had individuals who could easily analyze the reports and utilize the data, but other groups lacked the technical expertise to utilize the data. Overall, the reports left CDC and DOH officials impressed with the information that community groups had been able to assemble, but also with concerns over the lack of methodological rigor. Some groups used opportunistic sampling and data-gathering techniques (e.g., interviewing anyone that would consent to answer questions at a fair or social gathering) and would generalize and report the results as if it had been a random, anonymous sample. Statistical terms were also sometimes misapplied.

Most community groups recognized their weaknesses and wanted more technical support and skills development, but they also feared that the data-gathering efforts put the urban areas at a greater advantage over rural communities. Some groups also argued that focusing on numbers undervalued prevention and feared they would lose the few resources they had if the emphasis was on the numbers of people living with HIV and AIDS. A majority of Hawai'i's population resides on the island of O'ahu, specifically in the urban areas of Honolulu, where the number of HIV and AIDS cases is also high. Thus, community groups on the other islands feared an emphasis on numbers would be to their disadvantage and would downplay the special characteristics of rural areas. They argued that underreporting was more of a problem in rural areas because of privacy concerns and the fact that those who contracted HIV or AIDS often left the area. For example, on Kauai there were few cases of HIV and AIDS reported, but the group viewed the presence of a tester-counselor as critical to making residents aware of the risks. However, the Honolulu group and some public officials worried privately that focusing on a community planning process would weaken the emphasis on where the need was greatest. They emphasized that the resources should be channeled to those areas where the incidence of HIV and AIDS cases was highest. One government official voiced the concern that, "This community planning process may change priorities and move resources out to the communities but they may neglect to focus on where the risk is still highest."

There were definite problems, but also a number of positive outcomes in this case. Both the positive outcomes and the problems highlight the systemic issues that will have to be addressed if public processes are to truly involve citizens in decision making.

Community Input

The literature is replete with discussions about communities and community revitalization, community building, community assets, and so forth, but rarely is there any discussion on how community is defined or how community representation will be insured. Sometimes the word is used to refer to a city, a neighborhood, or an ethnic or interest group. Its definition will become a critical issue if community representation is to be taken seriously in Hawai'i and elsewhere. Who speaks for the community when institutions of community governance do not exist? The requirement for community input is usually satisfied by a public hearing or by asking members of a geographic area to serve or give feedback.

There was more attention to the question of community representatives in the HIV Community Planning Process in Hawai'i than is found in most efforts, despite the increasing rhetoric about involving the community. The CDC advocated measures to insure this from the initial-planning stage through the final-report stage. Although the term was used throughout the CDC guidelines, they left it up to the individual states to delineate the parameters of community and the specifics of the process.

In Hawai'i, community representation was problematic from the outset. As mentioned, there is the problem of very few identifiable communities and no institutions of community governance. Governance in Hawai'i, as in most states, takes place at a distance. It is rare that communities have the necessary infrastructure for governance. As efforts continue to mandate or promote "community input," it is important to consider more carefully how to promote the development of community infrastructure.

Implications

Most officials in the DOH, as well as other state agencies in Hawai'i, would admit that their efforts to promote citizen participation in decision making have been minimal. This is due in part to a long history where citizen participation was discouraged. From the time of the Hawaiian monarchy, into annexation and the provisional government in 1898, through the days of Hawai'i as a U.S. territory, and finally into statehood (1959) and a plantation economy, decision making has generally been centralized and top down. Hawai'i has never had political subdivisions below the county level, and many government functions that are municipal responsibilities in other jurisdictions are state responsibilities in Hawai'i. A common refrain in Hawai'i is the distance that citizens feel from those who represent them.

Hawai'i perhaps poses more hurdles than many other jurisdictions, but it is clear from the literature that the distance between citizens and decision makers is not uncommon. Daniel Yankelovich (1995) observes one of the most destructive trends—"the disconnect between leaders and the public is so deeply embedded in our modernist culture that as recently as a decade ago we were not even aware of its strength" (p. 12). He proposes that government institutions will have to change their culture in the interest of broader participation in decision making. The meaningful involvement of citizens will require fundamental change—both structural and cultural—in the relationships between citizens and government, in the process of participation, and in the way governance is often structured.

MODELS OF COMMUNITY GOVERNANCE

There are a number of neighborhood governance models that are being showcased as examples of where citizen participation is flourishing. Proponents of participatory democracy argue that developing local structures to provide meaningful involvement is essential for a strong democracy. Thomson, Berry, and Portney (1994) distilled lessons from the National Citizen Participation Development Project on hundreds of participation projects throughout the country, with a focus on five cities with the strongest participation systems they could find: Birmingham, Alabama; Dayton, Ohio; Portland, Oregon; San Antonio, Texas; and St. Paul, Minnesota. In each of the five core cities, they identified participation systems that were substantially different than the representative democracy that exists in most other American cities. Each city has made extensive, ongoing efforts to provide participation opportunities for every citizen. They argue that these cities can be viewed as models for other communities seeking to design new processes to renew civic engagement.

Lessons from the program initiatives such as budget advisory committees, neighborhood offices and staffing, community needs assessment and allocation processes, neighborhood newspapers, crime watch connections, early notification, and neighborhood group standing in zoning and policy decisions can be adapted in other cities. Although the participation systems in these five cities were designed to address neighborhood issues, they argued that these community groups could focus on citywide, statewide, and even national questions.

The resident-led Dudley Street Neighborhood Initiative (DSNI) is an example of how a community can help develop a new structure of governance (Medoff & Sklar, 1994). The Dudley Street neighborhood was Boston's most impoverished area. Redlined and neglected, it has become a model of how a community can revitalize itself and forge new relations with government. It began in the 1980s with a "Don't Dump on Us" campaign to clean up the vacant lots and close down illegal trash-transfer stations. The DSNI went on to organize hundreds of residents and forge a new sense of neighborhood identity and power, and forced city government to respond. DSNI did not try to influence the process driven by city government; instead they created their own "urban village" redevelopment plan and built an unprecedented partnership with the city to implement it. DSNI became the nation's first neighborhood group to win the right of eminent domain and began transforming Dudley's wasteland to wealth controlled by the community.

An ongoing problem-solving process emerged from a visioning project called Chattanooga Venture in Chattanooga, Tennessee (Lappe & DuBois, 1994). Chattanooga Venture launched a dialogue where they invited every person in the community to help create a plan and vision for a city that faced deteriorating properties, rising unemployment, and increasing racial tension. Dramatic and tangible change came from the public-private partnerships that tackled 34 goals, some addressing short-term needs (a shelter for abused women) and others long-term targets (a riverfront park). One of the important aspects of this process was the development of Chattanooga Venture into an ongoing all-community institution. Venture trained citizens to facilitate community dialogues and help organize neighborhood associations and has become a broad- based, diverse community organization.

In all of these examples of community deliberation and decision making there were administrators that were supportive of these efforts. As Berry et al. (1993) point out, many citizen-participation efforts fail miserably—that most programs are "empty rhetoric or lame efforts" (p. 294). They suggest that citizen-participation programs should not be tried unless cities are willing to turn over powers and have the authority to allocate significant goods and services in their communities. We must look critically at the instances where community input and decision making are proposed. If community decision making is to be taken seriously, it important that the mechanisms and institutions of community governance be taken seriously.

DEVELOPING A CULTURE OF PUBLIC PARTICIPATION

The role of public officials is changing. Mathews (1994) found that many officials still think of themselves as guardians of the public interest. However, that role is being questioned as citizens increasingly expect a greater role in decision making. As Perlman (1997) states, "Public officials can't pull the levers from behind a curtain and have their pronouncements stick. Citizens are less willing to accept policy decisions made from on high. They want to be involved in forming the policies that affect them" (p. 33). Administrators will have to develop new skills and mechanisms in order to be effective.

One of the issues that emerged from this case was the tension surrounding technical expertise. One of the concerns often voiced by public officials is that the issues are too technical for citizens to grasp all the implications of the various issues. They fear that making the process participatory will result in inferior decision making, as ignorance does not usually affect citizens' willingness to pronounce judgments. The tension between expert rule and public participation is not new. From Plato, who grappled with it in his idea of philosopher kings, to the American founders, the dilemma of how much citizen participation should be promoted has been debated. We still have conflicting views over the value of expertise.

The emphasis in the public sector on seeing citizens as customers or consumers may further drive us away from the notion of shared responsibility and shared governance. The idea of shared governance requires a shift in the models that appear to guide the way many citizens and public officials think about the role of government vis-à-vis citizens. The model that has been prevalent is one that views the citizen as consumer or what Hansell (1996) calls the "vending machine model." Hansell advocates a "barn raising" model in which all sectors of the community work together as they once did to help their neighbors raise a barn.

At the core of this problem is how we envision problem solving. What are the roles of public officials and citizens in community problem solving? Too often, government's role is seen as providing the expertise, with the community's role as giving feedback or input to the process. The process begins with a needs assessment, at which time citizens are sometimes asked for their input, but the problem identification is basically left to the experts. Rarely do citizens participate in the formulation of plans, but if they are involved in this stage, the choices are basically designated by the experts. This can ignore fundamental differences in the way a community might define the issue and the potential alternatives. The best alternative picked is usually far away from citizens' view, let alone participation. In the best of circumstances, the alternative is chosen on the basis of which has the most favorable ratio of benefits to costs. The evaluation of the plan is predicated on whether the plan has achieved its objectives. The whole process is predicated on the abilities of the government officials or their agents to analyze the problem and to act rationally in response.

Kretzmann and McKnight (1993) argue that governments need to "shift their role from defining problems and creating solutions to following community definitions and investing in community solutions" (p. 367). They suggest that government attempts to involve communities often dominate, stifle, and misdirect community efforts because government officials see themselves as the central actor in these efforts. McKnight (1995) proposes that government officials stop perpetuating actions that foster dependence and recognize and build on existing community assets. He suggests that the "needs" assessment approach perpetuated by government and universities disempowers communities and helps create self-fulfilling prophecies around the liabilities in communities. Although every individual and community has liabilities, they also have assets.

Public administrators need to ask whether policies and programs foster community as they are being designed and implemented. The reality is that, in most situations, if communities are ever considered, it is more often as a way to foster community acceptance. Community members are often consulted, but report that they feel manipulated because their feedback seemed to have little impact.

Some agencies are changing the way they have traditionally seen their role. Increasingly, agencies espouse missions and philosophies that embrace efforts to promote citizen participation and community capacity building. In a document from the Idaho Department of Health and Welfare on their 1996 public participation activities, they reported that they changed their philosophy to promote citizen participation in decision making and to build community capacity:

> The Department must be committed to working with communities to strengthen THEIR initiatives, rather than expecting them to work on ours. We learned that communities understand what work is worth doing and generally how to do it. (http://www.state.id.us/dhw/hwgd_www/famcomsv/96comsp1.html)

There are examples of agencies changing the way they have traditionally seen their role. Examples in "Connecting Government and Neighborhoods" (1996), a special section of *Governing* magazine, demonstrate ways some public officials are finding to promote community ownership of both problems and solutions. In Kansas City, Missouri, a broad-based collaborative effort led by Gary Stangler, Director of the Missouri Department of Social Services, created an innovative partnership called the Kansas City Local Investment Commission (LINC), whose mission is to move decision making away from remote bureaucracies. LINC is made up of a 20-member board that includes civic leaders from all segments of society not directly involved with social services. It is cited as a national leader in assisting welfare recipients to go to work without losing their benefits. They have also become a partner with five state agencies in an effort to improve the education of children.

In Little Rock, Arkansas, the vice mayor has been the leading advocate for neighborhood associations. This effort has helped foster another effort to promote decentralization of city government through the creation of Neighborhood Alert Centers. These centers are designed to bring together city services in partnership with neighborhoods throughout the city.

Baxter (1995) states that one of the keys to the success of these partnerships is the conscious effort to develop trust. Throughout the years, he says, citizens had developed a strong distrust of public officials. It was also evident that some public officials harbored resentment toward citizens as a result of protests, marches, and picketing over the years. Both sides managed to overcome these sentiments and form partnerships that reportedly are "making a difference." They began with small victories such as cleanups and gradually moved to innovative programs involving helping neighborhood groups to become community development corporations, community policing, and neighborhood revitalization initiatives. Another important ingredient was the sharing of power between government and citizen groups at all stages—from the problem-setting stage to taking credit for the successes.

TOOLS FOR PRACTICING PUBLIC PARTICIPATION

There are more and more manuals, articles, and tools being created for public managers to improve the interactions between public officials and the public. These range from texts on running public meetings to concerns for promoting participatory democracy. Some approaches are aimed at improving the skills or process without any fundamental change in the way decisions are made. Techniques to promote consensus building and collaborative problem solving are important skills for public officials. At the same time, it is important to understand how techniques can be used to mask manipulations designed to fulfill requirements or demands for citizen participation without responding in the spirit of meaningful participation.

It is important to assess the mechanisms and literature according to the degree to which citizens will share the decision-making power and the power to frame the issues or problems. Arnstein (1969) argues that "citizen participation is a categorical term for citizen power." She distinguishes among eight levels of citizen power in decision making with processes that result in "citizen manipulation at the lowest level and citizen control" at the top (p. 216).

In *Public Participation in Public Decisions*, Thomas (1995) proposes various strategies for involving citizens in government decision making. He argues that to achieve a strong democracy our decision-making processes must be reformed to accommodate more extensive and effective participation of citizens. He outlines actions for areas where the goal is involving the public for information only, involving the public to build acceptance, and where there is shared decision making. He concludes by stating,

> Following the recommendations of this book need not risk the "excess of democracy" that Huntington has warned threatens governmental effectiveness if the public becomes too involved in governance. Managers who heed the lessons of this book should not involve the public unnecessarily, and when they do involve the public, they should not permit the public to compromise essential agency quality standards. (p. 181)

Thomas offers many practical reasons for public managers "inviting public involvement," yet the tone is one of the public administrator as the key player. The use of facilitation and the other techniques help promote meetings and interactions that are civil, efficient, and productive. The techniques that are advocated can produce processes that will contribute to problem solving and to a sense by the participants that they have made a contribution. However, it is important to consider that any technique can be misused. The danger lies in the fact that skilled facilitators and managers can use techniques to design processes that do not promote high levels of citizen power sharing. Of course, such processes could be evaluated by some as manipulative and by others as efficient and productive.

Citizens complain that public officials often don't appear to be listening to their concerns. However, "good listening" will require changes in government processes as well as the development of skills. Public officials will need to develop facilitation, mediation, and collaborative skills. The benefit is that public administrators as facilitators and good listeners "offers the possibility for a real 'reinvention' of agency policy and management processes, one that vivifies the common space occupied by citizens and bureaucrats and offers prospects of substantive community" (Stivers, 1994, p. 368).

Lappe and Dubois (1994, p. 238) identify 10 skills as critical to participating in democratic decision making and action. They call these the arts of democracy:

- *Active listening*: encouraging the speaker and searching for meaning
- *Creative conflict*: confronting others in ways that produce growth
- *Mediation*: facilitating interaction to help people in conflict hear each other
- *Negotiation*: problem solving that meets some key interests of all involved
- *Political imagination*: reimaging our future according to our shared values
- *Public dialogue*: public talk on matters that concern us all
- *Public judgment*: public decision making that allows citizens to make choices they are willing to implement
- *Celebration and appreciation*: expressing joy and appreciation for what we learn as well as what we achieve
- *Evaluation and reflection*: assessing and incorporating the lessons we learn through action
- *Mentoring*: supportively guiding others in learning these arts of public life

There are a number of organizations around the country that are experimenting with efforts to promote these skills. Among them are the National Issues Forum and the Study Circles Resource Center. The goal of the former is to stimulate and sustain dialogue among and between citizens and between citizens and policy makers. The latter is based on the principle that our democracy requires the participation of an informed and concerned citizenry. Although each forum is organized locally by civic organizations, universities, service clubs, or membership groups, they are a part of a national network dedicated to deliberation and dialogue, and both seek to revitalize public discussions of issues.

The theory underlying these efforts is the essential role of deliberation in democracy. The culture of deliberation implies that citizens are actively engaged in the discussion of important issues and that this deliberation will result in a better understanding of those issues, greater dialogue between citizens and government officials, and ultimately, shared decision making. Mathew's (1994) contention is that the concept of "bodies politic"—public assemblies where views are formed—is missing in our picture of what is important in politics. This is a concept that John Adams and Thomas Jefferson understood well. Jefferson encouraged town meetings and public forums, arguing that "the voice of the whole people would be fairly, fully, and peacefully expressed, discussed and decided by the common reason of the society" (quoted in Mathews, 1994, p. 66). Not only are the opportunities for deliberation few, but the forums where groups deliberate long and seriously get little attention and less nurturing.

The principle of deliberation is central for many theorists of democracy. Pateman (1970) argues that widespread participation is critical for democracy because it transforms individuals into citizens. For some, the very definition of democracy requires deliberative listening and speaking. Gastil, Adams, and Jenkins-Smith (1995) studied the concept of deliberation and found a common definition in the writings of a number of scholars (Barber, 1984; Fishkin, 1995; Gastil, 1993; Mathews, 1994). Although they have different orientations and emphases, they share the same meaning of deliberation, "to weigh carefully both the consequences of various options for action and the views of others" (Mathews, 1994, p. 110).

It is important to create spaces for dialogue. There are places for people to complain or advocate, but few places where citizens come together to deliberate over issues. As Mathews (1994) states, deliberation is "a way of making a decision, it is of no use when a decision has already been made" (p. 182). Yet, that is what we often see in public hearings. Too often citizen input is requested after a decision is made. Deliberation begins by framing the issues, thus it is critical to consider carefully how issues are framed. In many cases, the solutions posed have been predetermined by the way the issues have been framed. In the rush to solve problems, it is easy to overlook the fact that an issue has been defined in such a way as to limit the potential solutions.

CONCLUSION

The rationale behind promoting citizen participation is theoretical—that citizen participation is critical to a self-governing democracy—and practical—that citizens are less willing to accept decisions when they have not been involved in the process. As we approach the 21st century, we are moving away from depending on government to solve our problems. There are many calls for decentralizing and empowering communities. Yet at the same time, for the most part, we haven't developed the structures and processes to support community governance or any kind of collective problem solving. The challenge is to develop structures and processes that will value technical and professional knowledge and integrate citizens into the governance process. This will involve more collaborative relationships and partnerships between citizens and public administrators. This partnership role emphasizes civic problem solving and civic capacity building with government increasingly acting as the facilitator of problem-solving processes rather than the problem solver.

Chapter 10

WORKING WITH CITIZENS

Breaking Down Barriers to Citizen Self-Governance

Richard C. Box and Deborah A. Sagen

It is now common knowledge that the contemporary American environment of public governance is often hostile and difficult. Citizens feel a sense of separation from their government, they are skeptical of collective (governmental) action, they resist providing the resources for public programs, and they are convinced that elected officials and public professionals are inefficient, corrupt, or both.

For many years, governments at all levels have made attempts to involve citizens in the process of making and implementing public policy (Ross & Levine, 1996, pp. 217-247). In the midst of the current forbidding environment, there is a hopeful and constructive trend that promises to reconnect people with their governmental institutions, allowing them to take control of their collective future through self-governance. This trend operates mostly at the smaller levels of government closest to the people. It can be described as a returning to these earlier American values about the role of the citizen and the government:

1. An emphasis on the local community as the place where citizens can have a meaningful impact on collective life.
2. Small and responsive government instead of large, bureaucratic, and remote government.
3. Public-service practitioners who help citizens achieve their collective goals, as contrasted with the career professional as the expert who controls public agencies.

As a field of study and practice, public administration has traditionally been concerned with technical efficiency and securing a sense of legitimacy in the broader legal and political context of society. Entering the 21st century, we are moving away from governmental practices that served well in building the administrative state but that stifle citizen self-governance. This requires a change in emphasis from seeking greater power or status for the field of public administration, to a concern with the impact public administration has on the quality of civic life and citizen commitment to social betterment. This concern can be seen, for example, in calls for "civism" (Frederickson, 1982), attention to "civic duty" (Newland, 1984), and emphasizing the administrator's role as that of a citizen, acting for other citizens (Cooper, 1984).

In this chapter, we write from the perspective of former local government administrators who now deal with the public sector from different vantage points. Richard Box, a former local government manager, teaches public administration to future and current public professionals and writes about the challenges facing public governance. Deborah Sagen, also a former local government manager, for several years directed a nonprofit agency that coordinates citizen efforts to improve their community. We argue that, in this turbulent and rapidly changing governance setting, the task of public administration as a field of practice is to break down the barriers to full citizen self-governance. Our intent is not to create a chaotic political free-for-all, but an open and welcoming environment for those who wish to govern themselves.

Moving toward this vision of our governmental future requires that we restore a public-service ethic of working with and for citizens. We think there are two primary barriers to citizen self-governance: control of the policy process by community elites and control of program implementation by public professionals.

Our purpose in this chapter is to advocate reorientation of professional roles and attitudes to meet the changing times and needs for self governance. This reorientation is based on returning to values of public service from an earlier era, an era when the gulf between the roles of citizens and public servants was not as great as it often is today (see Chapter 1). This does not mean returning to the social conditions of an earlier time, which in many cases were, by modern standards, oppressive toward minorities, women, and people on the lower end of the socioeconomic scale. Nor does it mean abandonment of the impressive and important advances made since the Reform Era of the early 20th century in efficient and effective delivery of public programs and services. Instead, it means returning to the notion of commitment to a public-service ethic, to the idea of the career public practitioner as a facilitator of citizen self-governance. Our focus is on the community, but our ideas apply to some extent at all levels of government. We seek a revitalization of the excitement and sense of discovery that come from the cooperative enterprise of citizens and public-service practitioners shaping the future together.

In what follows, Debbie Sagen describes her personal career journey as she discovered that her graduate school education and work in local government did not give her the skills to respond to the needs of citizens. From his work as a local government professional and a public administration academician, Richard Box examines the ways in which politically and economically powerful people influence the daily work of public professionals. We each write about our somewhat different perceptions of professional work in communities, but our experiences with citizens and public service lead us to the same conclusions about the future role of the public-service practitioner. At the end of the chapter, we conclude with ideas we believe are valuable to citizens and to practitioners as we face the challenges of the 21st century.

SAGEN: THE PRACTITIONER'S VIEW

From Theory to Practice

As a graduate student in public affairs, I chose to specialize in local government management because it was "closest to the people." Having completed college internships with a Wisconsin state legislator and a U.S. senator, I found the process of resolving specific constituent problems unrewarding—helping people navigate through large bureaucracies was a tortuous form of delayed gratification. A career in local government management held the promise of working directly with citizens to improve community life, which seemed tangible and immediate.

My graduate school studies were designed to make me a "skilled generalist." Although students joked about this (a skilled generalist, after all, is one who knows very little about everything), my training served me well as a local government practitioner. Developing analytical skills, learning basic research methods, and understanding policy development are essential to critical thinking. Looking back, however, I am surprised at how little time we spent in my graduate courses discussing the government professional's role as a facilitator of citizen interests in shaping and implementing policy. Citizens were described by their special interests; professionals were viewed as objective, value-free "keepers" of the public interest; and elected officials were regarded as "middle men" between the public and the rational bureaucrats.

What I did learn in graduate school about citizen involvement fueled my desire to pursue a career in local government. Each student was required to complete two years of policy research projects where, under the direction of our professors, teams of students were hired as consultants to government agencies. One of my "clients" was a council of governments, the other a city. In both cases, my colleagues and I interviewed citizens, researched issues, and presented findings and recommendations. Working with a mix of citizens, elected officials, and public managers challenged me the most, because each group had a different perspective and proposed alternative solutions. Reconciling differences between these groups was much more central to the success of our work than was the resolution of technical issues. This realization made me focus on insuring that citizens, elected officials, and government managers agree on which common goals to pursue before searching for perfect technical solutions.

After completing my graduate work, I served an internship with a progressive college town in northern Colorado. I was assigned a range of projects, from internal management issues like employee pay and benefits analyses, to staffing citizen boards and commissions. My work with citizens was the highlight of my experience in this city. Elected officials and volunteers alike were eager to learn about local government issues and were willing to spend the time to make thoughtful recommendations to improve service delivery and community life. The government managers who mentored me were surprised at my willingness to work with citizens. The only reprimand I faced during those years came from a mentor-manager who suggested that I was allocating too much of my time to my work with citizens and elected officials and working too hard to advocate citizen solutions to local issues. Because I saw myself as a public servant, I thought I had struck the right balance—dealing with the public first and completing the rest of my assignments as time allowed. My more senior colleagues made it clear that this was inappropriate. From their perspective, keeping the bureaucracy running efficiently was the most important task at hand because "that's what most citizens want." Interacting with citizens and responding to our elected officials' every question was something we got to when we had time on our hands.

Managing the Public

After more than two years in this position, it became clear that my local government career was becoming as stagnant as the Colorado economy.

Government cutbacks eliminated every middle management position I could apply for. I accepted a position as assistant to the city manager in a city in Oregon. The city is a large suburb of Portland, a rural farming town that had grown rapidly into a bedroom community. City officials were completing an annexation program that doubled the city's population and a state-mandated sewer connection project was forcing thousands of homeowners to pay to abandon their septic systems and connect to city sewers.

Although the annexation and public sewer connection programs met the theoretical criteria for the provision of urban services in a market-based model of management, these programs were implemented in such a way that citizens became openly hostile toward local elected officials and city staffers. Citizens living in unincorporated areas resisted annexation because they already received urban services without paying additional property taxes. The groundwater contamination caused by thousands of failing septic systems was an abstraction to the ordinary citizen faced with a five-digit sewer connection bill. Rather than taking the time to engage citizens in an educational process about why they were pursuing aggressive annexation and public utilities policies, elected officials chose to fast-track their decisions with few opportunities (beyond official public hearings) for public dialogue.

During my early tenure with this city, I worked hard with my manager counterparts to run government like a business. We kept taxes low, provided basic public services, and conducted ourselves as value-free bureaucrats. In terms of citizen involvement, we chose a path of managing the public. We kept citizen involvement to a bare minimum, choosing to work closely with city council members and a few key business leaders. Although many citizens served on advisory boards and commissions, their input arrived as recommendations to council with little support from city staff. Often, citizen recommendations were ignored or overturned. This was the way efficient government worked, and we accomplished many organizational goals in a short period of time.

Further, the professional network of local government managers in our region fostered an "us and them" attitude toward citizens. Tax-limitation measures were appearing on local ballots, challenges to the council-manager form of government were discussed in some communities, and long-standing city managers faced termination by new city councils. Although these managers were excellent technicians, they were at a loss to explain why citizens were not satisfied with community governance. Describing citizens as "the enemy of efficient government" became the topic of many of our professional networking sessions.

My transformation from local government manager to citizen-oriented practitioner occurred when the city began the periodic review of its comprehensive land use plan. The city hired a citizen involvement coordinator and hundreds of ordinary citizens were appointed to oversee the review process. Because comprehensive plan reviews touch every aspect of public service provision, this interaction with citizens led to many administrative and policy recommendations about how to improve the effectiveness of city services. In addition, the city's annexation program ended and several council members were elected from newly annexed areas of town.

The result? City employees could no longer embrace a policy of managing the public. Citizens demanded access to information and participation in policy setting. Changes in the planning system strengthened citizen participation in planning decisions, so several new neighborhood organizations formed to oppose large development applications. And the new city council believed strongly that our organizational goals should be rooted in larger goals developed and agreed to by the community.

As the director of community and economic development services during this time, my views about public involvement changed rapidly. I discovered that most citizens wanted to participate responsibly in setting and implementing city policy. Once armed with the facts, these citizens proposed reasonable solutions, were civil in their interactions with staff and elected officials, and were willing to negotiate with developers in order to attain common community goals. Curiously, these citizens responded best to those managers and employees who were not value free. Instead, citizens worked well with those employees who articulated common beliefs and values about how citizens should be treated and how the community should grow. The employees who tried hard to appear neutral were often characterized as uncaring or dishonest.

During my tenure as director, I tried to develop new skills in working with citizens. I learned to listen better and worked with my staff to do the same. I implemented recommendations from line staff designed to improve our citizen friendliness. For example, we opened our offices on weeknights so that citizens did not have to leave work to obtain building permits. With the council's blessing, we engaged hundreds of citizens in developing a collective vision for the city; our program won a national award. We hired staff to help homeowners who could not afford to hook up to city sewers under the state-mandated program arrange for low- or no-interest financing. We also worked closely with the police department to expand community-oriented policing to include code enforcement, building inspection, and public works employees who worked directly with citizens to resolve neighborhood problems.

My recollection of these days is that I was a very lonely manager. I became isolated from most of my colleagues (who continued to "manage the public"), who chided me for being too responsive to the needs of ordinary citizens. On the other hand, line employees and citizens appreciated my willingness to listen to their concerns about how city hall functioned.

A Citizen's Perspective

On moving back to Colorado, I began working for Citizens' Goals, a local nonprofit organization of committed volunteers working together to resolve critical issues and to mobilize citizens to take meaningful action to improve the region's quality of life. As executive director, my role was to bring citizens together to study issues, make findings and recommendations, and implement solutions. I interacted with local government officials daily, and found this role to be full of remarkable contrasts. First, I could be sympathetic to government professionals' fears about giving too much power to citizens because I've been there. Second, I could advocate openly for opening the doors at city hall to meaningful citizen involvement in civic life. Third, I appreciated the difficulties citizens face in gaining access to city hall because I've become one of them.

This position suited me well. I was able to help public administrators appreciate the role responsible citizens can play to improve city governance. I assisted citizens to understand the complexities of local government and develop the patience necessary to follow policy making from start to finish rather than stepping in to oppose individual city actions. I also explored new mechanisms for mobilizing ordinary people to take collective action.

The most inspiring part of my work was assisting citizens as they discovered the rewards of self-governance and observing public managers as they recognized the benefits of collaboration with citizens. I came to see myself as a translator between citizens and public officials, someone who can speak both languages and can help strengthen communication—and, hopefully, close the gap—between citizens and the administrators hired to serve them.

Returning to Public Service

My transformation from local government manager to public-service practitioner has been both troubling and challenging. Troubling, in that it has been a tremendously lonely journey with little support from colleagues or professional writing (most of which focuses on the "how to's" of citizen involvement rather than exploring the role of the administrator). Challenging, because I have learned how much better local government functions when citizens, elected officials, and practitioners work in partnership.

This transformation occurred when I came full circle and recognized that what brought me to local government service in the first place—being close to the people—defines the good public-service practitioner. For many years I followed the advice of mentors and colleagues who convinced me that my beliefs about public service were naive; public managers existed to serve bureaucratic interests, not community interests. As a result, I became an expert at managing the public.

Once I learned to trust my instincts—to recover my public-service ethic—I was able to focus my attention on how citizens felt about the quality, quantity, and cost of city services, and was able to reorganize people and resources to do the job better. I now believe that every public manager needs to rediscover an ethic of public service that puts the public first. My work as a nonprofit director allowed me the latitude, and gave me the perspective I needed to help my community on that journey.

BOX: WHOM DO WE SERVE AND FOR WHAT PURPOSE?

Who Controls Community Policy Making?

The process of working together to forge a community plan can be rewarding to citizens and a significant step forward for the community. After spending a number of years as a planner helping city and county citizens in planning processes, I have found that most people are willing and able to set aside negative or helpless feelings about government to accomplish a joint task. Americans innately understand how to balance individual liberty with collective action. Given information and opportunity, they do it well, that is, they demonstrate the capacity for self governance.

However, information and opportunity are sometimes hard to come by. Repeatedly, I have seen politically and economically powerful people seek to limit citizen access to the public-policy process in two ways. One is to control the number of citizen advisory bodies and their scope of responsibility. Another is to monitor the activities of public professionals and take action when they go "too far" in empowering citizens, that is, when the powerful believe that their financial interests might be threatened. Action taken against noncompliant public professionals may include a quiet word of warning, an effort to alter their spheres of responsibility, or attempts to terminate them.

This sounds more than a little dark and disturbing—powerful forces manipulating citizens and public professionals for their own benefit. But whether it is disturbing or a natural part of human behavior in organizations depends on your point of view. We should not be surprised to find

From the Conversation: Limits to Participation in the Current Political Economy

Delores: In Richard and Deborah's chapter they state that many people are willing and able to share the joint project. I find so few examples of this that I wonder how much the culture here [in Hawai'i] affects the low participation and the reluctance of both administrators and citizens to engage in dialogue. The most common reason given here is *the economy*—too many people have two and three jobs to survive. Some here see the highly centralized structure as a major part of the problem (nothing below the county level). But reforming the structure may not address many of the root problems. I fear that my emphasis on more mechanisms to promote deliberation will not have much effect if there isn't any change in the political economy.

that there are powerful people at the heart of the public enterprise of governing, at all levels of government. Virtually all human endeavor involves the formation of hierarchies of leaders and followers, a tendency that can be shaped or resisted, but rarely eliminated.

Commercial activity has always been a primary reason for the formation of urban centers. People whose lives and fortunes are invested in the economic success of a community can be expected to care deeply about the sorts of public policies that are enacted and how they might affect their affairs. Paul Peterson (1981) pointed out that people in local areas do not have much control over many of the forces affecting their communities, including state and federal public programs and the general economic environment. What they do control is the local use of land: development, redevelopment, planning for the future, and competing with other communities for new or expanding business.

Thus, the local political process naturally focuses on programmatic and resource issues related to basic, "hard" services such as streets, water and sewer systems, public safety, and an educational system that trains people to work in local businesses. "Soft" services such as health and welfare, esthetic and environmental improvement (air quality, landscaping and sign requirements, architectural review, etc.), liberal-arts education, parks and recreation, libraries, and human relations, are regarded as worthwhile if they help the community compete with other places to attract firms that bring jobs and a growing economic base. If soft services are not perceived as economically valuable but instead as blocking the economic goals of politically influential people, or as a resource drain on the economic vitality of the community, they become a target in the ongoing public-policy debate.

In some places, community members concerned about the human living environment will band together to counter business interests in the public-policy process. This takes a lot of time and effort, because public policies are formed through hundreds of incremental actions taken over a long period of time by many people, including public professionals, elected officials, citizen groups, and individuals (Logan & Molotch, 1987, p. 64). A single policy decision does not occur in a vacuum, but is built on a foundation of past decisions and events. For a person or group to change the community's course, they must be active participants over time, or rally overwhelming public opinion on a specific issue, or both.

The public-policy contest between economic interests and those of citizens concerned about the human living environment can produce a seesaw effect in which the balance of power in the local policy-making process shifts back and forth (Flentje & Counihan, 1984; Vogel & Swanson, 1989). In relatively rare situations, it may shift from economic interests toward concern for the human living environment in a way that seems permanent.

The Options Open to Practitioners

Like many public professionals, when I worked in local government I often found myself caught in the cross fire of this struggle between the values of the community as an economic marketplace and the community as a living space for people. I experienced pressure to go along with the status quo, with those who are dominant in the policy-making process, yet I felt a duty to do the "right" thing by assisting citizens in determining their own future. In this situation, I often found it hard to answer the enduring, key questions of public service: Whom do we serve, and for what purpose?

One way to approach these questions is to think about the evolution of today's corps of public-service professionals. In pre-Revolutionary America, most of the daily tasks associated with public life, such as keeping the peace, repairing roads, taking care of the needy, and keeping town records, were performed by citizens who volunteered their time (Cook, 1976). This pattern continued through the 18th century and into the 19th century, but was paralleled by increasing specialization in many places. As urban centers grew and the challenges of public administration became more complex, positions that had been filled by citizen volunteers often required more time and expertise than a volunteer could offer. Such positions came to be filled by people who were paid for their work, sometimes on a part-time basis, and eventually by full-time specialists.

By the late 19th century, the professionalization of the public service was well under way. Today, we expect public services to be operated by highly skilled people who devote their lives to their work, but this was not always the case. Taking the history of local public service into account, the contemporary public professional is in a very real sense a full-time citizen. Terry Cooper (1984) made this point, noting that that the "ethical identity" of the public professional is "that of the citizen who is employed *as* one of us to work *for us; a kind of professional citizen ordained to do that work which we in a complex large-scale political community are unable to undertake ourselves" (p. 307).

This view of the public professional is very different from the one we are most familiar with. Instead of the model of a value-neutral, skilled official in a remote bureaucratic organization, quietly implementing policies decided by elected legislators, the public professional becomes a sort of super-citizen, acting on behalf of the many people who cannot attend to public affairs because they are busy with their own lives. However, this view is intended to apply to all levels of government and some very large public organizations. At the community level, it is still possible for citizens to participate directly in shaping their collective future. This means that community public professionals have a broader range of action options available to them than do their counterparts in most state and national agencies.

One option is to model public administration after private business management. Parallel to the return to local action and small and responsive government, nationwide we can see a new focus on the technical aspects of management in initiatives to contract out services, privatize, benchmark, reinvent, be entrepreneurial, please the customer, rightsize, motivate employees to be more productive, and so on. This represents a transition for the public professional from the neutral bureaucratic model to a market-based model of management that can be helpful in dealing with resource scarcity and public concern about tax levels. It puts the public professional in the position of promoting a private-sector vision of managerial technique that yields the biggest bang for the buck. It also focuses on internal agency operations, emphasizing professional status and control in creating the best service-delivery system to serve the customers.

But this increased emphasis on market-like management ignores the political context of the public agency and leaves out the role of the citizen. It is a model sure to please those who view the community as a marketplace for economic enterprise, as well as those citizens who want nothing more from a community than an efficient and effective package of services, who want to pay their taxes and fees and leave the running of the collective community machinery to others. Not everyone is satisfied with such a consumer or customer role. Many people see themselves as integral parts of the community, willing and able to share with others the joint project of creating what they see as a better future.

Thus, another option open to the public professional builds on the history of the practitioner as citizen and the current trend toward localism and self-governance. This option emphasizes the role the practitioner plays in helping citizens achieve self-governance. It involves two elements. First, citizens must be given the knowledge and techniques they need to deal with public-policy issues in an informed and rational way. Second, they must be offered a forum for deliberation and decision making that is open and welcoming, that is, one that allows everyone who wants to participate the chance to do so without feeling intimidated, demeaned, or ignored.

The public professional who engages in this option of helping citizens works within a model of citizenship that Daniel Kemmis, former mayor of Missoula, Montana, identified as the "republican tradition." By republican, Kemmis (1990) referred not to a party, but to a concept of joint collective action that involves a "face-to-face, hands-on approach to problem-solving" (p. 11). Kemmis joined this model metaphorically with the traditions of farming communities, in which people help each other with the large and difficult tasks of life. He termed this collective activity "barn raising" (pp. 64-83).

Professionals who stay close to the neutral role of service to elected representatives and the established power structure may be able to remain safe and invisible as they give competent technical service. Professionals who adopt a market-like, entrepreneurial role may face resistance from citizens who demand greater influence over the policy process. Both neutral and market-management professionals answer the key public-service questions of whom they serve and for what purpose with the response that they serve recognized official power, for whatever purpose is valued by those in power. This purpose is often the marketplace goal of maximizing financial returns to influential people.

To highlight the difference between public professionals who focus on providing efficient technical services and those who, in addition, seek to help citizens govern, we might switch from use of the term *professional* to one that embodies the evolution of the citizen into the full-time practitioner—this is the *public-service practitioner.* Public service practitioners who seek to help citizens govern incur considerable risk. Powerful and influential people may take action against practitioners whose activities threaten the status quo, and citizens may reach conclusions about the future of the community that seem wrong to the practitioner. Some practitioners in the helping role may decide to modify their approach so they can reduce these risks, but their answer to the key questions continues to be that they serve citizens for the purpose of enabling them to govern themselves.

Finding the Right Balance

As a nation, we are moving away from the 20th-century reliance on government to solve our problems and toward greater reliance on collective action at the community level. With this change comes a new challenge to public professionals to reevaluate their relationships with citizens and elected representatives. Concepts of professional, value-neutral service and entrepreneurial efficiency are important to U.S. public administration, and skilled public professionals use these concepts in their daily work whenever appropriate. But they are only part of what it takes to do a good job in today's political, social, and economic environment.

In my work as a practitioner, I found that it was not enough to do things in a technically competent way. I found that the best results for the community and for myself came from working in partnership with citizens, giving them the information they needed to understand the issues and helping them to gain access to the decision-making process. Creating such partnerships could be time consuming. It could also draw fire from politicians and businesspeople who felt threatened by citizens who understood the issues and were ready to take part in shaping public policy and its implementation.

Despite these difficulties, I believe that if people whose full-time work is serving the public are to contribute to citizen self-governance, they need to move beyond reliance solely on neutral competence or market-like management, toward a balance between those models and helping citizens to govern themselves. This means worrying less about whether elected officials or citizens are micromanaging professionals, and more about whether practitioners are informing and educating them so they can make wise decisions. It means worrying less about whether taking time to discuss public matters with citizens detracts from efficient management and thinking more about encouraging open discourse on issues of importance to the community.

The problem for each of us, as practitioners and academicians in public administration, is how to find the right balance between competent technical or professional service and helping people reclaim responsibility for governing. At the level of daily tasks, this translates into finding a balance between responsiveness to the politically and economically powerful, and giving citizens the knowledge and access to the policy-making process they need to achieve the future they desire. Finding this balance is not easy for any of us. It is more likely to be a perpetual journey than a destination, as we seek our own personal answers, in each particular place and time, to the questions of whom we serve and for what purpose.

CONCLUSION

The contemporary public professional works in a general environment of public skepticism about government and a return to earlier American values of local action, small and responsive government, and the practitioner as a facilitator of citizen action instead of a controller of public agencies. At the community level, the professional working environment, as Richard Box says, is one of finding a balance between the value of the community as economic marketplace and the value of the community as living space for people.

Public professionals have several options available to them as they seek to answer the key public service questions: Whom do I serve? and for what purpose? They can stick to the traditional model of the value-neutral professional offering competent technical skills, they can adopt the market-based, business-like model of entrepreneurial provision of services to consumers, or they can help create an open and welcoming setting in which citizens can govern themselves. Over time, and in the complexity of specific events and issues, public professionals may move back and forth in the emphasis they place on each of these role options.

We think that the needs of communities and citizens as we enter the 21st century favor the role option of helper and facilitator, with due attention to the need for competent technical and managerial service as well. It is this role that allows public professionals to become true public-service practitioners, to develop an ethic of public service. We can identify three essential skills local government practitioners need to accomplish this transition. First, they need to learn to listen to citizens, becoming "the listening bureaucrat" (see sidebar below). Although citizens may not speak the technical language of government, their insights, perspectives, values, and goals for improving their communities are important for public-service practitioners to understand and respect.

Second, practitioners should conduct themselves in a technically competent way without pretending to be value free. The enterprise of governing communities is a subjective one—learning to articulate personal and organizational values helps citizens understand and trust public-service practitioners.

Third, practitioners should constantly seek new ways to view their work through the eyes of ordinary citizens. Effective public-service practitioners understand that the best way to serve the customer is to learn to observe the organization as citizens do, adjusting organizational policies and practices to help citizens achieve their goals for the community.

On a broader level, we believe that advocating for change in the role choices and behavior of individual practitioners may not be sufficient to meet the challenge of working with citizens in the 21st century. It may also be necessary to alter the way we train people for public administration, giving greater emphasis to awareness of the changing social and political environment and the need for recovery of an ethic of public service.

The Listening Bureaucrat[1]

Camilla Stivers

A number of years ago, Thomas Berger, a judge in Vancouver, British Columbia, was asked by the Canadian government to coordinate a series of hearings on the route of the Alaskan oil pipeline through the Mackenzie Valley. In a strategic use of his authority as hearing master, Berger insisted on supplementing the usual round of testimony by oil company executives and technical experts with testimony by residents of the native communities in the region. The hearing board traveled to every one of the 35 communities, bringing with them translators not only so the officials could understand the natives, but so the natives could have access to technical information. Through Berger's efforts, neglected voices were heard in what might have otherwise been a rather typical policy process. Native peoples became informed participants; all those involved were able to listen to one another on a much more equal footing. Almost single-handedly, Berger was able to democratize what would have otherwise been a rather routine process (Berger, 1977).

In the context of representative government, democratic public administration usually gets interpreted as adherence to formal accountability mechanisms (see Timney, Chapter 6): "I followed the law and the regulations." Or, "If anybody asks me, I'll be ready to give reasons for what I did." Or, "I'm accountable because, six levels above me in the chain of command, the agency head reports to an elected official." When administrators and firing-line workers in public agencies want something more than traditional, representative forms of democracy, when they want to work collaboratively with citizens, they sometimes find it hard to imagine how to build the necessary relationships. One element is so basic that it can be easily overlooked: developing the ability to listen. What is skillful listening and how can it help build collaboration with citizens?

Consider some basic aspects of listening. We have less control over what we hear than over what we see. We can shut our eyes easily, but we have to plug our ears, and even then some sound usually comes through. Therefore we are fundamentally open to sound. As we listen, sounds come into being and fade away. Whereas sight distances us from what appear to be fixed objects, sound penetrates the listener; it immerses and engages us.

In addition to being an experience of openness and engagement, listening is reciprocal. In dialogue, the listener is a participant in the speaker's emerging thought. The listener evokes the speaker's thought, paradoxically, by "standing aside and making room" (Fiumara, 1990, p. 144). At the same time, in sharing the speaker's language, the listener hears his or her own voice, while the speaker, hearing his or her own words, also hears in them the voices of others who speak the same language. "To listen to another is to learn what the world is like from a position that is not one's own; to listen is to reverse position, role, and experience" (Levin, 1989, p. 193).

Clearly, not all listening fulfills its potential. At the everyday level, much of the listening we do is pro forma. Either we scarcely notice what we are hearing, or we listen in an ego-driven way,

continued

shaping what comes to us so that it fits our desires, waiting impatiently for someone to finish speaking, shaping our reply in advance rather than attending to what he or she is really saying.

But with practice, we can move beyond these everyday modes to what Levin (1989) calls *skillful listening,* which involves slowing down, giving deliberate attention to the experience, and cultivating a welcoming receptivity that accepts others in their uniqueness. Levin argues that skillful listening is a "practice of the self": in other words, not mere self-development, but self-development that also changes society by altering the quality of interpersonal relationships, whether in private or public. He believes that skillful listening can join self and society, theory and action; it has this potential because it involves openness, engagement, letting-be, and reciprocity.

How can skillful listening help those in public agencies practice more democratically? First, it helps them to hear neglected voices, engage in truly reciprocal communication with stakeholders, and remain open to emerging perspectives. Also, it helps them deepen their understanding of complex situations, distinguish the impossible from the merely difficult, develop more workable problem definitions, and synthesize as well as they now analyze. Listening administrators and firing-line workers understand themselves as facilitators rather than manipulators or soloists, sensing the various themes sounding in their worlds, appreciating their harmony and their dissonance, creating occasions for the possibility of their interweaving.

The potential in good listening has recently been underscored by Daniel Kemmis (1990), mayor of Missoula, Montana. He argues that not much "public hearing" goes on at the typical public hearing; therefore, public officials must not only listen well themselves, they must also create alternative processes in which parties to contested issues can speak directly with and listen to one another. He cites several successful examples, including one in which a grassroots group that wanted to combine a community solar greenhouse with a laundromat (which would provide back-up heat and revenue) reached an accommodation with owners of existing laundromats. The mayor brought the parties together, but required them to negotiate their own settlement. Not only did he listen to them, but he encouraged them to listen to one another.

In public administration, as elsewhere, "democracy is paying attention" (Bellah, Madsen, Sullivan, Swidler, & Tipton, 1991, p. 254). Democratically minded administrators and firing-line workers may want to pay attention to their own listening abilities and to agency processes, in order that they personally, and their organizations, can pay better attention to the public.

NOTE

1. Adapted from Stivers (1994).

Chapter 11

TARGETED COMMUNITY INITIATIVE

"Putting Citizens First!"

Joseph E. Gray and Linda W. Chapin

In May of 1991, a newly elected county executive met with the residents of a small and impoverished rural community in Orange County, Florida. "I'm here to listen to your concerns," she said. "I want to help." The resulting torrent of hostility and resentment caught her by surprise. Citizens felt they had been neglected for so long by local government that they were unwilling to believe that anyone could be sincere about changing that relationship.

This chapter examines citizen involvement in practice in Orange County. In several central Florida locations, local government is working in partnership with citizens to build community, trust, and a new kind of interaction. The Targeted Community Initiative (TCI) provides evidence of hope for the coexistence of citizens and bureaucrats in the 21st century. This case study documents the ongoing struggle to maintain a balance between civic input and administrative responsibility in the governance process.

This unique, neighborhood-based community planning and development process began as a response to a public outcry for government assistance to deal with rising levels of juvenile crime in the tiny community of South Apopka in Northwest Orange County. The initiative has evolved into an effective model for neighborhood planning and community development. It has since been implemented in three other Orange County communities. We believe that it can be replicated in many other places as local governments attempt to improve blighted areas and rebuild confidence in the civic process.

175

SOUTH APOPKA PROJECT

The South Apopka Project was the beginning of a "community building" revolution in Orange County. An initial meeting was called to discuss the escalating juvenile crime problems that had plagued the area in recent years. In a local newspaper article published shortly before the meeting, the county sheriff referred to the community of South Apopka (approximately 5,000 residents), as the "juvenile crime capital of the county." According to local crime statistics, it was a well-deserved title. South Apopka constituted less than 2% of the county's total population, but nearly 25% of juvenile arrests.

County Chairman Linda Chapin first met with the citizens of South Apopka in the Phyllis Wheatley Elementary School cafeteria. As the chairman started to explain how they were "with the government, and here to help," the mood of the crowd turned sour. Once the booing and hissing subsided, the citizens began a litany of community needs and grievances that appeared to go well beyond the issue of juvenile crime. They expressed concern about jobs, housing, health care, child care, education, unpaved roads, and a lot of other things, including crime.

Following the meeting, Chapin created an interdepartmental team of county staff to identify the appropriate county role in South Apopka and develop a plan to address the community's needs. The team decided that a comprehensive problem solving-approach was required, with an emphasis on community empowerment. Department managers were asked to identify existing and proposed county projects in the area, develop ideas about ways that the county could further address the needs expressed by the South Apopka residents, and determine available resources and additional resources that would be needed.

In June of 1991, a month after the initial gathering, Chapin went back to South Apopka for a second town meeting. Again, more than 150 residents turned out. Chapin reported on the current programs and planned improvements. She also pledged her continued support, but challenged the citizens to show their support and commitment to their own community by organizing as a unified team to work in partnership with the county. There was no reason to separately negotiate the needs and priorities of all of existing community factions; too much work needed to be accomplished.

Community groups and churches had a long history of civic involvement in the South Apopka community. Organizations such as Concerned Citizens of Apopka, the Apopka Improvement Association, the Apopka South Side Improvement Society Task Force, the Justice and Peace Office, the Farmworker Association, and the Apopka Area Chamber of Commerce had long been involved in the struggle to revitalize the South Apopka community. Three factors hampered their efforts: lack of understanding and general disinterest on the part of local elected officials and government bureaucrats; no real cohesion between community groups; and citizen apathy.

South Apopka is a 2.1-square-mile area, representing less than 1% of the total county, and an equally small percentage of the county's overall population. The community is located in a semirural area of Northwest Orange County, outside of the urban service core. As a result of geography alone, few county services reached the area on a consistent basis. Portions of South Apopka are located within unincorporated Orange County, and the remainder is within the city limits of Apopka. This shared jurisdiction had proven to be a negative factor historically. The community is located quite literally on the "other side of the tracks" that separate the mostly white residents in the city of Apopka from the African American and farm worker (African American, Haitian, Hispanic) population of South Apopka. The lack of citizen participation in the political processes meant that elected officials were unresponsive. These factors, together with poor housing conditions, crumbling infrastructure, and an agricultural economy that had been devastated by the freezes of 1983, 1985, and 1989 contributed to the deterioration of the South Apopka community.

Sitting in the shadow of Disney World, the area suffered from a myriad of problems reminiscent of rural Mississippi. A mere 12 miles from downtown Orlando, the unpaved roads were lined with ramshackle houses with tin roofs, with little of the lush landscaping that seems so natural to central Florida. There were few public recreation facilities or parks, with the exception of the small John H. Bridges Community Center, which housed some county services but was used primarily for small neighborhood functions. The lack of recreational opportunities for youth provided at least a partial explanation for the juvenile crime problem. However, as evidenced by the lengthy list of grievances presented by the residents in the first town meeting, increased juvenile crime was merely a symptom of other problems.

The residents and organization leaders gathered several times after the second meeting with Chapin and, after much discussion, contacted county staff and agreed to take the Chairman up on her challenge. The residents and most of the existing community organizations united to form a new organization called the Apopka Coalition to Improve Our Neighborhood (ACTION, Inc.), which was subsequently incorporated as a not-for-profit corporation in 1992. Chapin assigned Ella Gilmore, who was at that time the manager of the county's Community Affairs Department, to coordinate county services and to facilitate the community organizing effort.

ACTION was to serve as an umbrella agency promoting the interests of the various churches, community groups, and citizens, through the co-ordination of volunteers, public, and private resources. It was also to serve as a central point for planning and implementing capital projects, service networks, and community-service projects. This arrangement was seen as an opportunity to work with all of the community groups and address individual citizen concerns through a single organization.

ACTION developed a working committee structure to identify community needs and priorities, and proposed action strategies. The group worked with county staff to develop a community action plan outlining long-range goals and short-term objectives. The plan was submitted to the Board of County Commissioners, which gave its unanimous approval. This was an especially significant accomplishment, considering that the Board consists of six commissioners, each representing a single member district. In essence, five of the commissioners were voting to target major county resources in someone else's district. This is representative of the support that the initiative has received from local elected officials.

During the past five years, the South Apopka community has experienced significant improvements as a result of the partnership. Roads were paved, 60-plus units of single-family affordable housing were built, a beautiful new community park was constructed, older houses are being rehabilitated, and a wide variety of new services are available to residents through a collaborative service network. The small community center was expanded into a state-of-the-art complex with four new buildings to supplement the original facility, which was also completely renovated. More than 200 trees were planted and additional landscaping was done on major roadways as well as in residential areas.

LESSONS LEARNED FROM SOUTH APOPKA

In spite of the many physical improvements that occurred in the South Apopka community, we failed in what was probably our primary objective: to fully engage citizens in the governance process. ACTION started out with a great deal of enthusiasm and momentum. The organization achieved national recognition and received the Presidential Points of Light Award, not to mention several other local and regional awards for community service and volunteerism. However, by the time the group had completed its application for nonprofit certification, the membership had dwindled down to a handful of die-hard board members who relied almost totally on county staff to plan and implement all of the organization's projects.

Many of the citizens who were considered community leaders and civic activists began behaving like the typical bureaucrats they had previously despised. They were more concerned with daily routines and processes than with finding creative approaches to community problems. Instead of being the umbrella organization that was originally envisioned, ACTION became another community faction, viewed by other community groups as a competitor for resources and attention. Chapin found herself spending considerable time refereeing between the various community factions, as well as between the project staff and ACTION board members.

ACTION complained that the staff was not being responsive to their needs; the staff accused ACTION of bossing them around while reneging on their commitment to recruit and coordinate volunteers for community-service projects. The staff also began to complain about being forced to work long hours and do all of the work in the community. Community Affairs staff dreaded being assigned to the project, objecting to what they referred to as the "24/7" work schedules (24 hours per day/7 days per week). In the meantime, few major projects were implemented and other county departments began to lose interest; service levels began to decline. Ella Gilmore's boss, the division director for Health and Community Services, was growing increasingly concerned about the amount of time she was spending on the project and the impact on the department's overall operation.

In 1992, Joe Gray was a program coordinator in the Community Affairs Department. That fall, Gilmore assigned him to serve as on-site coordinator for the project. His primary duties were to supervise the staff, coordinate the development of a comprehensive service network, and facilitate community organizing efforts. At that point, Gray had been with the county approximately 4 months, having recently relocated to central Florida from Illinois. He'd had considerable experience in community organizing and human services program administration back in Illinois, but was awestruck by both the available resources and civic involvement within the community and the high level of commitment by the county leadership to this community-building effort. He was also initially perplexed by the seeming lack of progress, given these apparently tremendous advantages.

It didn't take very long, however, to glean some of the obvious causative factors. In the county's well-intentioned haste to create a central contact point with which to engage the community, we assumed that the existing community groups and their leaders represented the collective community leadership and that the groups would lay down their swords and forget about turf issues to work toward the general public good. Wrong. We also assumed that by hiring staff from the community, we'd get a dedicated group of employees, willing to go above and beyond the call to serve their community. Wrong again. Finally, our focus on providing services caused us to overlook major infrastructure needs in the community. We were seeking to provide services primarily utilizing county staff and largely ignoring the wealth of service resources that already existed in the community. We were also failing to capitalize on the vast existing network of service providers in the central Florida area. We had effectively become another competing faction in the community, instead of a collaborative partner.

After some retooling and a few somewhat tense meetings between the ACTION board and Chairman Chapin, the South Apopka Project began to get back on track. Staff levels were reduced considerably, that is, employees assigned specifically to the project. However, the actual number of professional-services staff available at the center increased dramatically through internal and external collaboration. Instead of creating special recreation staff positions to provide after-school and summer activities for youth, the Parks and Recreation Department was co-located at the center in the new recreation building. Similar arrangements were made with more than 20 other local service providers. As a result, South Apopka residents can receive a wide variety of services and resources at one location ranging from child care, social services, and housing assistance, to karate, ballet, high school equivalency education, and regular community college classes. ACTION also has offices at the center and operates as an independent nonprofit community organization. Although not the umbrella organization originally envisioned, the organization is still a very positive force in the community. ACTION plays a key role in the planning and implementation of community-service projects and in coordinating citizen involvement in community-planning and decision-making activities.

The major lessons learned in South Apopka were as follows:

- In order to have an effective partnership, the roles of all partners should be clearly defined early in the process.
- It is easier, cheaper, and much more effective to develop collaborative service networks than to create and staff "special projects" in a community.
- Civic activists and community leaders should be encouraged and supported, but not necessarily coopted through the employment process.

- Building solid civic and physical infrastructure in distressed communities is the necessary foundation for successful community-revitalization efforts.

COMMUNITY BUILDING: FROM PROJECT TO INITIATIVE

From the time that the South Apopka Project was made public in several local newspaper articles, Chairman Chapin began to receive inquiries from other communities about the possibility that similar projects could be launched in their communities. Residents of the Bithlo community in East Orange County were particularly vocal in their request for what they deemed fair consideration in the allocation of tax dollars. Citizens in the Winter Garden community in the western end of the county were also making regular calls to the chairman and the commissioners' office. These other communities believed that targeting resources to a particular community was unfair to other distressed areas of the county. However, Chapin was determined to stick to her commitment to the residents of South Apopka. Besides, the South Apopka "experiment" had not run its course, and Chapin was not convinced that the model could be successfully replicated in other areas. She was especially concerned about what appeared to be deficiencies in the citizen-participation aspects of the model, aspects that she considered critical.

In the fall of 1994, Chapin decided to reexamine the notion of replicating the project in other Orange County communities. Gray was transferred to the chairman's office to coordinate the initiative. His charge was to refine the model and make the transition from *pilot project* to *county initiative*. The latter implies more of an institutional commitment to a certain policy course. Housing the initiative in the county chairman's office provided the necessary political and administrative clout to secure resources and ensure cooperation within the bureaucracy. However, finding a way to ensure meaningful citizen involvement and maximizing available resources through true collaboration was the real challenge.

In order to meet that challenge, Gray developed a revised implementation strategy for the new TCI. Chapin decided to launch the revised initiative simultaneously in both the Bithlo and Winter Garden communities. This would alleviate allegations of favoritism that were sure to come from either of those two communities if both weren't selected as target areas. The new systemic approach to community building, focusing on partnership and collaboration, would allow for the two projects to be implemented with limited staffing and resources.

Both communities met the criteria that Chapin decided should be key to the selection of targeted communities:

- Evidence of substantial economic and social distress
- Historic neglect relative to county services and resources
- Citizen interest in working in true partnership in any revitalization efforts

Bithlo and Winter Garden were both struggling with major economic and social problems that far exceeded available resources within the communities. Like South Apopka, both communities had major infrastructure deficiencies. Social maladies (crime, poverty, etc.) were also pervasive. It was clear that both had been neglected compared to the rest of the county when it came to the past distribution of county resources. And, most critically, in both communities, community leaders expressed a strong willingness to organize the necessary citizen participation to make the effort a true partnership between government and citizens.

Bithlo is a semirural, mostly Caucasian community in the eastern section of the county. Winter Garden is also a semirural, mostly African American community on the west side of the county. Bithlo is an unincorporated community under the sole jurisdiction of Orange County. A large portion of the targeted area in Winter Garden is within the Winter Garden city limits. The City of Winter Garden has been a major partner in the implementation of the initiative in that community, providing additional staff, services, and resources.

In both communities, the citizens have played a major role in shaping the futures of their communities. Citizens involved with the process received a crash course on bureaucratic process, and provided the bureaucrats involved in the effort insight into the needs and frustrations of the communities that they exist to serve. Along the way there were several almost violent exchanges between the two sides. However, as the planning meetings proceeded, both sides developed a deeper understanding and appreciation of the other side's position.

Citizens learned a great deal about available government resources and the processes for accessing those resources. Throughout the process, the limitations of government to solve community problems were stressed. Chapin and Gray continuously found themselves reminding citizens that "the government builds roads and buildings . . . it's up to citizens to build communities." What the bureaucrats learned most was how to listen and respond to citizen and community priorities and not to just carry out self-imposed bureaucratic mandates. We found that what the citizens in these distressed communities wanted and needed most of all from government was honesty and a sense of inclusion in the decision-making process.

THE TCI PLANNING PROCESS

In South Apopka we promised too much from government and expected too little from citizens. The revised planning process was designed to avoid repeating that mistake. We developed a work plan that clearly outlined the roles and responsibilities of everyone involved. A seven-step process was utilized to develop comprehensive Community Action Plans in each community. The steps included the following (see Figure 11.1 for a graphic depiction of the planning process):

- Town Meetings (steps 1, 2, and 6)
- Community Workshops (steps 3 and 5)
- Work-Group Meetings (step 4)
- Administrative Review and Board Approval of the Plan (step 6)
- Implementation of the Plan (step 7)

The revamped process began with a series of informal meetings with residents to determine if there was sufficient interest in the community to work with the county. This mainly involved meetings with typical community leadership figures such as local ministers and community-group representatives. The first formal step involved the organization of town meetings to introduce the initiative communitywide and obtain input from residents regarding community concerns and needs. Chairman Chapin attended the meetings along with the county commissioners whose districts included the Bithlo and Winter Garden communities, other top county officials, and in the case of Winter Garden, the mayor and other city officials.

These initial meetings served as a forum for residents to voice their concerns and vent their frustrations about community problems, needs, and long-term government neglect. In both communities, the citizens' expectations were low as a result of long histories of unfulfilled promises. In the second town meeting (also attended by the chairman, commissioners, and the mayor), county and city staff made presentations outlining initial responses to the community concerns voiced in the first meeting. Chapin deemed it critical that the county show the citizens that they meant business, not "business as usual." In many cases, staff were able to provide

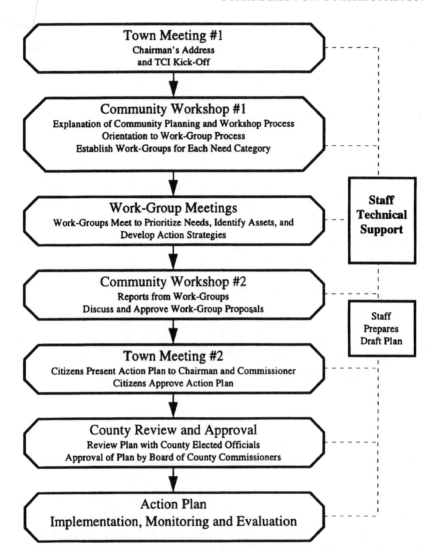

Figure 11.1. Targeted Community Initiative-Community Involvement Process

immediate remedies to community concerns with existing resources and within existing service-delivery frameworks. It was at this point that they realized that the problems that had led to the deterioration of communities were as much associated with education, awareness, coordination, and accessibility as with resources. The citizens were requesting services and resources that were readily available. They just didn't know whom to ask.

We discovered that passive and reactive government service systems were a big part of the problem in serving communities where civic involvement is low. Our task was to devise mechanisms to educate citizens about the governance process and to become better educated about the communities that we serve. The town meetings played a valuable role in that educational process.

The next step of the planning process involved the first of two community workshops. The workshops were intended to clarify the planning process. The first provided an opportunity to orient the community on the planning techniques to be utilized: visioning, goal setting, and devising realistic action strategies, budgets, and timelines. The workshops also included team-building exercises designed to reduce factionalism among various community groups that could hamper the planning process. These exercises also served to reduce the tension between the citizens and the staff.

Gray and other staff facilitators stressed the importance of comprehensive community planning, shared responsibility, and the need to set priorities. The citizens were encouraged to look at the needs of the entire community (not just the pothole on their street) when setting goals and assigning priorities. Effective goals were defined and the facilitators covered techniques for developing clear goal statements. They discussed the difference between needs and goals and explained how resource limitations dictate that not all needs are reasonable goals, thus the need to prioritize. The specific steps to be included in the planning process were discussed and agreed on. Most important, the workshops provided an opportunity to motivate citizens to participate in the planning and goal-setting process without feeling intimidated.

Facilitators guided the group through a visioning exercise where citizens drew pictures depicting their community as they viewed it at that point, replete with all of the perceived problems and deficiencies. The citizens then drew pictures of the community that they envisioned on the completion of the TCI development effort. The future visions would probably be considered modest by most standards. They included things like playgrounds, a community center, places to shop, and decent housing. To the residents of Bithlo and Winter Garden, these crude crayon drawings with stick figures represented their dreams. This was a very emotional and cathartic point in the process. The anger melted away as the citizen spokespersons presented their drawings at the end of the session. The session in Bithlo was especially poignant: The eyes of grown men welled with tears as they explained their current visions of hopelessness and despair, and their hopes and dreams for their children's future.

After the visions exercise, the citizens' attitudes softened considerably. It was as though the exercise made clear the opportunity being presented to the communities and the importance of taking advantage of anything that might offer a better future for their children. The citizens were ready to trade in their swords for plowshares, and staff clearly understood the importance of their mission. They could not let these people down after giving them such hope.

Staff reviewed the needs and concerns that were identified in the town meetings and divided them into categories. Those categories formed the basis for organizing planning work groups to outline specific goals and action strategies. The citizens were asked to sign up for one of the work groups at the conclusion of the meeting and to set initial meeting dates, times, and locations.

We were somewhat surprised that in spite of the differences between the two communities, the needs of both communities could be grouped into seven basic categories. The following work-group categories (not in order of priority) were developed based on the community needs identified by the citizens:

1. Crime and Safety
2. Code Enforcement and Land Use
3. Education
4. Health and Social Services
5. Housing
6. Parks, Recreation, and Youth Programs
7. Public Works

Each work group was charged with the development of a component of the Community Action Plan related to their work-group category. The groups further defined needs, goals, activities, and available resources. The groups also determined priorities and schedules for meeting goals. The roles and expectations of everyone involved (government, citizens, businesses, service agencies, churches, and community organizations) in the process were outlined in each of the component plans.

The work groups consisted of 10 to 20 individuals. They met biweekly during a two-month period. Community residents were the primary participants and took the lead in identifying community needs and determining priorities. County and city staff's primary role was to provide technical assistance to the groups during the planning process. The staff helped to facilitate the meetings and provided information about available government resources, services, and processes for accessing government resources.

Throughout the process, staff looked for opportunities to enhance citizen awareness of the many opportunities that exist for citizen participation in local government. Staff members were instructed to be forthcoming about budget issues. This was especially important as the citizens set priorities and timelines with budgetary implications. This is the area where staff members were initially most uncomfortable. Bureaucrats considered the idea of sharing internal budget information with citizens to be dangerous, perhaps even blasphemous. However, the sharing of budget information was probably one of the most important things public administrators could have done to build public trust. It also relieved staff from the burden of explaining to citizens why not all of their needs and expectations were realistic, given fiscal constraints. The staff was amazed at the citizens' ability to understand "these complex issues." They proved more adept at living within a balanced budget than the bureaucrats expected.

At the conclusion of the work-group planning process a second workshop was convened. The purpose of this workshop was to bring all of the work groups together to combine the component plans into a single Community Action Plan. Each group selected a representative to present its portion of the plan to the entire body. The individual proposals were discussed and a consensus was reached as to what should be included in the final Action Plan. Staff drafted the Action Plan document at the conclusion of the workshop.

The next step was the town meeting. This final meeting was mostly a celebration where the citizens presented the proposed Community Action Plan to the county chairman, the district commissioner, and in Winter Garden, to the mayor, as well as to the community at large. The proposed plans were then reviewed by the county administrator's office and other appropriate county and city (in Winter Garden) staff to ensure consistency with affected budgets, plans, policies, and procedures. This is the point where the involvement of staff throughout the process paid off. The plans went through the review process without any major modifications.

The plans were then presented to the Board of County Commissioners and the Winter Garden City Council for their approval in the form of a Resolution of Support. Specific elements of the plan (i.e., budget expenditures) would still have to go back to the board and council for approval as specific projects were completed. However, having the Board of County Commissioners and the City Council bless the plan in advance would make it difficult for them to veto specific projects that were clearly spelled out in the comprehensive plan.

IMPLEMENTATION: MORE LESSONS LEARNED

Overall, the implementation process has gone quite well. Major capital projects are underway in both communities. The citizens in both target areas are excited about new and refurbished community centers and service facilities, parks, housing improvements, road paving and sidewalk construction projects, landscaping, and other long overdue infrastructure improvements. New service collaboratives are providing a smorgasbord of services in the two communities, including tutoring services, cultural and recreation programs, adult education, drug treatment and mental health services, special programs and services for senior citizens, and a wide range of other services to address the community needs outlined in the plans. The vast majority of these services are provided by nongovernmental agencies eager to find customers.

The greatest challenge continues to be maintaining ongoing citizen involvement in the community-building process. Both the citizens and the bureaucrats have demonstrated a tendency to backslide to a "business as usual" approach once the plans are completed. The goal was for the citizens to continue to meet among themselves in the work groups to maintain the community-planning dialogue with their neighbors and to monitor and update the plans when necessary. Chairman Chapin stressed the need for staff to view the TCI approach as "a way of doing business" and not as another project. The lessons learned during this process were to guide our relationships with citizens from now on. Unfortunately, citizen participation in the monthly meetings declined. Staff viewed this as the reflection of lack of interest by the citizens in ongoing involvement in the governance process.

After several meetings with the citizens to discuss the issue, we came to the conclusion that a more formal permanent structure for citizen involvement was necessary. This was especially true in those communities where the civic infrastructure was weak. When staff members asked the citizens why they had stopped coming to the meetings, their answer was generally that "no one called or sent a notice." That was something that county staff had done during the planning process, but the understanding was that the work-group leaders would assume that responsibility after the plans were completed. However, the work groups had been informal, ad hoc committees without the necessary structure or resources to consistently do things that staff took for granted as being fundamental.

COMMUNITY ACTION TEAMS: THE EVOLUTION CONTINUES

Gray realized that he would have to devise more formal structures to achieve the kind of regular civic involvement necessary to build strong, stable communities. As he was planning to implement the initiative in the Taft community, he decided to shore up that part of the process. One of the things that he heard from the Bithlo and Winter Garden residents who had not participated in the process was that they didn't really know what was going on with the work groups until the plans were completed. They had seen the notices and flyers around the community, but they didn't know or care about things like "code enforcement and land use or public works," and so forth. It never occurred to him that such bureaucratic terms would fail to capture the interest of citizens. They were very interested in dealing with overgrown lots and getting roads paved, but what was this public works thing?

As Gray started the planning process in Taft, the first thing that he did was to propose changing the title of the work groups. It was decided not to even call them work groups, instead they would be referred to as Citizen Advisory Teams. That was a more formal title that would hopefully elevate the importance of the groups in the eyes of citizens. Instead of having government sounding titles like *public works,* the teams were given titles such as Streets, Sidewalks and Drainage, Housing Improvements, and Landscaping and Beautification. The process was formalized to include a Citizen Advisory Council that would be comprised of a representative from each of the teams, and that would meet monthly with county staff to discuss the progress of the plan implementation as well as other community issues that the team needed county input on or assistance with (see Figure 11.2).

We arranged meetings with the citizens from Bithlo and Winter Garden to discuss the proposed changes and to gauge their interest in adopting the new format for citizen involvement. In both communities, the citizens agreed nearly unanimously to make the changes. The citizens in Taft also embraced the format, and the planning process in Taft was completed in record time. After several months, the revised format appears to be working quite well in all three communities. Citizen involvement in the Advisory Team meetings is stronger than ever, with new citizens joining the teams on a regular basis. The citizens from the target communities are participating

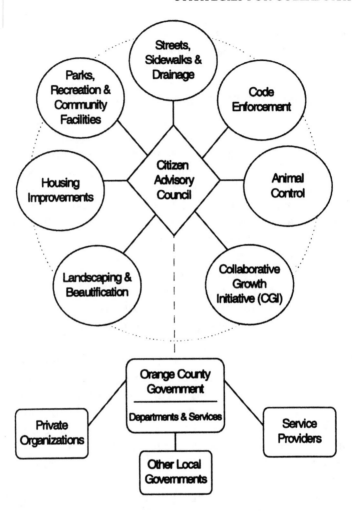

Figure 11.2. Citizen Advisory Teams and Council

in a wide range of additional civic endeavors such as other local government advisory boards. Most important, they are involved in community building in their communities through a wide range of community-service projects, and just being good neighbors.

CONCLUSION

In this age of decreasing public resources and increasing citizen demand for accountability, the development of effective partnerships between citizens and government to take full advantage of existing resources is critical. The cry for additional services and resources in distressed communities can only begin to be addressed through the development of creative, efficient, and well-coordinated service-delivery and infrastructure-development strategies. Citizens have only recently begun to be recognized as viable partners and communities are just starting to be mined for the valuable resources that most contain in great abundance, such as facilities, volunteers, creative ideas, and expertise. They are definitely the experts when it comes to knowing what "they" (communities) want.

Citizens' distrust of government and staff disdain for anything other than token civic inclusion in the administrative decision-making process made for an uneasy partnership, at least in the initial stages of the TCI. Once the planning process begins, however, both the citizens and bureaucrats usually come to realize that they are more alike than different. By openly involving citizens in the capital budget review process, bureaucrats expose citizens to the reality of the budgetary and legislative constraints that bureaucrats face. Administrators grow to appreciate the frustration that citizens are confronted with in their attempts to deal with government bureaucracy and to understand widespread apathy among fellow citizens. Public administrators develop a clearer understanding of the political value of involving citizens in the prioritization of capital projects. That way they aren't guaranteed public support, but at least have minimized pressures to meet unrealistic community expectations. County commissioners and other local political leaders have embraced the initiative as a means of garnering major resources for their constituencies in a process that is devoid of the usual political maneuvering and potential public backlash.

The initiative has provided a tremendous learning experience for bureaucrats and citizens alike. As a result of their involvement, citizens are learning to trust those heretofore nameless, faceless individuals who collectively compose the previously despised public bureaucracy. Public administrators, in turn, are learning to appreciate the value of partnering with an enlightened citizenry, especially when it comes to making the difficult decisions associated with the prioritization of increasingly limited public resources. As a result of this experience, both sides are learning valuable lessons about the importance of mutual trust and shared responsibility in the governance process.

Interview with Joe Gray, Manager, Orange County (Florida) Public Affairs Department

What is it like to be this kind of administrator? It's the best part of my job; if I did this all the time, my job would be wonderful. This is the best thing that has ever happened in my career. I have received more credit and personal satisfaction than I ever could have had sitting in an office, stamping papers. When you work with the public, it elevates you to a different kind of status that you can't achieve with all the office politicking in the world. All of sudden, all the internal evaluations mean nothing. What matters is what the people outside think of what you are doing.

Working with citizens is always a surprise. I gear myself up for confrontations but, even when things are controversial, the bottom line is that people are thinking just what I am. There is the fear of the unknown; both citizens and administrators go into things with preconceived notions. But we find out that people are people—we end up talking about our kids, or the same things I talk about with people in my neighborhood.

The initial organizing of the communities is kinda awkward—it's like going out on a date with someone for the first time—you don't know each other, putting your best foot forward and not really communicating because you are just trying to impress each other. We use a visioning exercise to disarm people. Asking people to draw pictures of their hopes for their community's future gets them thinking about things that they don't normally get to think about—it lets them dream. It is a very humbling experience for bureaucrats. You are not working with a depersonalized mandate or rule; you have a real person in front of you and you have to answer them. You can't just send them an e-mail from behind your desk and say "well, this is why your dreams are shattered."

Also, when we give the citizens the information they need to decide, for example, which pothole to fix when they can't fix them all, they begin to understand where we are coming from. They begin to understand why we do what we do in government. Citizens don't always get what they want, but including them personalizes the work we do—connects public administration to the public. And this connection leads to understanding for both citizens and administrators.

Sometimes it is frustrating; I have to check myself to keep from saying "the nerve of these people." I'm out here working hard, giving up my nights and weekends, and they don't appreciate it. But I know this is not true. I recently was attacked by a resident in one of our communities. He came after me, hurling racial slurs and attempting to harm me. However, afterwards, the whole community embraced me. They wanted me to know that he didn't speak for the community.

It is actually more frustrating to work with staff than with the citizens. It's hard to get staff to break out of traditional bureaucratic roles; to try to solve problems without relying on the "old way" of doing things. For example, I recently had a long argument with the county engineers who argued against erecting some "Slow, Children at Play" signs at the request of community members. The engineers said that we couldn't put up the signs because of liability issues; if a child was injured in the area, the county could be sued because the signs created a false sense of confidence that the children were actually safe. This is ridiculous; this kind of thinking does not lead to good relationships with citizens.

I wasn't ever a "traditional bureaucrat." I guess we are all a product of our experiences. I grew up dependent upon the government. In one way or another, we were either dependent upon a program or a politician. As the middle child, I was the one who went with my Mom to help her fill out the forms. Time after time, she would be in tears from some administrator who would humiliate her for asking for help. I've always had that picture of my mom's face in my head—the only time I ever saw her cry, except for when my grandma died, was when she had to deal with the government. I've always been fighting the bureaucrats from the outside; now I'm fighting from the inside.

We were able to secure the resources for TCI because the chairman has a personal interest in citizen governance. She gets satisfaction from doing this, knowing she is doing the right thing. Now we are trying to teach the bureaucrats to do things right. This is the more efficient way to run the railroad. We recently had a community project in Taft where community members and volunteers painted and repaired a number of homes some of which were about to be cited for code violations. It cost the county $300 to do this. Sears paid for the paint and supplies and members of the community did the work. We were there just as cheerleaders. If the county would have condemned the homes, or done the work ourselves, it would have cost us several thousand dollars in staff time, supplies, equipment, and legal fees.

Most of the money devoted to this work is not new money. It is simply a matter of coordinating existing resources. We went to the department heads who were turning back money because they had no customers, and helped connect the citizens to the resources and opportunities that already exist. Unless you tell people what you can do for them, they will never know. How many people do you know who know how to get their sidewalk repaired or how easy it is for them to get a new streetlight on their street?

The rest of the communities in Orange County are jealous. They want TCI in their communities too. The affluent communities have been very quiet. We thought we would get some backlash. Since they pay all the taxes, why are their tax dollars going to communities who don't pay taxes to the same degree. However, we were wrong. The affluent communities seem to be happy; they seem to recognize that the rising tide brings everyone up. The key is to not take resources away from other communities.

The only people who are complaining are some of the staff. We are making them work harder. We are working hard, however, to make this transition easier. We do lots more training, have all kinds of internal campaigns to get people to be more citizen focused, and have revamped the payroll system to tie merit increases to citizen-first attitudes. Employees automatically get a COLA increase; however, they can receive additional merit increases if they demonstrate a committment to the "citizens first" philosophy and related organizational strategic goals.

(continued)

What's going to happen when the Chairman leaves? Hopefully we will create enough momentum so that the work will continue far after she's gone. Her goal has always been that this can't be a project, it is a way of business. Also, empowered citizens don't easily become disempowered again—they will make sure that things continue. They now know how to organize and the power they have. Really, much of what we have done is to help citizens acquire the citizenship skills they need to work with us to meet their goals.

Chapter 12

CONCLUSION

Strategies for an Anti-Government Era

Cheryl Simrell King and Camilla Stivers

In a time of anti-government paranoia, potential images of public administration and public administrators are constrained by anti-government rhetoric. No matter how or why one works in government, the current context seems to evoke few, mostly negative, images of public service (see Chapter 1). In an argument that parallels ours, Larry Terry (1997) suggests that public administrators can be only villains, victims, or heroes. As he indicates, these models are too simplistic, incomplete, and potentially dangerous: "The villain is incapable of positive action; the hero lacks an understanding of the limitations to power; and the victim is ignorant of responsibility" (p. 59).

Administrators and front-line workers can be more than passive victims, heinous villains, or hegemonic heroes. They can work to change citizen perceptions by collaborating with citizens; they can, in effect, democratize public administration.

Democratizing public administration means creating the conditions under which citizens and public servants can join in deliberating about, deciding, and implementing the work of public agencies. What we mean by *Government is Us* is a democratic public administration that involves active citizenship and active administration. By *active administration* we mean not an enhancement of administrative power, but the use of discretionary authority to foster collaborative work with citizens. The active administrator is one who acts creatively to direct administrative prerogatives toward active citizenship in administrative contexts.

195

As a group, the collaborators of this book agree that there are ways to move toward more active citizenship and active administration. They are united in calling for a more facilitative, less expertise-driven approach to administrative practice, for balancing scientific and technical approaches with experience-based knowledge, and for personal skills like listening. Each also has specific insights. Hummel and Stivers point to the gap between the lived knowledge of citizens and the abstract knowledge on which governance in predicated. Timney roots her analysis in the fundamental difference between government for and government by the people. Foley emphasizes the development of mediation skills. Zanetti recommends using critical lawyering techniques to organize and empower citizens. Box and Sagen recommend a "public service" frame of mind. Kovalick and Kelly draw our attention to the importance of administrative and agency realities and of organizational and structural changes to support partnership efforts with communities. Finally, Gray and Chapin describe a situation in which they successfully put into practice much of what this book advocates: They listened, responded, gave up administrative control, made the needed organizational changes, and tied organizational goals to citizen goals. Most of all, they made a complete commitment to active citizenship and active administration.

We have seen that there are barriers to the practice of democratic public administration. They include individual habits of mind, administrative practices, and the larger political-economy within which administrative governance takes place. As we bring this exploration toward its conclusion, we will reflect briefly on each of these barriers to active citizenship and administration. Our goal is to suggest tangible steps that administrators and front-line workers, the rank and file of bureaucracy, can take in order to democratize public administration through collaborative relationships with citizens.

HABITS OF MIND

Active citizenship is different from voting, paying taxes, or using government services. It means sharing the authority on the basis of which administrative agencies carry out legislated mandates. As Aristotle (1981) suggested long ago, in active citizenship, citizens rule and are ruled in turn. Active administrators create conditions that foster opportunities for citizens to "rule," that is, to exercise authority. A basic new habit of mind for active administrators is thinking of citizens as citizens rather than as voters, taxpayers, consumers, or customers.

From the Conversation: Government Is Different

Lisa: I never thought of myself as a public administrator. I thought of myself as a *public servant*, which has an entirely different connotation. And as I enter the academy, I think of myself as contributing to the education of current and future public servants. I don't think of my role as one that involves churning out B-school clones. Paul Appleby said it best: "Government is different."

Advocates of a substantive role for citizens have argued that participation in governance develops capacities and skills important to effective public affairs. In order to live fully, human beings need the experience of wrestling with problems larger than their own private interests. Their capacity to learn and grow as a result of experience is what ensures that a government run in some meaningful sense by citizens will be run well. More important, though, the education citizens thus receive is a moral education:

> [The citizen] is called upon, while so engaged, to weigh interests not his own; to be guided, in case of conflicting claims, by another rule than his private partialities; to apply, at every turn, principles and maxims which have for their reason of existence the common good. (John Stuart Mill, in Acton, 1972, p. 233)

Active citizenship, its proponents argue, fosters many of the very qualities that ensure its successful practice: a sense of connection with other people, a perception that the fates of individual human beings are intertwined, a feeling of the possibility of community. By thinking of citizens as citizens, active administrators lay the groundwork for effective collaboration.

In a complex turn-of-the-millennium world dominated by global systems and giant organizations, the practice of active citizenship can often seem like a pipe dream. In such a world, citizens would feel a sense of alienation from government even in the best of circumstances and, as we have argued in this book, circumstances are far from the best. Even so, we have suggested, public servants can do much to promote active citizenship. With citizenship as a continuing habit of mind, active administrators foster opportunities to work collaboratively with citizens. They inform citizens, deliberate with citizens, learn from citizens' experience, and put in place administrative practices and processes that build, or rebuild, public trust and a sense of connection with government.

The traditional administrative habit of mind emphasizes managerial control over administrative processes. In contrast, the idea of active citizenship and active administration suggests moving, to the extent possible, away from hierarchical and elitist views of administration. The active administrator is willing to reduce personal and organizational control over problem definition, decision making, and implementation strategies for the sake of active citizenship, trusting in the collaborative process itself to evoke the necessary control. Terry Cooper, a key architect of citizenship theory in public administration, puts this in terms of horizontal authority, or "power with" relations. Such a habit of mind fosters a collaborative rather than chain-of-command approach. Cooper (1991) notes that horizontal authority relations require administrators to look both to legislators and to the citizenry as a whole for guidance. Drawing on Mary Parker Follett, he suggests that,

> "power with" involves a collaborative integrating of desires among participants in a decision-making process, instead of a quest for dominance by some. It grows out of circular behavior in which participants have a genuine opportunity to influence each other. . . . Information, judgment, and advice flow back and forth around the circle of political authority. (p. 140)

In giving up a measure of personal and organizational control, however, administrators are not risking ultimate chaos and disorder. As Follett argued, they are making it possible for order to emerge from, rather than being imposed on, the situation.

Processes of integration require administrators to give up reliance on professional norms. The professional habit of mind privileges agency technical and scientific knowledge and knowledge processes over the experiential knowledge of citizens. In contrast, the active administrator's habit of mind takes an egalitarian approach to knowledge that views both science and lived experience as vital to the development of dependable bases for action. Although expertise and efficiency are important, they are inappropriate norms to guide public servants in their efforts to develop working relationships with citizens.

In summary, the active administrator's habits of mind include the following:

- See citizens as citizens.
- Share authority.
- Reduce personal and organizational control.
- Trust in the efficacy of collaboration.
- Balance experiential with scientific and professional knowledge.

From the Conversation: The Self and Relationship

Cheryl: Here's the big problem for me: Authentic relationships involve a great deal of good will, good intentions, commitment, transcendence of the self, work, willingness to be reflexive and to work on the self, skills, passion, desire, and energy. If we do all this, good things will emerge most of the time. Unfortunately, most of us are not very good at relationship and many of us are not willing to do the work, don't have the time, don't "believe," etc. If we want to shape more authentic relationships, we will have to be very different people than we are now, or maybe just be the people (private selves) we are in our public life. Or, is this dangerous?

Cam: I would say that there are not "selves" but "selves-in-relationship." In other words, relationship isn't outside the self.

Lisa: It seems to me that the individuated self must come before the relationship, if the relationship is to be a balanced, egalitarian, nonexploitative one. From a feminist perspective, it seems that if I do not have a distinct sense of self I risk becoming defined first as someone's daughter, wife, mother—rather than as myself. Certainly I am all those things, but not first. Without the individuated self, one is more likely to become either subsumed by the relationship, or incapable of forming relationship in the first place. Cam, I read your comment to suggest that there is no self outside of relationship to people or environments. Is that a correct reading? Agreeing with Cheryl here, citizens don't perceive themselves as such—in other words, they don't have that distinct sense of self as citizen that is necessary for the relationship with government.

Richard: In an odd way, I guess I don't really think there is an "I" prior to the collective shaping of personality and consciousness. When you say you want the space to move away from predetermined identities like daughter or wife, it seems to me you do so in reaction to something perceived, not as a result of prior self constructed in pristine isolation.

Cam: Both social constructivist and feminist theory have much to say about the self being an impossible concept without others. There is no human being in the absence of other human beings, beginning with birth. That's what the Tarzan story is all about. . . . On citizens being able to "see themselves," there have to be some enabling conditions for the practice of citizenship. This is one thing I think administrators can foster perhaps more than they do.

ADMINISTRATIVE PRACTICES

Most administrative practices can be reshaped in order to promote collaboration with citizens, as several of our stories show. Many routines and procedures are typically introduced and justified on the basis that they contribute to the achievement of agency goals. Within this goal-achievement structure of public organizations, citizenship values tend to become instru-

---

The Purpose of Citizen Partipication

Mary Timney

Administrators must reflect on what the purpose of citizen participation is and what their role should be in facilitating meaningful participation. To address these issues, we must first ask *what do citizens want?* Drawing from 25 years of experience as a citizen activist, I believe that citizens have four goals:

1. To be heard in a meaningful way, to be treated as if their opinions and information mattered;

2. To influence problem definition as well as proposed policies;

3. To work with administrators and policy makers to find solutions to public problems;

4. To have an equal voice in the policy process.

I have known some environmentalists over the years who do fit the popular stereotype of radical tree hugger. But I know more who also genuinely care about the economy and the disadvantaged in our society. For these citizens, the aim of participation is to change the definitions of environmental problems from a choice between jobs and the environment to the development of an economy within a healthy environment for the benefit of all members of society. Such a goal will likely be seen as a challenge to agency autonomy, but it may also be an opportunity for the agency to rethink its own assumptions.

What citizen activists want most is to be heard.

---

ments for the inducement of greater cooperation and organizational effectiveness. As instruments, their value depends on whether they promote organizational purposes; if they turn out not to serve these ends, they are generally abandoned. All the contributors argue that collaboration with citizens does indeed positively contribute to agency objectives; this, however, should not be the sole reason to work toward active citizenship and administration. Active citizenship must take care not to fall into the trap of selling itself only on the basis of organizational effectiveness, as current managerialism does. The significance of active citizenship and administration goes far beyond agency effectiveness and the achievement of agency objectives; it reaches, as Mary Timney holds, to the very heart of our understanding of governance in the United States—to the question of who rules.

As the stories in this book suggest, administrative practices that need immediate attention include the following:

- Routine procedures for getting citizen input, such as relying solely on traditional public hearings and notices.

- Defining problems and issues before asking citizens what they think, thus constraining possible ways of understanding the situation and possible solutions.
- Convening "advisory" committees whose advice is then ignored.
- Holding meetings when most people are working, or in locations that are hard to get to.
- Not providing child care for meetings.
- Failing to facilitate conversation at meetings, thus letting the proceedings turn into a series of monologues.

These administrative "don'ts" imply a corresponding list of suggested actions for revamping administrative practices:

- Allocate resources to support participation efforts.
- Reward administrators for working with citizens.
- Create ongoing project teams of citizens and administrators that follow a project through from conception to implementation.
- Hold meetings at more convenient times and places.
- Bring citizens in when the agenda can still be shaped.
- Have roundtable discussions instead of serial monologues.
- Avoid one-shot techniques like surveys or biased approaches like boards or panels, which raise the issue of representation without being able to solve it (see also King, Feltey, & Susel, 1998).

This list of administrative "do's" has some of the flavor of trendy organization reforms like total quality management and reinventing government. In contrast to these movements, we offer this list for political rather than managerial reasons. Although we recognize the importance of agency effectiveness, out aim is to reshape the way administrative governance takes place, not primarily to improve the way that agencies function.

THE POLITICAL-ECONOMIC CONTEXT

The current political-economic context and its implications for active citizenship and administration are vexing issues. Active citizenship and active administration are not enough in and of themselves to change the power dynamics implicit in the distribution of wealth, to reshape how many and what kinds of jobs are available, or to improve the economic security of those employed in them. As Barbelet (1988) notes, the exercise of citizenship cannot modify the material relations between economic classes, particularly as long as the economic and political spheres are considered in isolation from one another. American political philosophy continues to reconcile formal political equality (the right to vote) with increasing economic inequality, limiting what we as a society are able to envision.

Yet in American history the idea of citizenship had economic as well as political origins. In the civic republican framework that helped to shape American political ideas, both slavery and an idle aristocracy were political anomalies because the ethical basis of citizenship was what Shklar (1991) calls "self-directed earning" (p. 92). In civic republican thinking, citizenship involved not just formal rights but also the ability to earn: "A good citizen is an earner, because independence is the indelibly necessary quality of genuine, democratic citizenship" (p. 92). One who is unemployed or underemployed, who cannot get a job that makes a basic level of economic independence possible, is a second-class citizen who has not only lost self-respect but also public respect and standing.

Much of the recent bemoaning of the loss of "civic virtue," such as is found in Robert Putnam's widely cited article "Bowling Alone" (1995), has diverted attention from disastrous conditions in poor city neighborhoods and rural areas, where lack of work and a range of social problems make community building not only difficult, but a poor substitute for government-supported efforts to deal with deep-seated conditions (Lemann, 1996). The era of big government may be over, as President Bill Clinton has said, but no amount of volunteering is going to ameliorate these deep-rooted economic and social problems. Involving citizens can contribute to fundamental economic reform, but cannot be thought of as a substitute for it.

Perhaps the kind of society implied in ideas of active citizenship and active administration is one that affords to all citizens able to work the opportunity to earn a living wage and thus to attain the level of independence, self-respect, and public respect that makes practices of active citizenship viable. Active administrators, then, are aware of the interrelation between political and economic factors, understand how they affect the work of their particular agencies, and are critical of agency policies that undercut the economic basis of citizenship.

GOVERNMENT (OF THE PEOPLE) IS US

The images of active administration set forth in this book—*transformative, facilitative, public-service practitioner, task-oriented but inclusive and bal-*

anced convener, and *listening bureaucrat*—are all predicated on the notion that the administrator actively works with citizens to shape and reach agency and citizen ends. Our notion of "government *of* the people," based on collaboration or integrative participation, is one in which active citizens and administrators work together on administrative and citizenship needs, goals, and objectives in ways that allow new perspectives and approaches to emerge from the deliberative situation. In doing so, administrators' work will be organized around creating the conditions that enable these new directions to come forth. Doing so will require administrators to do the following:

- Actively create opportunities for people to come together and deliberate: be the maker and shaper of the space for community participation.

- Employ skills and techniques not typically associated with administration: facilitation, active listening, deliberation, negotiation, empathy, and creative conflict resolution.

- Work to be inclusive in these efforts, not only with regard to demographics, but also to ensure that all interests get to the table (see also Chrislip & Larson, 1994).

- Give up some control, take some risks, learn from situations, move toward collaborative rather than chain-of-command type relations.

- Identify the gap between citizen knowledge and technical knowledge and work to bridge or close the gap; help citizens understand technical information; let citizens help administrators understand what their experience has taught them.

- Provide citizens with access to administrative processes and the work of implementation.

- Gain support from leadership as well as adequate resources to achieve collaborative or integrative participation.

- Make needed organizational structural changes to ensure that active citizenship and administration live on after the original implementors leave.

We are aware that we are advocating approaches that may seem radical or impractical to some who practice (or theorize about) public administration. Our stories, however, reveal possibilities for more active citizen and administrative roles and speak to the importance of the suggested practices. There are many other stories out there.

As we have argued, in important respects the entire history of the United States has been an anti-government era. If so, the distinctiveness of the current situation may not lie in the level of public criticism, but instead in the opportunities to which it can awaken us, if we have ears to hear them. We are convinced that not only Americans' feelings about their government, but the very future of governance in the United States, rest on the need for a more involved, active citizenry and for active administration that has at its center the nurturance of citizenship.

References

Academy for Educational Development. (1994). *Handbook for HIV prevention community planning*. Washington, DC: Centers for Disease Control.

Acton, Harry Burrows. (Ed.). (1972). *John Stuart Mill's utilitarianism: On liberty and consideration of representative government*. London: Dent/Everyman's Library.

Adams, Guy B. (1992). Enthralled with modernity: The historical context of knowledge and theory development in public administration. *Public Administration Review, 52*(4), 363-373.

Alinsky, Saul D. (1971). *Rules for radicals: A pragmatic primer for realistic radicals*. New York: Vintage.

Alway, Joan. (1995). *Critical theory and political possibilities*. Westport, CT: Greenwood.

Apple, R. W., Jr. (1995, May 28). Voters may feel powerless but they're not frightened. *New York Times*, pp. A1, A13.

Arendt, Hannah. (1968). *Between past and future: Eight exercises in political thought*. New York: Viking.

Arendt, Hannah. (1978) *The life of the mind*. New York: Harcourt Brace.

Arendt, Hannah. (1982). *Lectures on Kant's political philosophy* (Ronald Beiner, Ed.). Chicago: University of Chicago Press.

Aristotle. (1981). *The politics* (T. A. Sinclair, Trans.). New York: Penguin.

Arnstein, Sherry R. (1969). A ladder of citizen participation. *Journal of the American Institute of Planners, 35*(3), 216-224.

Bailey, Mary Timney. (1992). Do physicists use case studies? Thoughts on public administration research. *Public Administration Review, 52*(1), 47-55.

Ban, Carolyn, & Riccuci, Norma M. (1991). *Public personnel management: Current concerns—future challenges*. New York: Longman.

Barbelet, J. M. (1988). *Citizenship: Rights, struggle and class inequities*. Minneapolis: University of Minnesota Press.

Barber, Benjamin. (1984). *Strong democracy: Participatory politics for a new age*. Berkeley: University of California Press.

Baxter, Charley. (1995). Partnerships: Good citizen/government relations. *Journal of Housing and Community Development, 52*(5), 34-37.

Bell, Daniel. (1974). *The coming of post-industrial society*. London: Heinemann.

Bellah, Robert N., Madsen, Richard, Sullivan, William M., Swidler, Ann, & Tipton, Steven M. (1991). *The good society*. New York: Knopf.

Berg, Bruce L. (1995). *Qualitative research methods for the social sciences* (2nd ed.). Boston: Allyn and Bacon.

Berger, Thomas. (1977). *Northern frontier, northern homeland: The report of the MacKenzie Valley pipeline inquiry.* Toronto: Lorimer.

Berkowitz, Edward D., & McQuaid, Kim. (1992). *Creating the welfare state: The political economy of 20th-century reform* (Rev. ed.). Lawrence: University of Kansas Press.

Berman, Evan. (1997). Dealing with cynical citizens. *Public Administration Review, 57*(2), 105-112.

Berry, Jeffrey M., Portney, Kent E., & Thomson, Ken. (1993). *The rebirth of urban democracy.* Washington, DC: Brookings Institute.

Bezich, Louis S. (1997). N.J. county shows citizens what's in store. *PA Times, 20*(3), 1-2.

Big onion award for greed, sloth, and exceptional idiocy by the people whose salaries you pay. (1997). *Chicago Magazine, 46*(2), front cover.

Bronner, Steven E. (1994). *Of critical theory and its theorists.* Cambridge, MA: Blackwell.

Buchanan, Ruth, & Trubek, Louise G. (1992). Resistances and possibilities: A critical and practical look at public interest lawyering. *Review of Law and Social Change, 19,* 687-719.

Buchler, Justus. (Ed.). (1955). *Philosophical writings of Peirce.* New York: Dover.

Carroll, William K., & Ratner, Robert S. (1994). Between Leninsm and radical pluralism: Gramscian reflections on counter-hegemony and the new social movements. *Critical Sociology, 20*(2), 3-26.

Carson, Rachel. (1962). *Silent spring.* Greenwich, CT: Fawcett.

Cassidy, John. (1995, October 16). Who killed the middle class? *New Yorker, 71*(32), 113-124.

Causey, Mike. (1997, April 27). The vanishing bureaucrats. *The Washington Post,* p. B2.

Chrislip, David D., & Larson, Carl E. (1994). *Collaborative leadership.* San Francisco: Jossey-Bass.

Connecting government and neighborhoods. (1996). *Governing, 10*(2), 2-8.

Cook, Edward M. (1976). *The fathers of the towns: Leadership and community structure in eighteenth-century New England.* Baltimore: Johns Hopkins University Press.

Cooke, Jacob. (Ed.). (1961). *The federalist papers.* Middletown, CT: Wesleyan University Press.

Cooper, Marc. (1997, July 14). A town betrayed: Oil and greed in Lima, Ohio. *The Nation, 265* (2), 11-15.

Cooper, Terry L. (1984). Public administration in an age of scarcity: A citizenship role for public administrators. In Jack Rabin & James S. Bowman (Eds.), *Politics and administration: Woodrow Wilson and American public administration* (pp. 297-314). New York: Marcel Dekker.

Cooper, Terry L. (1991). *An ethic of citizenship for public administration.* Englewood Cliffs, NJ: Prentice Hall.

Crosby, Ned, Kelly, Janet M., & Schaefer, Paul. (1986). Citizen panels: A new approach to citizen participation. *Public Administration Review, 46*(2), 170-178.

de Tocqueville, Alexis. (1945). *Democracy in America* (2 vols.). New York: Vintage. (Original work published 1830)

Diggins, John Patrick. (1994). *The promise of pragmatism: Modernism and the crisis of knowledge and authority.* Chicago: The University of Chicago Press.

Egan, Timothy. (1995, May 15). Unlikely alliances attack property rights measures. *New York Times,* p. A1.

Fishkin, James S. (1995). *We the people: Public opinion and democracy.* New Haven, CT: Yale University Press.

Fiumara, Gina Corradi. (1990). *The other side of language: A philosophy of listening* (Charles Lambert, Trans.). London: Routledge.

Flanigan, William H., & Zingale, Nancy H. (1994). *Political behavior of the American electorate.* Washington, DC: CQ Press.

Flentje, H. Edward, & Counihan, Wendla. (1984). Running a "reformed" city: The hiring and firing of city managers. *Urban Resources, 3*(2), 9-14.
Foley, Dolores. (1994). *HIV prevention community planning process: Evaluation report* (Prepared for the Department of Health, State of Hawaii). Unpublished manuscript.
Follett, Mary Parker. (1918). *The new state: Group organization, the solution of popular government.* London: Longmans, Green & Co.
Follett, Mary Parker. (1924). *Creative experience.* New York: Longmans, Green & Co.
Forester, John. (1989). *Planning in the face of power.* Berkeley: University of California Press.
Fox, Charles J., & Miller, Hugh T. (1995). *Postmodern public administration: Toward discourse.* Thousand Oaks, CA: Sage.
Frankus, Sylviann. (1995). *Twenty-First Century League of Women Voters: Opportunities in new technology, new strategy, and the changing social reality.* Unpublished master's thesis, the Evergreen State College, Washington.
Frederickson, H. George. (1982). The recovery of civism in public administration. *Public Administration Review, 43*(6), 501-508.
Gastil, John. (1993). *Democracy is small groups.* Philadelphia: New Society.
Gastil, John, Adams, Gina, & Jenkins-Smith, Hank. (1995). *Understanding public deliberation* (Prepared for the Kettering Foundation). Albuquerque: University of New Mexico, Institute for Public Policy.
Gaventa, John. (1980). *Power and powerlessness: Quiescence and rebellion in an Appalachian valley.* Chicago: University of Illinois Press.
Gaventa, John. (1993). The powerful, the powerless, and the experts: Knowledge struggles in an information age. In P. Park, M. Brydon-Miller, B. Hall, & T. Jackson (Eds.), *Voices of change: Participatory research in the United States and Canada* (pp. 21-40). Toronto: OISE Press.
Gay, Lance. (1995, December 29). Many upset about paying idle workers. *Plain Dealer,* p. 12-A.
Gendlin, Eugene. (1973). Experiential phenomenology. In M. Natanson (Ed.), *Phenomenology and the social sciences* (pp. 281-319). Evanston, IL: Northwestern University Press.
Giddens, Anthony. (1984). *The constitution of society: Outline of the theory of structuration.* Berkeley: University of California Press.
Giddens, Anthony. (1985). Jürgen Habermas. In Q. Skinner (Ed.), *The return of grand theory in the social sciences* (pp. 121-139). Oxford: Cambridge University Press.
Giroux, Henry. (1988). *Schooling and the struggle for public life: Critical pedagogy in the modern age.* Minneapolis: University of Minnesota Press.
Goodwyn, Lawrence. (1978). *The populist moment.* Oxford: Oxford University Press.
Gramsci, Antonio. (1971). *Selections from the prison notebooks* (Q. Hoare & G. Nowell-Smith, Trans.). London: Lawrence & Wishart.
Gramsci, Antonio. (1985). *Selections from cultural writings* (William Boelhower, Trans.). Cambridge, MA: Harvard University Press.
Guba, Egon G., & Lincoln, Yvonna S. (1994). Competing paradigms in qualitative research. In N. Denzin & Y. Lincoln (Eds.), *Handbook of qualitative research* (pp. 105-117). Thousand Oaks, CA: Sage.
Habermas, Jürgen. (1972). *Knowledge and human interests* (J. J. Shapiro, Trans.). Boston: Beacon.
Habermas, Jürgen. (1975). *Legitimation crisis* (T. McCarthy, Trans.). Boston: Beacon.
Habermas, Jürgen. (1996). *Between facts and norms.* Cambridge: MIT Press.
Haddam, Jane. (1996, January 29). Promote the general welfare! *The Nation,* pp. 18-20.
Hansell, William. (1996). A common vision for the future. *National Civic Review, 85*(3), 5-13.
Harmon, Michael. (1995) *Responsibility as paradox: A critique of rational discourse on government.* Thousand Oaks, CA: Sage.
Head, Simon. (1996, February 29). The new, ruthless economy. *New York Review of Books,* 47-52.

Heidegger, Martin. (1962). *Being and time* (John Macquarrie & Edward Robinson, Trans.). San Francisco: Harper.

Hobbes, Thomas. (undated). *Leviathan, or The matter, form and power of a commonwealth ecclesiasticall and civil* (Michael Oakeshott, Ed.). Oxford: Basil Blackwell. (Original work published 1651)

Hochschild, Jennifer L. (1995). *Facing up to the American dream: Race, class and the soul of the nation.* Princeton, NJ: Princeton University Press.

Hollinger, David A., & Capper, Charles. (1989). *The American intellectual tradition, Volume II.* New York: Oxford University Press.

Holub, Renate. (1992). *Antonio Gramsci: Beyond Marxism and postmodernism.* New York: Routledge. (http://www.state.id.us/dhw/hwgd_www/famcomsv/96comsp.1.html)

Hummel, Ralph P. (1991). Stories managers tell: Why they are as valid as science. *Public Administration Review, 51*(1), 31-41.

Hummel, Ralph P. (1994). *The bureaucratic experience* (4th ed.). New York: St. Martin's.

Hunt, Alan. (Ed.). (1993). *Explorations in law and society.* New York: Routledge.

Husserl, Edmund. (1970). *The crisis of European sciences and transcendental phenomenology: An introduction to phenomenological philosophy* (David Carr, Trans.). Evanston, IL: Northwestern University Press. (Original work published 1937)

Janovsky, Michael. (1995, May 15). The far right rallies in quiet New England. *New York Times,* p. A6.

Johnston, David Cay. (1997, April 18). More U. S. wealth sidestepping I.R.S. *New York Times,* pp. A1, A12.

Jones, Brian. (1981). Party and bureaucracy: The influence of intermediary groups on urban public service delivery. *American Political Science Review, 75*(Nov), 688-700.

Kant, Immanuel. (1781). *Kritik der reinen Vernunft* [Critique of pure reason] (1st ed.). Riga: Johann Friedrich Hartknoch.

Kant, Immanuel. (1787). *Kritik der reinen Vernunft.* [Critique of pure reason] (2nd ed.) Riga: Johann Friedrich Hartknoch.

Kant, Immanuel. (1987). *Critique of judgment* (Werner S. Pluhar, Trans.). Indianapolis, IN: Hackett. (Original work published 1790)

Kearney, Richard J., & Sinha, Chandan. (1988). Professional and bureaucratic responsiveness: Conflict or compatibility. *Public Administration Review, 48*(5), 571-579.

Kemmis, Daniel. (1990). *Community and the politics of place.* Norman: University of Oklahoma Press.

Kemmis, Daniel. (1995). *The good city and the good life.* Boston: Houghton Mifflin.

Kettering Foundation. (1991). *Citizens and politics: A view from main street America* (Report prepared for the Kettering Foundation by the Harwood Group). Dayton, OH: Kettering Foundation.

Kettner, Kenneth Laine. (Ed.). (1995). *Peirce and contemporary thought.* New York: Fordham University Press.

Kilbourn, Peter T. (1995, July 3). Even in good times, it's hard times for workers. *New York Times,* pp. A1, A7.

Kincheloe, Joe L., & McLaren, Peter L. (1994). Rethinking critical theory and qualitative research. In N. Denzin & Y. Lincoln (Eds.), *Handbook of qualitative research* (pp. 138-157). Thousand Oaks, CA: Sage.

King, Cheryl Simrell, Feltey, Kathryn M., & Susel, Bridget O'Neill. (1998). The question of participation: Toward authentic public participation in public decisions. *Public Administration Review.*

Kleinfield, N. R. (1996, March 4). The company as family, no more. *New York Times,* pp. A1, A12-A14.

Kolakowski, Leszek. (1978). *Main currents of Marxism.* Oxford, UK: Clarendon.

Kolata, Gina. (1995, December 12). New administrator is "not an administrator." *New York Times,* p. C1.

Kretzmann, John, & McKnight, John. (1993). *Building community from the inside out.* Chicago: ACTA.

Krislov, Samuel. (1974). *Representative democracy.* Upper Saddle River, NJ: Prentice Hall.

Lappe, Frances Moore, & Du Bois, Paul Martin. (1994). *The quickening of America.* San Francisco: Jossey-Bass.

Lasch, Christopher. (1994). The revolt of the elites: Have they canceled their allegiance to America? *Harper's Magazine, 289*(1734), 39-49.

Lemann, Nicholas. (1996). Kicking in groups. *Atlantic Monthly, 277*(4), 22-26.

Letcher, Robert A. (1994). *Practical political economy: Public planners, practical actions, and the construction of political-economic institutions.* Unpublished doctoral dissertation, Cornell University, New York.

Levin, David Michael. (1989). *The listening self: Personal growth, social change, and the closure of metaphysics.* London: Routledge.

Lincoln, Yvonna. (1995, September). *At the querulous edge.* Paper presented at the University of Tennessee, Knoxville.

Lipsky, Michael. (1992). Street level bureaucracy: The critical role of street-level bureaucrats. Reprinted in J. Shafritz & A. Hyde (Eds.), *Classics of public administration* (3rd. ed., pp. 476-484). Pacific Grove, CA: Brooks/Cole.

Logan, John R., & Molotch, Harvey L. (1987). *Urban fortunes: The political economy of place.* Berkeley: University of California Press.

The "lost" mercury at Oak Ridge. (1983, July 8). *Science, 221,* 130-132.

Lukes, Steven. (1974). *Power: A radical view.* London: Macmillan.

Lustig, R. Jeffery. (1982). *Corporate liberalism: The origin of modern American political theory.* Berkeley: University of California Press.

Lynch, Jim. (1995, December 4). Angry patriots. *Spokesman Review,* pp. H1-H4.

MacNair, Ray H., Caldwell, Russell, & Pollane, Leonard. (1983). Citizen participation in public bureaucracies: Foul-weather friends. *Administration and Society, 14,* 507-523.

Marin, Peter. (1996). An American yearning: Seeking cures for freedom's terrors. *Harpers, 293*(1759), 35-43.

Mathews, David. (1994). *Politics for people.* Urbana: University of Illinois Press.

McKinley, James C. (1995, June 22). Major haulers of garbage are indicted in Mafia plot. *New York Times,* p. B16.

McKnight, John. (1995). *The carless society: Community and its counterfeits.* New York: Basic Books.

Medoff, Peter, & Sklar, Holly (1994). *Streets of hope.* Boston: South End Press.

Merrifield, Juliet. (1993). Putting scientists in their place: Participatory research in environmental and occupational health. In P. Park, M. Brydon-Miller, B. Hall, & T. Jackson (Eds.), *Voices of change: Participatory research in the United States and Canada* (pp 65-84). Toronto: OISE Press.

Mills, C. Wright. (1959). *The sociological imagination.* London: Oxford University Press.

Missouri Statewide Energy Study (May 1992). Environmental Improvement and Energy Resources Authority, State of Missouri Department of Natural Resources: Author.

Mladenka, Kenneth R. (1981). Citizen demands and urban services; The distribution of bureaucratic response in Chicago and Houston. *American Journal of Political Science, 25*(Nov), 693-714.

Morin, Richard. (1996, January 29). Who's in control? Many don't know or care. *Washington Post,* pp. A1, A6-A7.

Morin, Richard, & Balz, Dan. (1996, January 28). Americans losing trust in each other and institutions. *Washington Post,* pp. A1, A6-A7.

Morone, James A. (1990). *The democratic wish: Popular participation and the limits of American government.* New York: Basic Books.

Morris, William. (Ed.). (1971). *The American heritage dictionary of the English language.* Boston: American Heritage.

Mosher, Frederick C. (1982). *Democracy and the public service.* New York: Oxford University Press.

Murphy, John P. (1990). *Pragmatism: From Peirce to Davidson.* Boulder, CO: Westview.

Myers, Steven Lee. (1995, July 9). City hall's going retail in wholesale fashion. *New York Times,* p. E-2.

Nasar, Sylvia. (1995, June 11). The bureaucracy: What's left to shrink? *New York Times,* p. A2.

National Research Council, Committee on the Institutional Means for Assessment of Risks to Public Health, Commission on Life Sciences. (1983). *Risk assessment in the federal government: Managing the process.* Washington, DC: Author.

National Research Council, Committee on Risk Assessment of Hazardous Air Pollutants, Board of Environmental Studies and Toxicology. (1994). *Science and judgment in risk assessment.* Washington, DC: Author.

National Research Council, Water Science and Technology Board and Board on Radioactive Waste Management, Commission on Geosciences, Environment, and Resources. (1994). *Alternatives for ground water cleanup.* Washington, DC: Author.

Nelson, Michael A. (1982). A short, ironic history of American national bureaucracy. *Journal of Politics, 44,* 749-778.

Newland, Chester A. (1984). *Public administration and community: Realism in the practice of ideals.* McLean, VA: Public Administration Service.

Nigro, Lloyd C., & Nigro, Felix A. (1994). *The new public personnel administration.* Itasca, IL: F. E. Peacock.

Nigro, Lloyd C., & Waugh, William L. (1996). Violence in the American workplace: Challenges to the public employee. *Public Administration Review, 56*(4), 326-333.

Office of the President, National Performance Review. (1993). *From red tape to results: Creating a government that works better and costs less.* Washington, DC: Government Printing Office.

Osborne, David, & Gaebler, Ted. (1992). *Reinventing Government.* Reading, MA: Addison-Wesley.

Parr, John, & Gates, Christopher. (1989). Assessing community interest and gathering community support. In International City Management Association (Eds.), *Partnerships in local governance: Effective council-manager relations* (ICMA Handbook). Washington, DC: International City Management Association.

Pateman, Carole. (1970). *Participation and democratic theory.* Cambridge, UK: Cambridge University Press.

Pearlstein, Steven. (1996, January 30). Angry female voters a growing force. *Washington Post,* pp. A1, A5.

Pennock, J. Roland. (1979). *Democratic political theory.* Princeton, NJ: Princeton University Press.

Perlman, Ellen. (1997). The consensus industry. *Governing, 10*(4), 33-34.

Peterson, Paul E. (1981). *City limits.* Chicago: University of Chicago Press.

Pitkin, Hanna Fenichel. (1967). *The concept of representation.* Berkeley/Los Angeles: University of California Press.

Pollitt, Katha. (1996). French lessons. *The Nation* (February 19), 9.

Putnam, Robert. D. (1995). Bowling alone: America's declining social capital. *Journal of Democracy, XX*(1), 65-78.

Rabe, Barry G. (1994). *Beyond NIMBY: Hazardous waste siting in Canada and the United States,* Washington, DC: Brookings Institute.

Reich, Robert. (1991). *The work of nations: Preparing ourselves for 21st century capitalism.* New York: Knopf.

Ricci, David M. (1984). *The tragedy of political science.* New Haven, CT: Yale University Press

Robbins, Jim. (1997, June 1). Montana landowners fight public on trout streams. *Cleveland Plain Dealer,* p. 21-A.

Roelofs, H. Mark. (1976). *Ideology and myth in American politics: Portrait of a national political mind*. Boston: Little, Brown.

Roelofs, H. Mark. (1992). *The poverty of American politics: A theoretical interpretation*. Philadelphia: Temple University Press.

Rohr, John A. (1986). *To run a constitution: The legitimacy of the administrative state*. Lawrence: Kansas University Press.

Roper, Burns W. (1993). Democracy in America: How are we doing? We're doing our best to make the answer "Badly." *The Public Perspective, 5*(1), 3-5.

Rose, Stephen J. (1992). *Social stratification in the United States*. New York: The New Press.

Ross, Bernard H., & Levine, Myron A. (1996). *Urban politics: Power in metropolitan America* (5th ed.). Itasca, IL: F. E. Peacock.

Sabine, George H., & Thorson, Thomas L. (1973). *A history of political theory* (4th ed.). Hinsdale, IL: Dryden.

Schell, Jonathan. (1975). *The time of illusion*. New York: Vintage.

Schmidt, Mary R. (1993). Grout: Alternative forms of knowledge and why they are ignored. *Public Administration Review, 53*(6), 525-530.

Schneider, Keith. (1992, Feb 29). EPA is called lax with contractor. *New York Times*, p. A6.

Schrag, Peter. (1994). California's elected anarchy: A government destroyed by popular referendum. *Harper's, 298*, 50-58.

Selden, Sally Coleman. (1997). *The promise of representative bureaucracy: Diversity and responsiveness in a government agency*. Armonk, NY: M. E. Sharpe.

Selznick, Phillip. (1949). *TVA and the grass roots*. Berkeley: University of California Press.

Sharp, Elaine B. (1980). Citizen participation: The co-production concept. *Midwest Review of Public Administration, 14*(June), 105-119.

Shklar, Judith N. (1991). *American citizenship: The quest for inclusion*. Cambridge, MA: Harvard University Press.

Skowronek, Stephen. (1982). *Building a new American state: The expansion of national administrative capacities, 1877-1920*. Cambridge, UK: Cambridge University Press.

Sloan, Allen. (1996, February 26). The hit men. *Newsweek, 127*(9) 44-48.

State of Missouri Department of Natural Resources. (1992). *Missouri statewide energy study* (Volume VI: Public participation). Jefferson City, MO: Environmental Improvement and Energy Resources Authority.

Stever, James A. (1986). Mary Parker Follett and the quest for pragmatic administration. *Administration and Society, 18*(2), 159-177.

Stever, James A. (1990). The dual image of the administrator in progressive administrative theory. *Administration and Society, 22*(1), 39-57.

Stewart, Thomas R., Dennis, Robert L., & Ely, David W. (1984). Citizen participation and judgment in policy analysis: A case study of urban air quality policy. *Policy Science, 17*(May), 67-87.

Stivers, Camilla. (1988). *Active citizenship in the administrative state*. Unpublished doctoral dissertation, Virginia Polytechnic and State University, Blacksburg.

Stivers, Camilla. (1990a). Active citizenship and public administration. In G. L. Wamsley, R. N. Bacher, C. T. Goodsell, P. S. Kronenberg, J. A. Rohr, C. M. Stivers, O. F. White, & J. F. Wolf (Eds.), *Refounding public administration* (pp. 246-273). Newbury Park, CA: Sage.

Stivers, Camilla. (1990b). The public agency as polis: Active citizenship in the administrative state. *Administration and Society, 22*(1), 86-105.

Stivers, Camilla. (1993). *Gender images in public administration: Legitimacy and the administrative state*. Newbury Park, CA: Sage.

Stivers, Camilla. (1994). The listening bureaucrat: Responsiveness in public administration. *Public Administration Review, 54*(4), 364-369.

Superfund Amendments and Reauthorization Act, Title III. (1986). *Emergency Planning and Community Right-To-Know Act of 1986*. Washington, DC: United States Congress.

212

GOVERNMENT IS US

Targeted community initiative [Videotape]. (1997). Orange County, FL: Orange County Florida Health and Communities Services Division, Community Affairs.

Tauxe, C. S. (1995). Marginalizing public participation in local planning: An ethnographic account. *Journal of the American Planning Association, 61*(4), 471-481.

Terry, Larry D. (1997). Public administration and the theater metaphor: The public administrator as villain, hero, and innocent victim. *Public Administrative Review, 57*(1), 53-62.

Thomas, John Clayton. (1995). *Public participation in public decisions.* San Francisco: Jossey-Bass.

Thompson, Dennis. (1970). *The democratic citizen.* Cambridge: Cambridge University Press.

Thomson, Ken, Berry, Jeffrey M., & Portney, Kent E. (1994). *Kernels of democracy.* Boston: Lincoln Filene Center at Tufts University.

Timney, Mary M. (1996, July). *Overcoming NIMBY: Using citizen participation effectively.* Paper presented at the 57th National Conference of the American Society for Public Administration, Atlanta, GA.

Tolchin, Susan J. (1996).*The angry American: How voter rage is changing the nation.* Boulder, CO: Westview.

Tremblay, Paul. (1990). Toward a community-based ethic for legal services practice. *UCLA Law Review, 37,* 1101.

Uchitelle, Louis, & Kleinfield, N. R. (1996, March 3). On the battlefields of business, millions of casualties. *New York Times,* pp. A1, A26-A29.

Unocal will settle suits for $80 million. (1997, April 15). *San Francisco Chronicle,* p. A1.

U.S. Environmental Protection Agency. (1997, February 27). *Memorandum on agency reorganization.* Washington, DC: Author.

U.S. Environmental Protection Agency, Chemical Emergency Planning and Preparedness Office. (1991, January). *Public knowledge and perceptions of chemical risks in six communities: Analysis of a baseline survey.* Washington, DC: Author.

U.S. Environmental Protection Agency, Office of Administration. (1993, January). *Oral history interview—1, William D. Ruckelshaus.* Washington, DC: Author.

U.S. Environmental Protection Agency, Office of Administration and Resources' Management. (1971-1996). *EPA Telephone Directories.* Washington, DC: Author.

U.S. Environmental Protection Agency, Office of Policy, Planning and Evaluation. (1992a, February). *Environmental equity: Reducing risks for all communities.* Washington, DC: Author.

U.S. Environmental Protection Agency, Office of Solid Waste and Emergency Response. (1992b). *CERCLA/Superfund orientation manual.* Washington, DC: Author

U.S. Environmental Protection Agency, Science Advisory Board. (1990). *Reducing risk, setting priorities and strategies for environmental protection.* Washington, DC: Author.

U.S. Government Accounting Office. (1994, September). *Issues pertaining to an incinerator in East Liverpool, Ohio.* Washington, DC: Author.

U.S. Office of Management and Budget. (1996, January 11). *Economic analysis guidance of federal regulation under Executive Order 12866.* Washington, DC: Author.

Van Meter, E. C. (1975). Citizen participation in the policy management process. *Public Administration Review, 35*(6), 804-812.

Van Riper, Paul P. (1958). *History of the United States civil service.* New York: Harper & Row.

Ventriss, Curtis. (1987). Two critical issues of American public administration: Reflections of a sympathetic participant. *Administration and Society, 19*(1), 25-47.

Ventriss, Curtis. (1995). Modern thought and bureaucracy. *Public Administration Review, 55*(6), 575-580.

Vick, Karl. (1995, October 20). A cutback, literally. *Washington Post,* p. C1.

Villa, Dale. (1996). *Arendt and Heidegger: The fate of the political.* Princeton, NJ: Princeton University Press.

Vogel, Ronald K., & Swanson, Bert E. (1989). The growth machine versus the antigrowth coalition: The battle for our communities. *Urban Affairs Quarterly, 25*(3), 63-85.

Volcker, Paul A. (1989). *Leadership for America: Rebuilding the public service* (Report of the National Commission on the Public Service). Lexington, MA: Lexington Books.

Waldo, Dwight. (1948). *The administrative state.* New York: Ronald Press.

Waldo, Dwight. (1984). Response. *Public Administration Review, 44*(6), 107-109.

Wamsley, Gary L. (1990). Introduction. In G. L. Wamsley, R. N. Bacher, C. T. Goodsell, P. S. Kronenberg, J. A. Rohr, C. M. Stivers, O. F. White, & J. F. Wolf (Eds.), *Refounding public administration* (pp. 19-29). Newbury Park, CA: Sage.

Wamsley, Gary L., Bacher, Robert N., Goodsell, Charles T., Kronenberg, Philip S., Rohr, John A., Stivers, Camilla M., White, Orion F., & Wolf, James F. (Eds.). (1990). *Refounding public administration.* Newbury Park, CA: Sage.

Weinstein, James. (1968). *The corporate ideal in the liberal state.* Boston: Beacon.

White, Lucie E. (1987-1988). Mobilization on the margins of the lawsuit: Making space for clients to speak. *Review of Law and Social Change, 16,* 535-564.

Wiebe, Robert H. (1967). *The search for order, 1877-1920.* New York: Hill & Wang.

Wiebe, Robert H. (1995). *Self-rule: A cultural history of American democracy.* Chicago: University of Chicago Press.

Wilson, James Q. (1989). *Bureaucracy.* New York: Basic Books.

Wilson, Woodrow. (1887). The study of administration. *Political Sciences Quarterly, 2*(June), 197-222.

Wolin, Sheldon. (1996, April 22). Democracy and counterrevolution. *The Nation, 262*(16), 22-24.

Yankelovich, Daniel. (1995, Fall). Three destructive trends. *Kettering Review,* pp. 6-15.

You know you're a bureaucrat if . . . (1997). *Readers' Digest, 150*(898), 12.

Zanetti, Lisa A., & Carr, Adrian. (1997). Putting critical theory to work: Giving the administrator the critical edge. *Administrative Theory and Praxis, 19*(2), 208-224.

Zinsmeister, Karl.(1995, September/October). Payday mayday. *The American Enterprise, 6*(5), 44-48.

Index

About the Collaborators

Richard C. Box is Associate Professor in the Graduate School of Public Affairs, University of Colorado at Colorado Springs. He served for 13 years as a land-use planner, department head, and city manager for local governments in Oregon and California before completing his doctorate at the University of Southern California. He is particularly interested in issues of community power, citizenship, the administrative role, and democratic governance.

Linda W. Chapin is serving her second term as Orange County Chairman. As Chairman, she is the Chief Executive Officer for Orange County, and is responsible for managing the daily operations of all divisions and departments, along with chairing the Board of County Commissioners. A Florida native, she graduated from Michigan State University before returning to Orlando. She has focused much of her time in public life on issues affecting children and families and is the founder of the Citizens' Commission for Children. She has overseen the development of Orange County's Economic Action Initiative, has championed the purchase of environmentally sensitive lands, and promotes water resource issues.

Dolores Foley is Assistant Professor in the Public Administration Program at the University of Hawai'i. She teaches organizational theory, qualitative methods, and collaboration. Her research and writing interests are in the areas of citizen participation and organizational change strategies. She is active in numerous community building and visioning efforts and is the

Project Coordinator of the Hawai'i Democracy Forum, a project to revitalize citizenship and democracy through the dialogue of local issues.

Joseph E. Gray is Manager of the Orange County Community Affairs Department and is responsible for managing the daily operations of the department and supervising nearly 400 staff members. The department serves as the focal point for many of the county's community-outreach efforts, including the operation of community centers and coordinating community-development initiatives. A native of the state of Illinois, he graduated from Southern Illinois University and spent a number of years working in state and local government in Illinois, as well as directing non-profit community-based organizations before moving to Florida.

Ralph P. Hummel is trying to develop a philosophical basis for public administration in the theory of knowledge. In recent years, he has taught organization theory, personnel, work policy, qualitative methods, and existential political thought at the University of Oklahoma and the University of Akron. Summers, he functions as codirector of the Institute of Applied Phenomenology, Spruce Head Island, Maine. His latest work, with David C. Carnevale, is a knowledge analytic of the modern organization: *Why Management Reforms Fail.*

Margaret M. Kelly coordinates the regulatory aspects of a new concerted effort at the EPA to prevent health and safety risks to children. Prior to this, she was detailed to organize and facilitate the Petroleum Refining Sector of the "Common Sense Initiative"—an EPA project to redesign the Agency's approach to achieving environmental goals. She has also held the position of Deputy Director of the Technology Innovation Office in the EPA's Office of Solid Waste and Emergency Response. She has worked, over several years, in EPA programs that include developing regulations to remove lead from gasoline, modeling the effects of acid rain, cost-benefit analysis for pesticide use, and has held a number of analytical and management positions in the EPA's Office of Solid Waste and Emergency Response.

Cheryl Simrell King teaches public administration and urban studies at the University of Akron. She is trained in psychology and public administration and has published book chapters and articles on gender issues in public administration, leadership, organizational behavior, and public administration theory. Before joining academe, she held a number of positions in community-based organizations and in the private sector. She continues her community activism by serving as a volunteer with several local and state-level community organizations in Ohio.

Walter W. Kovalick, Jr. manages an office chartered to act as champion for the introduction of more innovative remediation technologies in the cleanup of abandoned waste sites under "Superfund" and corrective action under the Resource Conservation and Recovery Act. He served during the Clinton Administration transition period as the Acting Deputy Assistant Administrator for the Office of Solid Waste and Emergency Response. For 5 years prior to that, he was the Deputy Director of the "Superfund" program, where he shared leadership responsibilities for a nationwide program to respond to hazardous substance releases. Since joining the EPA in 1970 from one of its predecessor agencies, he has represented the EPA on hazardous waste and chemical issues to several international organizations, served as a consultant to the United Nations Environment Program, and worked for the last 11 years on a NATO project to share information on remediation technologies.

Renee Nank is a doctoral student at the Levin College of Urban Affairs at Cleveland State University. Her current research interests include citizen participation, gender and public administration theory, spatial differences in women's occupations and earnings, and capacity building in nonprofits.

Deborah A. Sagen served for four years as Executive Director of Colorado Springs Citizens' Goals, a nonprofit organization that facilitates citizen research and action on issues of community concern. Before coming to Citizens' Goals, she worked in local government for 8 years as a lobbyist, labor negotiator, policy analyst, and director of community development. She is an advocate for local government that encourages citizen involvement and self-governance. She is now Director of Corporate Workforce and Economic Development at Pikes Peak Community College.

Camilla Stivers is the Albert A. Levin professor of urban studies and public service at Cleveland State University. For nearly two decades, she was a practicing manager in community-based nonprofit and government organizations. She is the author of *Gender Images in Public Administration: Legitimacy and the Administrative State,* as well as a variety of articles and book chapters on citizenship in the administrative state and other topics in normative public administration theory.

Mary M. Timney is Professor and Chair of the Department of Public Administration at California State University at Hayward. She teaches courses in public administration theory and environmental policy. She was president of the Ohio Environmental Council from 1993 to 1996. She has published articles in *Public Administration Review, Administrative Theory and Praxis,* and *Public Productivity Review,* and is coeditor of the book *Public Management in an Interconnected World.*

Lisa A. Zanetti teaches public administration at the University of Missouri-Columbia. Her research interests include critical theory, nonbehavioral research methodology, democratic and administrative theory, and ethics. She has published articles and essays in *American Review of Public Administration, Administrative Theory and Praxis, Public Management and Productivity Review,* and *Public Voices.* Before entering academia, she was employed at the U.S. Department of Commerce and the U.S. International Trade Commission.